AUGUSTINE

Against the Academicians
The Teacher

AUGUSTINE

Against the Academicians
The Teacher

Translated, with Introduction and Notes, by
Peter King

Hackett Publishing Company, Inc.
Indianapolis/Cambridge

Augustine: 354–430

Copyright © 1995 by Hackett Publishing Company, Inc.

Printed in the United States of America

00 99 98 97 96   2 3 4 5 6

For further information, please address

Hackett Publishing Company, Inc.
P.O. Box 44937
Indianapolis, Indiana 46244-0937

Cover design by Listenberger & Associates

Text design by Dan Kirklin

Library of Congress Cataloging-in-Publication Data

Augustine, Saint, Bishop of Hippo.
    [Contra academicos. English.]
    Against the academicians; The teacher/Augustine, translated, with
    introduction and notes by Peter King.
        p.   cm.
    Includes bibliographical references and index.
    ISBN 0-87220-213-5   ISBN 0-87220-212-7 (pbk.)
    1. Skepticism—Controversial literature—Early works to 1800.
    2. Knowledge, Theory of—Early works to 1800.   3. Philosophy
    and religion—Early works to 1800.   I. King, Peter, 1955– .
    II. Augustine, Saint, Bishop of Hippo.   De magistro. English.
    III. Title.   IV. Title: Teacher.
    B655.C62E5 1995
    189'.2—dc20   95-32851
                                                                                    CIP

∞

Contents

Introduction

Augustine's early works *Against the Academicians* (386) and *The Teacher* (389) belong together. In the former, which is directed at Cicero's *Academica*, he defends the possibility of knowledge against the skeptical arguments of the New Academy;[1] in the latter, directed at Plato's *Meno*, he offers his theory of illumination to explain how knowledge is acquired. As a pair, they present Augustine's alternative to the pose of ironical detachment fashionable among late Roman intellectuals.

In late antiquity, philosophy was more a way of life than an academic discipline. Philosophers were organized into schools (*secta*), each with a venerable tradition and its own worldview — one that included specific arguments and points of view as well as positions on such major questions of general interest as the number of stars in the heavens and the nature of God. Some philosophical schools also held esoteric doctrines that were revealed in secret to a novice after he had served the requisite apprenticeship. Philosophers often lived together in communities, adhered to the dictates of a common rule based on their doctrines, and wore distinctive clothing (the philosopher's mantle) to indicate the school of philosophy to which they belonged. It was not uncommon for people to "withdraw from the world" to pursue philosophy — especially if they had experienced a conversion of some sort. Thus philosophical schools were to all intents and purposes like religious orders.

In Augustine's view, (Christian) religion and (Platonist) philosophy were engaged in the same enterprise, namely the quest for knowledge: "Just as the Hebrews were prepared for Christianity by the law and the prophets, so too the Gentiles were prepared by Plato and Aristotle. And just as Christianity is the fulfillment of the Old Covenant, so too it is the fulfillment of Greek philosophy."[2] The difference between them is that Christian doctrine suc-

---

1. Augustine identifies the 'New Academy' as the successors of Plato, who endorsed skepticism: see *Against the Academicians* 2.5.13–2.6.15.

2. Spade [1985] Chapter 7.

ceeds where unaided platonism fails. Hence Augustine could summarize his views as follows:

> I've renounced all the other things that mortal men think to be good and proposed to devote myself to searching for wisdom . . . no one doubts that we're prompted to learn by the twin forces of authority and reason. Therefore, I'm resolved not to depart from the authority of Christ on any score whatsoever: I find no more powerful [authority]. As for what is to be sought out by the most subtle reasoning — for my character is such that I'm impatient in my desire to apprehend what the truth is not only by belief but also by understanding — I'm still confident that I'm going to find it with the Platonists, and that it won't be opposed to our Holy Writ. [*Against the Academicians* 3.20.43.12–24]

Truth is one, however. It is reached through authority by means of belief and through reason (philosophy) by means of understanding. Philosophy thus proceeds autonomously to attain whatever truth it can. But the internal Teacher[3] is the final arbiter of truth regardless of its source. When Augustine says, then, that he will devote himself "to searching for wisdom," he is committing himself to a life of philosophizing along platonist lines in the service of Christianity.

In support of this vision of the philosophical way of life, Augustine could look back to a long tradition of Christian platonism: Simplicianus and Ambrose in Milan, Marius Victorinus before that, and Origen and Justin Martyr earlier still. Moreover, his apparently extravagant claims for platonism were largely in keeping with a philosophical consensus that was already a century old, for philosophical inquiry over the ages had reached the conclusion that platonism — especially of the sort defended by Plotinus — was the correct view. (Philosophical thought in Augustine's day "was 'post-Plotinian,' much as that of our own age is 'post-Freudian.'")[4] That is why Augustine does not draw a

3. The 'internal Teacher' is Christ operating within us to provide knowledge: this is the core of Augustine's theory of illumination, discussed in *The Teacher*.

4. Brown [1967], p. 102. Augustine describes this consensus in concluding his survey of the history of philosophy in *Against the Academicians* 3.18.41.41–3.19.42.10: "Plato's visage, which is the most pure and bright in philosophy, shone forth once the clouds of error had been dispelled —

sharp distinction between philosophy in general and platonist philosophy in particular.

The consensus on platonism, combined with the view that Christianity is platonism perfected, led Augustine to adopt a tolerantly dismissive attitude toward most other philosophical schools: the Peripatetics really have the same system as the Platonists, one that leads to Christianity when improved by philosophical argument; the Cynics can be dismissed because of their lax morality, and the Stoics and the Epicureans dismissed because of their materialism.

Yet there was one philosophical school that claimed to hold no doctrines and that criticized other schools — including the Platonists — for their dogmatism, namely the Academicians. Standing apart from the clash of dogmatic philosophies, these thinkers prided themselves on their restraint and detachment, and on their avoidance of the error into which others had raced headlong. In addition, their school had the sanction of Cicero, who was venerated as the Latin master of literary, legal, rhetorical, and philosophical writing. The late Roman intellectual who claimed to be a Ciceronian skeptic must have been a familiar sight.

Thus for Augustine the live options were Ciceronian irony and philosophical commitment. In his early works they are what engage his philosophical interest.

When Augustine became disillusioned with Manichaeanism in 383, he despaired of finding the truth and went through a period of being a skeptic.[5] Consequently, he had an insider's knowledge

---

and above all in Plotinus. This Platonic philosopher is considered to be so like Plato that they seem to have lived at the same time .... there is, in my opinion, one system of really true philosophy. It has finally emerged after many centuries and many controversies, because there have been acute and clever men who taught in their disputations that Aristotle and Plato agree with each other (although they did so in such a way that to the unskilled and inattentive they seemed to disagree)."

5. Some scholars have questioned this claim, pointing out that from Augustine's autobiographical remarks in *The Happy Life* 1.4 (Appendix 1) and *Confessions* 5.14.25 (Appendix 5), for example, all we may infer is that Augustine was impressed by the Academicians, not that he was an adherent of their doctrines; his "despair at finding the truth" (*desperatio veri inveniendi*), as described in *Against the Academicians* 2.1.1, *Revisions* 1.1.1 (Appendix 11) and *Enchiridion* 7.20 (Appendix 7), need not involve any

of skepticism, though he never apprenticed himself to any skeptical school. Eventually his reading of "platonist books" convinced him that skepticism was mistaken. In 386 he resigned as court rhetorician, broke off his engagement to be married, gave up life on the fast track, and went in philosophical retirement to a country-house in Cassiciacum.[6] *Against the Academicians* is the first fruit of this retirement, containing, among other things, Augustine's explanation of why he abandoned public life. It is a manifesto

---

philosophical allegiance to the Academicians. Yet Augustine was more than sympathetic to them. He writes in *Against the Academicians* 3.15.34.17–20 (emphasis added):

> When in my retirement in the country I had been pondering for a long time just how the plausible or the truthlike can defend our actions from error, at first the matter seemed to me nicely protected and fortified, as it usually seemed *when I was peddling it.*

Augustine thus defended the view of the Academicians, and did so publicly. This conclusion is reinforced by such remarks as *Confessions* 5.10.19: "There also arose in me the thought that the philosophers called the Academicians had been more prudent than the rest, since they held that everything should be doubted, and made the amount of truth that man is able to apprehend disappear." It is understandable that Augustine should later want to minimize his attachment to the Academicians, as he does in *Confessions* 5.14.25, but we need not follow his example.

 6. Verecundus lent his villa at Cassiciacum, near Milan, to Augustine. But since Augustine did not have the wealth to support himself, he had to take in private pupils in addition to members of his household. He introduces most of his companions in *The Happy Life* 1.6.139–146:

> In the first place there was our mother [Monnica], to whose merit, I believe, I owe all that I am; my brother Navigius; Trygetius and Licentius, fellow-citizens and my students; my cousins Lartidianus and Rusticus — although they had not even been trained in grammar, I didn't want them to be absent, for I thought their common sense necessary to the enterprise I was attempting. My son Adeodatus was also with us. He was the youngest of all, but his abilities promise something great (if my love doesn't blind me!).

Another member of the household was Alypius, Augustine's close friend who had followed him into retirement and who took a leading role in most of the dialogues written at Cassiciacum, including *Against the Academicians.*

written by a former skeptic presenting himself for the first time as a platonist and a Christian.

Book 1 is devoted to a debate between Licentius, an Academician, and Trygetius, a non-Academician, about the merits of their respective ways of life. Despite many digressions, which justify Augustine's later characterization of their discussion as "elementary" (1.9.25.39–43), they do manage to explore a challenging topic, namely the nature of happiness and the bearing of error and wisdom on it. But the main business of the dialogue begins in Book 2, with Augustine's own detailed exploration of skepticism and its development within the Academy.

Augustine takes the core of skepticism to consist in two theses, first formulated by Arcesilaus and justified in a particular way.[7] These theses are:

(1) Nothing can be known.
(2) Assent should always be withheld.

(1) was justified by appeal to Zeno's account of truthful perception. Zeno claimed that a perception is truthful when (*a*) it accurately reflects the way the world is, and (*b*) it could not be caused by anything other than its actual cause. The skeptics argued that (*a*) could not be satisfied because things are naturally obscure and so cannot be accurately represented, and that (*b*) could not be satisfied because two things may resemble each other too closely to be reliably distinguished as causes. If (*a*) and (*b*) could be satisfied, why, they asked, would there be so many errors and disagreements? They concluded that since no perceptions satisfy (*a*) and (*b*), nothing can be known. (2) was then derived from (1) with the aid of two other premises:

(3) The wise man should not risk error.
(4) Giving assent to what is not known risks error.

Two refinements were later made to this core skeptical position by

7. Augustine's presentation of skeptical doctrine relies heavily on Cicero. The doctrine, as well as its historical development, is more complex than Augustine makes it out to be. See the Recommended Reading for more information about ancient skepticism.

Carneades. First, (1) was restricted to philosophical or theoretical matters; it didn't apply to ordinary everyday concerns. Understanding (1) in this restricted way enabled the skeptic to avoid many of the more offensively counterintuitive consequences of his position. For example, he could now claim to know that he was not a bug!

The second refinement came about as follows. It was objected to (2) that if one assents to nothing, one also will never do anything. Carneades replied that a skeptic can be guided in his actions by "what is plausible (*probabile*)" or "what is truthlike (*verisimile*)."[8] In other words, he adopted the following thesis:

(5) The wise man follows the plausible or truthlike.

Thus the new refined Academician emerges as above all an anti-dogmatist — iconoclastic as regards competing explanatory theories, careful to believe no more than the evidence warrants, free of philosophical commitments. He can comment on other philosophical systems, relieved of the burden of having to defend any himself.

Augustine's arguments against this skeptical position are a mixed bag. His main contention is an attack on the relative plausibility of (1) — he argues at length that it's at least as plausible that the truth can be found as that it cannot[9] — but his conclusion

8. See the Remarks on the Translations regarding these technical terms.

9. Augustine describes to Alypius in 2.13.30.34–43 the conclusion he wants to establish:

> Therefore, the question between us is whether the arguments [of the Academicians] make it plausible that nothing can be perceived and that one should not assent to anything. Now if you prevail, I'll gladly yield. Yet if I can demonstrate that it's much more plausible that the wise man be able to attain the truth and that assent need not always be withheld, then you'll have no reason, I think, for refusing to come over to my view.

Earlier, in 2.3.8.39–40, Augustine says that he wants to persuade Romanianus that his views against the Academicians are plausible. He states the conclusion of his argument in 3.5.12.43–44 in the same terms — "It's enough for me that it's no longer plausible that the wise man knows nothing." He emphasizes several more times that this is his conclusion:

depends on rejecting the distinction between 'Jones knows that *p'*
and 'It seems to Jones that he knows that *p*.' Philosophers have
found Augustine's supplementary attempt in *Against the Academicians* to identify instances of genuine knowledge more promising.
He identifies three kinds of knowledge impervious to skeptical
doubts. First, there are logical truths, and in particular disjunctive
truths, about the world: we know, for instance, that either it is raining or it is not raining. We know the truth of such disjunctions even
without knowing which of the disjuncts is true, if the disjuncts are
mutually exclusive and exhaustive.[10] Second, there are pure
appearance-claims. Rather than asserting that something *is* the case
I can say that it *seems to me* to be the case, and such propositions are
directly known to be true. While "There is a book in front of me"
may be false, the pure appearance-claim "It seems to me that there
is a book in front of me" is unaffected by the unreliability of sense-
perception and perceptual illusion, the possibilities that one is
dreaming or insane, and so on.[11] Pure appearance-claims, Augustine tells us, are all that perceptual knowledge ever warrants, and
we cannot go wrong if we restrict ourselves to what seems to us to
be so. Third, there are mathematical truths, which are also independent of sense-perception. They hold whether one is dreaming or
awake, hallucinating or clear-headed. (The account of how we
know these nonperceptual truths is given in *The Teacher*.) In his

---

3.14.30.20–21, 3.14.31.45–49, and at the close of his monologue (3.20.43.2–
3). See Heil [1972] and Mosher [1981] for the importance of this fact.

10. If the skeptic objects that we have to *know* that the disjunctions are
exclusive and exhaustive, Augustine can reply that this is determined by
their logical form. If the skeptic charges that truths about the world pre-
suppose the existence of the world, which is not itself known, Augustine
replies that he calls 'world' whatever seems to appear to him — so there
is no substantive presupposition at stake here.

11. Apparently the skeptical arguments relied a great deal on undermin-
ing the trustworthiness of sense-perception. Augustine begins his discussion of knowledge in *The Trinity* 15.12.21 (Appendix 6) by pointing this
out and then setting aside sense-perception as a source of knowledge; he
does likewise in *The City of God* 11.26 (Appendix 8). However, he notes
that the senses are not so unreliable as the skeptic makes them seem: an
oar partially submerged in the water 'appears' bent — but, Augustine
adds, that's precisely how a straight oar *should* look in the water, and the
same could be said for many other cases (3.11.26.46–56).

later works Augustine adds a fourth kind of indubitable knowledge, anticipating Descartes: namely the knowledge that one exists and that one is alive, even in the teeth of skeptical challenges: "If I am deceived, I exist" (*Si fallor, sum*) — see Appendices 6–8.

Augustine concludes his discussion in *Against the Academicians* by asking how anyone could take skepticism seriously when all one has to say to a skeptic is: "It seems to me that someone can know the truth" (3.16.36.60–62). He reasons that the Academicians were too clever not to have recognized the force of this refutation, and, therefore, they could not have held the skepticism they publicly professed. In fact they held a secret doctrine, namely platonism![12] His inference was no doubt credible in a world of warring philosophical sects some of whom did have secret doctrines, but it has found no support among modern scholars.

The upshot of *Against the Academicians*, then, is that knowledge is possible. In *The Teacher* Augustine explains how knowledge is acquired by means of a philosophically improved 'Christianized' version of Plato's theory of recollection, known as the theory of illumination.

---

12. Augustine is careful to say that he does not *know* this to be the case but only *thinks* it to be so (3.17.37.3–4); it is a view he finds plausible, but none of the philosophical points he has been making depends on it (3.20.43.1–3). He apparently held this view for the rest of his life. It is the topic of his first extant letter (translated in Appendix 3). And writing to Dioscurus in 410/411, more than twenty years after completing *Against the Academicians*, Augustine declares that "the Academicians held the same views as the Platonists" and narrates a compressed version of the history recited in *Against the Academicians* 3.17.37–3.19.42 (*Letter* 118.16–21). He concludes his survey there as follows (118.20.22–28):

> Therefore, since the Platonists held views of the sort that couldn't be taught to men given to carnal pleasures, and since they didn't have great enough authority among the people to persuade them that their [platonist] views ought to be believed, then, until the spirit is brought to take hold of what had captured them, they chose to hide their doctrine and to argue against those who claimed that they had found the truth, since these men postulated the very discovery of truth in the bodily senses.

The Academicians, therefore, embraced skepticism as a defense against the 'empirical' schools of philosophy!

According to Plato's theory of recollection, all instances of learning are merely apparent. Learning is in reality the soul's "recollection" (ἀνάμνησις 'un-forgetting') of truths it already possesses: recollection is "recovering knowledge by oneself that is in oneself" (*Meno* 85d4 and 85d6–7).[13] Plato supports his theory of recollection by the vivid example of the dialogue between Socrates and a slave, complete with a running commentary to Meno (82b–85b). Socrates sets the slave, who is ignorant of geometry, the problem of constructing a square with an area twice the size of a given square. The slave suggests that a square with sides of double length will have twice the area; recognizing his mistake, however, he proceeds to generate the correct construction, which is obvious from simple diagrams. During the conversation the slave has come to see why his first answer is wrong and why the correct answer is correct. Socrates later tells us that beliefs, even true beliefs, are "not worth much until they are tied down by reasoning about the explanation (αἰτίας λογισμῷ) — and this is recollection, as we previously agreed" (*Meno* 98a3–5).[14] The slave has acquired knowledge by coming to understand the reasons behind the proof. And that, as Plato concludes, is a process internal to the slave.

Plato and Augustine do not hesitate to draw the consequences of this insight. Whatever 'grasping reasons' may be, it is not the result of an external causal process: some students in the classroom understand the teacher's explanation of the proof and some students don't; the difference is internal to each student, not found in their identical external circumstances.[15] Teaching as it is usually understood, namely as a process by which knowledge is

13. Plato argues that such knowledge must have been acquired by the soul before its present incarnation in this life; Augustine, though he remained neutral on the possibility of the soul's preexistence, finds the latter part of this doctrine dispensable, and accordingly he dispenses with it.

14. Socrates remarks at 85d7–e1 that if the slave-boy were interrogated "many times and in many ways," in the end "his knowledge would be as accurate as anyone's." See Nehamas [1985] for an account of recollection.

15. It doesn't help to say that the difference is in the intelligence of the receptive students (an attempt to resurrect the causal account): intelligence may be what allows people to grasp the truths they do grasp, but their grasp of truths is and remains a purely internal matter.

transferred from one person to another, is therefore not possible.[16] Learning is a purely internal matter. Consider the following example. You recite to yourself the steps of a mathematical proof while attempting to understand it, but without understanding it: you're merely parroting the proof. Yet in thinking it through you suddenly have a flash of insight and see how the proof works — you comprehend it, and thereby recognize its truth. There is a real difference between your situation while not understanding the proof and your situation after understanding it. We commonly describe this difference with visual metaphors — the 'flash' of insight, 'seeing' the truth, 'enlightenment,' and so on. Augustine calls it *illumination*.[17] It is an internal event whereby we 'see' the truth.[18] The power that reveals the truth to us, Augustine maintains, is Christ as the Teacher operating within us (*The Teacher* 11.38). The very understanding we have testifies to God's presence in the world, since the mind is illuminated with knowledge by the inner Teacher.[19]

16. This characterization of 'teaching' is not limited to formal teaching situations. It is broad enough to cover any transfer of information. See n. 19 below.

17. Augustine, following Plato, explains the metaphor of illumination as involving the direct grasp of special objects (*i.e.*, Forms) in a public realm only accessible to the mind. Plato held that this took place prior to the soul's incarnation; Augustine, that it happens during this life — see Book 2 of *The Free Choice of the Will*. Augustine's account of illumination is the distant but direct ancestor of Descartes's 'natural light of reason.'

18. This formulation is neutral on the disputed question whether for Augustine illumination is that by means of which we are able to exercise our cognitive powers to grasp the truth (as sunlight is that by means of which we can exercise our perceptual faculties to see objects) or the actual comprehension of the truth itself (as seeing itself grasps objects). There are texts on both sides of the question, and *The Teacher* does not resolve it. The same ambiguity pervades our everyday metaphors: in a "flash of insight," the flash is like something we see by, whereas the insight is like the seeing itself.

19. The theory of illumination is at its most plausible with mathematics, where the objects of knowledge are necessary truths that typically deal with ideal objects, such as perfect circles. How far it extends is disputed. (The dispute is exacerbated by disagreement over what should count as knowledge in the first place.) The view that it is fully generalizable to all

Plato presents us with the dialogue between Socrates and the slave in the *Meno* to draw attention to such underlying issues, but he undermines his case. When Socrates emphasizes to Meno that he isn't telling the slave anything but merely asking questions (*Meno* 82e2–3 and 84d1–2), generations of readers have immediately countered with the objection that information can be conveyed through leading questions.[20] Therefore, so the objection goes, Socrates does teach the slave — that is, he provides him with knowledge he did not previously possess: Socrates *transfers* information to the slave, thinly disguised in interrogative form. Augustine describes this commonsense alternative, the 'information-transference account' of teaching, in his *Homilies on John the Evangelist* 37.4.14–24 (commenting on John 8.19) as follows:[21]

> When there is an idea in your heart it differs from [any] sound, but the idea that is in you seeks out the sound as though it were a vehicle to come across to me. Therefore it clothes itself in the sound, somehow gets itself into this vehicle, travels through the air, comes to me. . . . You've said what you were thinking and uttered those syllables so that what was hidden inside you would come to me; the sound of the syllables conveys your thought to my ear; through my ear has your thought descended into my heart.

You encode your thoughts into language and utter the appropri-

---

instances of knowledge is called 'general illumination,' and the view that it is needed only for special cases, such as advanced knowledge in the various disciplines, is called 'special illumination.' The scope of divine activity in illumination is also problematical. Does God have to directly act in each instance of knowledge, or merely ordain the world in such a way that humans can be knowers? These matters are discussed in Nash [1969].

20. According to Plato and to Augustine, the impossibility of teaching has as a consequence that even directly telling the slave the correct answer doesn't count as teaching. This begs the question, of course, if Plato's example is construed as an argument — but that's a good reason for not taking it as an argument at all.

21. See also *On Christian Doctrine* 2.2.3 (Appendix 10): "The only reason for our signifying, *i.e.*, giving signs, is to bring forth and to transfer into another's mind what is happening in the mind of the person giving the sign." In the translation 'idea' renders *verbum*, since Augustine is talking about his theory of the inner mental Word.

ate sounds; I hear your utterances, and, knowing the language, I decode them back into ideas. That is how knowledge can be transferred from your mind to mine. Why subscribe to Plato's theory of recollection when the information-transference account explains the mistake in his argument and is plausible in its own right?

Augustine takes on the information-transference account of teaching by offering an analysis of *language*, the medium through which knowledge is said to be transferred. The result of Augustine's semiotic investigations in *The Teacher* is that language is inadequate to the task. We come to know linguistic facts through language — that two words mutually signify one another, say — and we acquire beliefs about nonlinguistic items through language, from the testimony of others. That's all. We can't acquire knowledge about nonlinguistic items through language. Without language to serve as a medium, the information-transference account cannot work, and so Augustine is free to present and argue for his alternative, namely the theory of illumination. Most of *The Teacher* is given over to the analysis of language, including our abilities to know items through language and independently of it. Language, therefore, is the topic of *The Teacher* and explains the structure of the dialogue.[22] The importance of the theory of illumination, and especially of Christ the inner Teacher, shouldn't obscure this fact.

Language, according to Augustine, is a system of *signs*. Signs include a wide range of linguistic and nonlinguistic items: words, inscriptions, gestures, symbols, icons, statues, flags. Three elements are involved: the *sign*, which may be any sort of object; the semantic relation of *signifying*, which is what a sign does, roughly like our notion of meaning; and its *significate*, which is the item signified by the sign.[23] Therefore, a sign signifies its significate —

22. I have adopted the analysis of the structure of *The Teacher* presented in Crosson [1989]. Augustine's roundabout method — for which he apologizes in 8.21, and which he explains in 12.40 — has pedagogical motivations: his audience must be properly prepared before it can understand and accept the theory of illumination.

23. In Latin as in English there is a tempting word to use in connection with signs: *significatio*, signification. This term is ambiguous, referring either to the property possessed by the sign in virtue of its activity of signifying, or to the significate (or class of significates) of a sign. Augustine

when a word is linked to a thing, the word becomes a sign, the thing its significate; and the linkage is accomplished by the semantic relation of signifying. The paradigm case of signs is proper names: a proper name (sign) names (signifies) its bearer (significate), so that meaning is taken to be a kind of labeling of things.[24]

Augustine's main argument against the information-transference account of teaching is initially posed as a version of the learner's paradox: I cannot know that a sign is a sign unless I know what it signifies — but then I learn nothing from the sign; my knowledge of its significate is presupposed in its being a sign in the first place (*The Teacher* 10.33). Knowledge is derived from things directly. Nor can ostensive definition help us to break out of this paradox, since ostension is equally a conventional sign and so presupposes knowledge. Words can at best prompt us to look for things, from which we derive our knowledge (11.36).

It might be objected that I do learn from others, namely by their reports and their descriptions. Augustine argues that this is mistaken on two counts (11.37). First, what is signified by the words in a narrative account must already be known to us; if not, the words don't enable us to know the things. Second, and more telling, from narrative description all we get is belief rather than knowledge. Hence teaching cannot succeed in conveying knowledge from one person to another, as the information-transference account of teaching holds.

Augustine proposes his theory of illumination and Christ as

---

uses 'signification' in both senses in *The Teacher*. He doesn't define 'signifying' in *The Teacher*, but does so implicitly in *On Christian Doctrine* 2.1.1 (Appendix 10): "A *sign* is a thing that of itself causes something else to enter into thought beyond the appearance it presents to the senses."

24. The attempt to construe meaning solely in terms of naming, using the model of proper names, has serious difficulties. (This is the account Gilbert Ryle derisively called the 'Fido'-Fido account of language: the dog's name 'Fido' picks out the actual dog Fido itself, a claim that works for pets and not much else.) See Burnyeat [1987] and Kirwan [1989], Ch. 3 for a discussion of Augustine's proposal in modern terms. Even Augustine seems to be aware that not all he wants to say can be said with this model in mind, for at one point he introduces an element that looks suspiciously like the *meaning* (intension) of a sign; see the note to *The Teacher* 7.20.55–57.

the Teacher within (11.38–12.40) as an alternative. The test of truth is inside, Augustine argues. What gets conveyed from one person to another are at best putative knowledge-claims that each recipient judges for himself. In items perceived by the senses, we have knowledge when the sensible object itself is present to us.[25] In items perceived by the mind, we look upon these "immediately in the inner light of Truth" and know them. Roughly, each person grasps conceptual truths, to the extent he or she is able, without recourse to experience or external testimony.

Augustine offers several further counterexamples to the information-transference account of teaching, cases in which the speaker is not transferring his thoughts to the hearer: mishearings, deception, slips of the tongue, misunderstandings, and the like. Yet even if we put these cases aside and allow that the speaker's thoughts are known to the hearer, Augustine remarks, the hearer does not thereby learn whether what the speaker has said (or thought) is true. The test of knowledge is still within each person; signs can at best lead to knowledge only of other signs, not of signifiable things that are not signs. Only illumination can serve as the test of truth, which is an essential ingredient in knowledge. Augustine closes his monologue by declaring that his theory of illumination should be self-validating: you can recognize its truth by looking within!

Taken together, *Against the Academicians* and *The Teacher* offer complementary sides of a single extended argument for the possibility of genuine knowledge, one that mattered crucially to Augustine at the beginning of his constructive exploration of platonism and Christianity. They lay the foundation for a new intellectual type of late antiquity: the committed nondogmatic philosopher. But neither Augustine nor his successors could live the life so brilliantly sketched in these early dialogues. The classical world was disintegrating, and it needed people like Augustine

---

25. Augustine is puzzled over the case of 'past sensibles': how can we know things that happened in the past, given that the objects themselves are not present but only their representations are? His tentative answer is that we know past objects *as* past through these (present) representations of them, but this knowledge must be individual. This is an intimation of problems that will be dealt with in the *Confessions*; see O'Daly [1987].

in public life. They were not enough in the end. Augustine died while Hippo, the town of which he was the bishop for nearly forty years, was under siege by the Vandals. It was left to later generations to explore and develop Augustine's account of knowledge, and by then a new conception of (dogmatic) philosophy had arisen.

The texts translated in the Appendices have been selected to illustrate or corroborate features of *Against the Academicians* or *The Teacher*. They are arranged in approximate chronological order of composition. Appendix 1 (*The Happy Life* 1.4) describes Augustine's progress from Manichaeanism to Christianity via skepticism and platonism. Appendix 2 (*The Happy Life* 2.13–16) is the 'missing conclusion' to the discussion in Book 1 of *Against the Academicians*, written, if we are to believe Augustine, between the composition of Book 1 and Books 2–3 of *Against the Academicians*. Appendix 3 (*Letter* 1) was written at the end of 386 and is independent testimony for Augustine's claims about the Academicians' secret platonism. Appendix 4 (*On Dialectic* 5.7–8) is now accepted as a fragment of Augustine's abortive project of writing a textbook series for his new way of life. Written in 387, it reveals an earlier stage of thinking about the theory of signs than is found in *The Teacher*. Appendix 5 (*Confessions* 5.14.25) dates from 397/398 and briefly describes Augustine's relation to skepticism. Appendix 6 (*The Trinity* 15.12.21) is a later treatment of the Academicians (before 419). Appendix 7 (*Enchiridion* 7.20) from 423 and Appendix 8 (*The City of God* 11.26) from 426 are two late treatments of skepticism, the latter containing Augustine's famous anticipation of Descartes with *Si fallor, sum*. Appendix 9 (*On Christian Doctrine* 1.2.2) and Appendix 10 (*On Christian Doctrine* 2.1.1–2.4.5) are part of Augustine's general semiotics and consistent with the theories of *The Teacher*; they were likely written by 397, but the whole text was abandoned and then redrafted in 427. Finally, Appendix 11 (*Revisions* 1.1.1–4) contains Augustine's late reflections on *Against the Academicians*, written in 427/428.

Preface

The Biographical Index contains brief entries for everyone mentioned by name outside of this Preface, including Augustine's interlocutors. I have provided the interested reader with a Recommended Reading list and a Select Bibliography that can be used as starting points for further investigation.

Readers may want to skip the dedicatory sections of *Against the Academicians* the first time through; although they contain much of interest, they obscure the course of the argument. Those who are primarily interested in Augustine's own anti-skeptical arguments will want to concentrate on Book 3, perhaps to the extent of focusing on 3.9.18–3.16.36 above all else. Appendix 6 and Appendix 8 also include anti-skeptical arguments. Arguments over the place of wisdom in the happy life appear in Book 1 and Appendix 2.

Those reading *The Teacher* in conjunction with *Against the Academicians*, or readers who are short of time, may want to pick up Augustine's argument with the discussion of Division [2(*a*)] in 10.29. Material revelant to the history of logic, semantics, and semiotics is discussed in *The Teacher* 1.1–4.7, Appendix 4, and Appendices 9–10.

Autobiographical material is found in *Against the Academicians* 2.2.3–5, Appendix 1, Appendix 5, and Appendix 7.

Each of Augustine's works fits well with other readings: *The Teacher* is well paired with Plato's *Meno*, and *Against the Academicians* can be read in conjunction with selections from Sextus Empiricus or Descartes. Augustine's works can profitably be read against the background of his own writings, especially his *Confessions* and the other dialogues written at Cassiciacum.

I owe more than I can say to Anna Greco, whose criticism, advice, and encouragement have been invaluable at all stages of this project. Many students have also helped me, willingly or otherwise. I first began to work on *The Teacher* with Patrick Barker, Kate Nolan, and Cornel Owesny in a graduate classics course on Augustine. Drafts of my translations have been field-tested in several graduate and undergraduate courses, some of which I have given, others given by my colleagues Calvin Normore and Ivan Boh. The Classics Reading Group at the University of Toronto offered advice and comments on the penultimate version of *The Teacher*. The comments of C.D.C. Reeve on an earlier version of the Introduction were invaluable.

Finally, I owe a debt of gratitude to Brian Rak in particular and Hackett Publishing in general for their patience and flexibility, and for the high critical standards they set. The faults that may remain here are entirely my responsibility.

Remarks on the Translations

When clarification of Augustine's works is called for, I have tried to provide it in his own words, and above all in writings that are roughly contemporary with *Against the Academicians* and *The Teacher*. Hence the early letters and the other dialogues written at Cassiciacum figure prominently in the notes; later works are sometimes adduced to show that Augustine continued to hold an earlier position. I have also tried to supply cultural references that Augustine could take for granted his audience would recognize. All translations are mine.

A work of Augustine's is traditionally subdivided into books, chapters, and sections. *Against the Academicians* consists of three books; *The Teacher*, one. The appropriate numbers are given in the outside margin. Line numbers correspond to the lines of the Latin text — *not* the English translation — and are given in arabic numerals in the outside margin; they are sequential within each chapter. Internal references and cross-references are given in the standard manner to the chapter, section, and line numbers — e.g., 'The Teacher 5.12.40' refers to Chapter 5, Section 12, line 40 of *The Teacher*.

I have rendered certain philosophical terms in a uniform way, a procedure that seems appropriate when the terminology is technical in nature. For *Against the Academicians*, these are words that have to do with assent, doubt, appearance, seeming, and the like:

approbare	to give approval	*consentire*	to consent
assensio	assent	*perceptio*	perception
assentiri	to assent	*percipere*	to perceive
comprehendere	to apprehend	*probabile*	plausible
comprehensio	apprehension	*probare*	to approve
consensio	consent	*verisimile*	truthlike

For *The Teacher* these are words that have to do with semantics, teaching, and memory:

commemorare	to remind	*notitia*	conception
commemoratio	reminding	*ostendere*	to show
demonstrare	to point out	*significare*	to signify
docere	to teach	*significatio*	signification
enuntiare	to enunciate	*significatum*	significate
indicare	to indicate	*valere (vis)*	to mean (meaning)
monstrare	to exhibit	*verbum*	word
nomen	name	*vocabulum*	term
notare	to mark out		

I have made some minor alterations in the translation in the service of having the content match the English. For example, when Augustine refers to the number of syllables of a word in *The Teacher*, I have matched the number of syllables of the English translation rather than the original Latin. Likewise, when his discussion turns on the number of words in a phrase or the ordinal number of a given word, I have given the number corresponding to the English translation. When the act of uttering a word is under discussion, I have given the word uttered in italics and broken it down into syllables. Single and double quotation marks are used in accordance with philosophical conventions, so that when a word or its utterance is mentioned rather than used, it is given in single quotation marks.

Four terms have resisted my efforts to render Augustine's Latin into standard English: 'perception' (*perceptio*), 'truthlike' (*verisimile*), and the pair of 'name' (*nomen*) and 'word' (*verbum*). Each calls for some comment.

First, 'perception' is meant to have cognitive overtones; it has little to do with ordinary sense-perception. It is the sense in which Sherlock Holmes says that he *perceives* that Dr. Watson has been in Afghanistan. We may perceive through our senses, but the relevant faculty here is the intellect. This is the term used for the way things naturally seem to someone — for example, Jones might perceive that the cat is on the mat. (One part of doing this might be to formulate the proposition that the cat is on the mat.) It may even be true that the cat is on the mat. If so, we can say that Jones has perceived a truth. But has he perceived it *as* a truth? This is one of the points debated by the Stoics and the Academicians.

The term 'truthlike' is a literal rendering of *verisimile* (what-is-like-truth). Part of Augustine's argument in *Against the Academicians* turns on this word, as opposed to its synonym 'plausible,' being literally composed of elements indicating that it is like the truth. I have nominalized it as 'the truthlike' and helped myself to the abstract form 'truthlikeness'; all I can plead in my defense is that 'verisimilitude' is hopeless in English, and no other suggestion comes anywhere close.

The pair 'name' and 'word' pose a different sort of problem. They could equally well be translated 'noun' and 'verb,' but no one rendering will do for all contexts, and using different renderings would obscure the fact that Augustine is talking about one and the same thing in different contexts. Since the grammatical categories only emerged later and split off from earlier usage, I have kept to 'name' and 'word' in almost all cases, except when the strain in English is too great — in which case I mention it in a footnote.

Against the Academicians

[Book 1]

[First Dedicatory Introduction]¹

Romanianus—   [1.1.1]

I wish virtue could keep the man who's suited for it away from
bad fortune, the way it keeps bad fortune from taking any man
away from itself! Virtue would then have already set its hands
upon you. It would have declared you to be rightfully its own
and put you in possession of the most secure goods, not allowing   5
you to be a slave to chance, even when chance was favorable.
However, either because we deserve it or because it's necessary
by nature,² it has been ordained that the harbor of wisdom never
gives entry to our divine spirit³ while it is united to our mortal
bodies (a harbor where it would be unmoved by the favorable
and unfavorable winds of fortune), unless good fortune itself, or   10
fortune that merely seems bad, should lead us to this harbor.
Accordingly, we're left with nothing to do for you but pray. With
our prayers to God, Who has these matters as His concern, we
shall, if we can, successfully entreat Him to restore you to yourself — for He will thereby return you to us as well — and to permit your spirit, which has been waiting to take a deep breath for
a long time now, to come forward at last into the fresh air of true 15
freedom.

Perhaps what is commonly referred to as 'fortune' is governed
by some hidden order, and we only call 'chance' those events in

---

1. Augustine's dedicatory introduction to Romanianus is highly rhetorical in character. The dialogue proper begins in 1.2.5.

2. See *Revisions* 1.1.2 (Appendix 11).

3. "Divine spirit": *divinus animus*. See Cicero, *Tusculan Disputations*
5.13.38: "The human spirit has been derived from the Divine Mind and
can be compared with nothing save God Himself, if it be permitted to say
so." Augustine uses the same figure of speech at 1.1.3.65.

the world whose reason and cause are concealed:[4] nothing advantageous or disadvantageous happens in any part that isn't suitable
20   to and in harmony with the totality.[5] Philosophy promises that
this view to which I'm inviting you, elicited from the precepts[6] of
the most fruitful teachings and the farthest removed from the
understanding of the uninitiated, will show itself to its genuine
lovers. Don't belittle yourself, then, when many things unworthy
of your spirit happen to you. If Divine Providence extends all the
25   way to us (and this should hardly be doubted!), then believe me:
it's appropriate that you be treated as you are being treated.

The reason is this.[7] You entered upon this human life, which is
filled with all kinds of errors, with so much natural talent obvious
from your early youth, when the imprint of reason is weak and
faltering, that I'm always lost in admiration. Riches were show-
ered upon you from every side. They began to engulf your youth-
ful spirit, leading you to the eager pursuit of whatever appeared
30   beautiful and worthwhile in their seductive whirlpools. When
you were practically drowning, you were snatched away by those
winds of fortune that are considered unfavorable.

[1.1.2]   Yet if the enthusiastic applause of the Circus always came to
you for providing our citizens with exhibitions of bears and other
35   sights never seen there before; if you were praised to the skies by
the united and unanimous cries of foolish men (of whom there is
a huge throng!); if nobody dared to be unfriendly to you; if munic-

---

4. Augustine takes this suggestion from Cicero, *Academica* 1.7.29: "The
[followers of Antiochus] call it 'fortune' when many operations are
unforeseen and unexpected by us because of their obscurity and our ignorance of the causes." Augustine later repented of his use of 'fortune' at all,
citing this passage in particular: see *Revisions* 1.1.2 (Appendix 11).

5. See Plotinus, *Enneads* 3.2.3.13. The whole of *Enneads* 3.2 is known as
the "Treatise on Providence" (Περὶ προνοίας). Augustine refers to it
explicitly in *The City of God* 10.14.

6. "Precepts": *oracula*, a favorite word used to talk about the Bible,
divine revelation and inspiration, the Christian mysteries, and the like.

7. The 'reason' begins here and ends in the first paragraph of 1.1.3:
Romanianus should be grateful for the good fortune that saved him from
the seductive whirlpool of indulgence, and also for the bad fortune that
allowed people to approach him about true happiness and to open him to
philosophy.

ipal plaques[8] designated you in bronze as the patron not only of
the citizens but also of the neighboring peoples; if they erected
statues of you, poured honors on you, and added privileges to   40
increase your civic position greater than is customary; if the finest
delicacies were provided liberally at your daily banquets; if someone were confidently to ask you for whatever he needed, or even
for whatever pleasures he longed for, and have confidence in
obtaining it; if many things were lavished upon people who didn't   45
even ask for them; if your household, carefully and faithfully
looked after by your people, proved itself to be adequate for such
great expenditures; if you were meanwhile enjoying life in the
most exquisite and pleasurable of buildings, in the splendor of the
Baths, in those games of chance that an upright man does not dis-
dain, in hunting expeditions, and at banquets; if you were spoken
of by your clients, by the citizens, and finally by the people gener-   50
ally as the most cultured, most generous, most refined, most fortunate man — well, then I ask you *who*, Romanianus! Who would
dare to mention another happy life to you, one that alone is the
happy life? Who could persuade you that not only were you not
happy, but that you were especially unhappy in seeming to your-   55
self not unhappy at all? How rapidly you have come to realize this
now, with the many great misfortunes you have endured! You
don't need to be convinced by examples of other people how fleet-
ing and fragile and full of misfortunes are all the things mortal
men think of as goods, since now you have had thorough experience of them in this regard, and, as a result, we can convince oth-   60
ers by your case.

Therefore, that divine element in you, whatever it may be —   [1.1.3]
the element because of which you have always sought after what
is fitting and worthwhile; because of which you have preferred to
be generous rather than wealthy; as a result of which you have
never wanted to be more powerful rather than to be more just; the
reason you have never given in to adversities and improprieties
— that element, I say, which has been lulled to sleep by the leth-   65
argy of this life, a hidden Providence has decided to awaken by
the various hard reverses you have suffered.

8. A Thagaste inscription [COR]NELIVS ROMANIANVS survives
(*Corpus inscriptionum latinarum* tom.8 suppl. #17226), likely one of the
"plaques" Augustine mentions here.

Wake up! Wake up, I beg you! Believe me, you'll be grateful
that the gifts of this world have hardly entranced you at all with
70 the successes by which they ensnare the unwary. They tried to
catch me while I was daily singing their praises, until the pain in
my chest compelled me to cast aside my puffed-up profession and
to flee to the bosom of philosophy.[9] Now philosophy nourishes
and sustains me in that retirement we have so much hoped for. It
has freed me completely from the superstition into which I had
75 thrown you headlong with myself.[10] Philosophy teaches, and
teaches truly, that nothing whatsoever that is discerned by mortal
eyes, or that any of the senses[11] comes into contact with, should be
worshipped. Instead, everything of the sort must be despised.[12]

9. Augustine taught rhetoric in Milan before his withdrawal to Cassiciacum. He tells us that he was prompted to resign his post as court rhetorician in Milan because of chest and throat trouble, though there were
other reasons, philosophical and religious, as well — a fact Augustine
explicitly notes in *Confessions* 9.5.13. See Augustine's remarks about his
delicate health at 3.7.15.18–26, at *The Happy Life* 1.4.105–7 (Appendix 1),
and in *Confessions* 9.2.4: "During the summer [of 386], as a result of exces-
sive labor in teaching literature, my lungs had begun to weaken. It was
difficult to breathe; pains in my chest were symptoms of the lesion; it prevented me from speaking more clearly or at greater length." In *On Order*
1.2.5.36 Augustine cites pain in his stomach (!) as the cause of his retirement, not respiratory problems, leading some scholars to question the
veracity of his reports and others to suppose that he was a hypochondriac.

10. The "superstition" is Manichaeanism, to which Augustine had converted Romanianus, still an adherent when Augustine wrote this dialogue in 386.

11. Augustine later held that this should be emended to "other senses *of
our mortal body*": see *Revisions* 1.1.2 (Appendix 11).

12. Augustine gives a lucid explanation of this platonic claim in a letter
written to Zenobius (the dedicatee of Augustine's *On Order*) shortly after
the completion of *Against the Academicians* in 386 (*Letter* 2.1): "We have correctly agreed, I believe, that nothing our bodily senses come into contact
with can remain unchanged for even a single moment, but rather passes
away, flowing along, preserving nothing at present — that is, to speak
plainly, it does not exist. Therefore, the true divine philosophy cautions us
to restrain and calm our love for these things, a love that is terribly destruc-
tive and abounding in penalties, so that even while the mind is involved
with the body it may intensely and ardently pursue those things that are
always in the same state and do not please with a transient beauty."

Philosophy promises that it will display the true and hidden God, and now and again deigns to show us a glimpse of Him through the bright clouds, as it were. 80

Our Licentius enthusiastically shares this way of life with me. [1.1.4] He has so wholeheartedly turned toward philosophy and away from the seductive pleasures of youth that I confidently dare to propose him as a model for his father to imitate. No age has any reason to complain that it is excluded from the breasts of philosophy![13] Though I'm well acquainted with your thirst for philoso- 85 phy, I wanted to send along a foretaste to incite you to cling to it and suckle the more eagerly. I implore you that I do not hope in vain, and that this will be most agreeable and, I might say, an enticement to you.

I have for this reason sent you a written version of a debate between Trygetius and Licentius. Military service had taken 90 Trygetius away for a little while, as if to relieve him of any distaste for studies. It has returned to us one who is eager and avid for the high and noble arts. Just a few days had gone by after we came to live in the countryside [at Cassiciacum], and, while I was exhort- 95 ing and encouraging them to their studies, I saw that they were prepared beyond what I had hoped for, and enthusiastic as well. I wanted to test what they could do at their age, especially since Cicero's *Hortensius* seemed already to have largely won them over to philosophy. Therefore, having employed a stenographer *so that the winds might not blow away our labor*,[14] I didn't allow anything to 100 be lost. You're going to read in this book, then, the issues and views discussed by these two young men, along with my words and Alypius's.

[10 November 386]

When at my invitation we were all gathered in a place that [1.2.5] appeared to be suitable for this purpose, I said: "Do you have any doubt that we ought to know the truth?"

"Hardly!" said Trygetius. The others showed by their expressions that they agreed with him.

"Well," I said, "if we can be happy while not apprehending 5

---

13. Augustine uses the same image in *Letter* 1.3 (Appendix 3).

14. Vergil, *Aeneid* 9.312.

the truth, do you consider the apprehension of the truth to be necessary?"

At this point Alypius interposed: "I think it's more prudent for me to be a referee in this investigation. Since it has been arranged for me to go into the city,[15] it's appropriate that I be relieved of the
10 burden of taking up either side. I can also pass along to another the role of referee more easily than the role of defendant, for either side. Accordingly, from this time onwards you shouldn't expect anything from me on behalf of either side."

When all had granted Alypius's request and I had repeated my question, Trygetius said: "*Surely we wish to be happy.*[16] If we can
15 reach this condition without the truth, we don't need to search for the truth."

"What's this?" I said. "Do you believe that we can be happy even though we haven't found the truth?"

Then Licentius ventured: "We can if we're searching for the truth."[17]

I solicited the view of the others by nodding my head. Navigius
20 said: "I'm impressed by what Licentius has said. Perhaps to live in the search for the truth can itself be to live happily."

"Then define," Trygetius said, "what the happy life is, so that I may gather from your definition what would be suitable to say in reply."

I said: "What else do you think living happily is, if it isn't living in accordance with what is best in man?"

25 "Let me not toss words around loosely," he replied. "I think you ought to define for me what that best element is."

I answered: "Who would doubt that what is best in man is anything but the ruling part of his spirit? Anything else there is in man ought to comply with it. Furthermore, this part — lest you

15. Alypius leaves for Milan at 1.3.8.41–42, to return for the discussion reported in the later books.

16. Cicero, *Hortensius* frag. 36 (Müller). Cicero alludes to this view in *Tusculan Disputations* 5.10.28. Augustine took it to be self-evident: see *The Teacher* 13.46.25–27 and *The Trinity* 13.4.7.

17. Cicero, *Academica* 2.41.127: "There is delight in the mere investigation of matters that are very important and very obscure at the same time, and, if something strikes us that seems truthlike, our spirit is filled with a pleasure that is supremely human."

demand another definition — can be called 'mind' or 'reason.'[18] If   30
this isn't clear to you, ask yourself how you would define either
the happy life or what is best in man."

"I agree," he replied.

"What then?" I said. "Let's return to the case at hand. Does it   [1.2.6]
seem to you that anyone can live happily if he's only searching for
the truth and hasn't found it?"

"I repeat my view," Trygetius replied; "it hardly seems so."[19]

"What's your opinion?" I said to the others.   35

Here Licentius volunteered: "It certainly seems so to me. Our
ancestors, for example, whom we agree to have been wise and
happy, lived well and happily for the sole reason that they were
searching for the truth."[20]

"I'm grateful," I stated, "that you have appointed me a referee
with Alypius.[21] I had already started to envy him, I admit. Since,   40
therefore, it seems to one of you that the happy life can consist in
the mere search for truth and to the other only in finding the truth,
and Navigius indicated a little while ago that he wants to move
over to your side, Licentius, I'm eagerly watching what kind of
defenders of your views you can prove yourselves to be. The sub-

18. Augustine probably derives this definition from Cicero, *Republic*
1.38.60: "If there is any regal power in the spirits of men, it should be the
governance of a single element, namely reason (*consilium*), for this is the
best part of the spirit." Augustine means for this definition to be uncon-
troversial wisdom common to all the philosophical schools. Plato and
Aristotle assert this to be the nature of the happy life, each in his own way.
Furthermore, in 1.4.9.85–86 a life in accordance with reason is said to be
one lived in accord with nature (a Stoic commonplace for the good life).
In *Revisions* 1.1.2 (Appendix 11), Augustine regrets that he didn't define
the happy life as one lived in accordance with God.

19. Trygetius has not explicitly stated this, but it follows from his initial
response to Augustine's question at 1.2.5.3–4, so that he is "repeating" his
first answer.

20. See Cicero, *Academica* 2.41.128: "Your wise man and ours are both
investigating these matters [in physics], but your wise man does so in
order to assent, believe, and assert, whereas our wise man does so in
order to be afraid of recklessly forming opinions and to hold that all goes
well with him if in matters of this kind he discover something truthlike."

21. Alypius was appointed referee at 1.2.5.7–12, but Augustine's
appointment as referee hasn't been mentioned previously.

45   ject is important and deserves a careful discussion."

"If it's an important subject," exclaimed Licentius, "it calls for important men!"

"Don't search," I replied, "especially in this country-house, for something difficult to find anywhere in the world. Instead, explain why the opinion you have stated — not carelessly, I think — seems to you to be so. When the most important subjects are
50   investigated by insignificant men, they typically make these men important!"

[1.3.7]   "Since I see that you're trying your best to get us to argue the question with one another," Licentius ventured, "which I'm sure you want for some good reason, I ask: why can't someone who searches for the truth be happy, even if he were never to find it?"[22]

5   "Because," replied Trygetius, "we hold the happy man to be a wise man, perfect in all matters. Anyone who is still searching isn't perfect. Therefore, I don't see at all how you can assert that he is happy."

Licentius asked: "Does the authority of our ancestors carry any weight with you?"

"Not of all of them," answered Trygetius.

"Which of them, then?"

"Obviously, the authority of those who were wise."

10   Then Licentius said: "Doesn't Carneades seem wise to you?"

"I'm not a Greek!" Trygetius said. "I don't know who this Carneades was."

"Well then, what do you think of our own Cicero?" asked Licentius.

After Trygetius had been silent for a while, he replied: "Cicero was a wise man."

15   "His view on this matter, therefore, has some weight with you?"

"Yes."

"Then listen to what it is, for I think it has gotten away from you. Cicero held that a person searching for the truth is happy,

---

22. In *The Happy Life* 4.25, Augustine argues that the wise man is not made unhappy by the presence of evils he cannot avoid, and his happiness consists in doing what he does "on the basis of some precept of virtue or divine law of wisdom."

even if he hasn't been able to arrive at the discovery of it."[23]

"Where did Cicero say this?" asked Trygetius.

"Doesn't everyone know," Licentius responded, "that Cicero
emphatically declared that man cannot perceive[24] anything and   20
that the only thing left for the wise man to do is to search for the
truth carefully? If the wise man assented to uncertain matters
then, even if they perhaps were to be true, he couldn't be free from
error, and this is the greatest fault in a wise man. Consequently, if
we must believe that the wise man is necessarily happy and that   25
the perfect employment of wisdom is the mere search for the
truth, why do we hesitate to believe that the happy life can itself
be achieved as such by the very search for the truth?"

At that point Trygetius asked: "Is it at all permitted to return to   [1.3.8]
points that have been conceded carelessly?"

Here I declared: "People who are stirred into debating to give   30
a childish display of their cleverness rather than by any desire to
discover the truth typically don't allow this request. Yet I not only
grant it (especially since you still need to be nurtured and
instructed), I also want you to take it as a rule that you must return
to those points needing discussion that have been conceded incau-
tiously."

"I think there is no little progress in philosophy," Licentius   35
remarked, "when a disputant despises victory in comparison with
the discovery of the just and the true. Therefore, I freely abide by
your rules and views. I permit Trygetius to return to what he
thinks he has conceded carelessly — for this issue falls within my
rights."[25]

Alypius then interrupted, saying: "You yourselves realize with   40
me that it isn't yet time for the powers of the referee's role I have
undertaken. But my trip, which has been arranged for some time
now, forces me to break away. My fellow-referee will therefore not
refuse a doubling of his power, taking over my job as well, until

23. Cicero, *Hortensius* frag. 101 (Müller).

24. The term 'perceive' is used here much the way Sherlock Holmes
used it in exclaiming, upon first meeting Dr. Watson, "You have been in
Afghanistan, I perceive!" To perceive something in this technical sense is
to have an immediate cognitive grasp of it. See the Notes on the Translation.

25. Cfr. Cicero, *Hortensius* frag. 60 (Müller).

my return. I see that your debate is going to go on for a long time!"

45   After Alypius had gone, Licentius asked: "What have you conceded carelessly? Tell us!"

Trygetius replied: "I carelessly granted that Cicero was a wise man."

"So Cicero was *not* a wise man? The one who began philosophy in the Latin language and brought it to perfection?"

"Even if I concede that Cicero is a wise man," said Trygetius, "I still don't approve all his views."

50   "Well, you need to refute many other views of his not to seem impudent in rejecting the one in question now!"

"What if I'm prepared to affirm that this is the only point he hadn't judged correctly? What matters to you, I think, is only the weight of the reasons I bring in to support what I claim ought to be maintained."

55   "Go ahead," said Licentius. "What do I dare to venture against someone who declares that he opposes Cicero?"

[1.3.9]   At this point Trygetius said: "I want you, as our referee, [Augustine], to pay attention to the way you defined the happy life above. You said that the person who lives according to the part of his spirit that properly commands the rest is surely happy

60   (1.2.5.26–30). And you, Licentius, I want you now to concede to me — for I've now cast off the yoke of authority in accordance with the freedom that philosophy above all else offers to secure for us — I want you to concede that the person who is still searching for the truth isn't perfect."

After a lengthy silence, Licentius replied: "I do not concede this."

65   "Please explain why!" said Trygetius. "I'm ready, and I'm dying to hear how it's possible for a man to be perfect while he's still searching for the truth!"

Licentius answered: "I admit that someone who hasn't gotten all the way to his goal isn't perfect. I think that God alone, or

70   maybe the human soul once it has abandoned the dark prison that is the body, knows the truth![26] Man's goal, though, is to search perfectly for the truth. We're searching for someone who is perfect

26. The description of the soul being 'imprisoned' in the body here is derived from Vergil, *Aeneid* 6.734. The theme is a commonplace in Platonic thought, derived from the spurious *Alcibiades I*, but with some

but still a man."

"Then man can't be happy," Trygetius asserted. "How could he be, since he can't attain what he desires so greatly? Yet man can live happily if he can live according to the part of his spirit that by right should rule in man (1.2.5.23–31). Therefore, he can find the truth. Otherwise, he should come to his senses and not desire the truth, to avoid the necessity of being unhappy because he hasn't been able to attain it."[27]

"This *is* human happiness," responded Licentius, "to search for the truth perfectly! This is to get to a goal we can't go beyond. Therefore, anyone who searches for the truth less insistently than he should doesn't get to the goal of man. Anyone who takes pains to find the truth, to the extent that a man can and should, is happy — even if he were not to find it. He's doing everything he can do, as he is fit by nature. If he fails to find the truth, it's because nature didn't equip him to find it.[28] Finally, since man must be either happy or unhappy, isn't it sheer madness to say that someone is unhappy who spends his days and nights, as far as he can, searching for the truth? Thus, he'll be happy.

"Next," Licentius continued, "the definition [of the happy life] supports me well, I think. If someone is happy, as is the person who lives according to the part of his spirit that properly governs the rest (this part is called 'reason'), then I ask: doesn't anyone searching for the truth perfectly live according to reason? If this is ridiculous, why do we hesitate to call a man happy in virtue of the mere search for the truth?"

"It seems to me," responded Trygetius, "that anyone in error neither lives according to reason nor is happy at all. Someone who is always searching and not finding anything is in error. Accordingly, you need to show one of two things: either (*a*) someone in error can be happy; or (*b*) anyone who is searching for what he never finds isn't in error."

"The happy man can't be in error," Licentius stated. Then, after

75

80

85

90

95

[1.4.10]

5

---

justification: see *Cratylus* 400C, *Gorgias* 493A, *Phaedo* 82E and 114B-C, and *Phaedrus* 250C.

27. Kirwan [1989], pp. 17–20 discusses the argument given here by Trygetius.

28. Cicero, *Academica* 2.10.32: "Is that our fault? Blame nature for having hidden truth away completely — 'in an abyss,' as Democritus says."

he had been silent for a while, he said: "Well, a man isn't in error when he's searching, because he's searching so as not to be in error."

Trygetius countered: "He's searching so as not to be in error, but he's in error when he doesn't find it. You thought it counted in your favor that he doesn't want to be in error — as though no one were in error against his will, or as though anyone at all were in error except unwillingly!"

After Licentius had hesitated for a while about what to say in reply, I interposed: "You need to define what error is. You can see its confines more easily now that you've entered into it deeply."[29]

"I'm not suited to define anything," said Licentius, "although it's easier to define error than to confine it."

"I'll define it!" Trygetius declared. "It's easy for me — because of the strength of my position rather than any cleverness of mine, to be sure. To be in error is always to be searching and never to find."

"For my part," Licentius asserted, "if I could refute that definition with any ease at all, I wouldn't have failed in defending my position a long time ago. Either the subject is difficult in itself, or it appears to be so to me. So I petition you to postpone the question until tomorrow morning if I'm unable to come up with anything to say in reply today, once I've thought it over carefully."

I thought that this petition should be granted, with no dissent from the others. We got up to walk around, and Licentius was transfixed in thought while we talked about many different things among ourselves. When he realized how fruitless his thoughts were, he chose to give his mind a rest and to mix in with our conversation. Later, when evening came, they returned to the same debate. I imposed moderation and persuaded them to allow it to be postponed to another day. Then we went to the baths.

[11 November 386]

[1.4.11]   On the following day, once we had sat down together, I said:

---

29. The ambiguity in Augustine's final remark is present in the Latin: does he mean that Licentius has a better theoretical understanding of error than before, or that Licentius is now in the midst of errors (so he can have a better look at them)?

"Carry on with what you started yesterday."

"Unless I'm mistaken," replied Licentius, "we postponed the debate at my request, since the definition of 'error' was difficult for me."

I said: "You're clearly not in error on this point! I sincerely hope this will be a good omen for you of what follows."[30]

"Then listen," Licentius said, "to what I would have said yesterday, too, had you not intervened. Error seems to me to be the approval of a falsehood as a truth.[31] Now anyone who believes that the truth is always to be sought doesn't fall afoul of this [definition] in any way. After all, someone who doesn't approve anything can't approve a falsehood, and so he can't be in error. Yet he can easily be happy.

"We have an example even without going very far afield. If we were allowed to live each new day as we were allowed to live yesterday, I see no reason we should hesitate to call ourselves happy. We lived in great mental tranquility, keeping the spirit free from every stain of the body; and, far removed from the raging flames of desire, we were taking pains, as far as man is allowed, to cultivate reason[32] — that is, to live according to the divine part of the spirit — and this we agreed yesterday was by definition the happy life (1.2.5.23–31). Yet so far as I know, we didn't *find* anything. Instead, we only searched for the truth. Hence man can reach the happy life with the mere search for the truth, even if he never finds it.

"As for your definition — see how easily it is put aside by our common concept [of error]! You said that to be in error is always to be searching and never to find (1.4.10.17–18). What if a man weren't searching for anything and were asked, for instance, whether it now is daytime, and he straightaway carelessly forms the opinion that it is night and gives that as his answer? Doesn't

30. Augustine regretted his use of 'omen' here: *Revisions* 1.1.2 (Appendix 11).

31. The definition of 'error' given here has affinities with Cicero's remark that to approve falsehoods as though they were truths is "supremely disgraceful": *pro veris probare falsa turpissima est* (*Academica* 2.20.66).

32. Augustine's language here is reminiscent of Vergil, *Aeneid* 6.46. See also the note to 1.3.9.70.

he seem to you to be in error? Your definition, then, doesn't include even this horrible kind of error.[33]

"What if it also includes people who aren't in error? Can any definition be worse? For example, if someone were searching for Alexandria and set out to travel to it along a direct road, you can-
60   not, I take it, call him in error. What if he spends a long time on that very road, hindered by various causes, and death comes upon him on the way — hasn't he always searched and never found, and still was not in error?"

"He wasn't *always* searching," replied Trygetius.

[1.4.12]   "You're right," said Licentius, "and your remark is a good one, for
65   then your definition is completely irrelevant to the matter at hand. After all, I wasn't the one to say that the person who *always* searches for the truth is happy. This can't even happen! First, because a man doesn't always exist. Second, because a man can't search for the truth when he begins to exist, since his age prevents him.

"Alternatively, if you think by 'always' we mean that he
70   doesn't allow any time to be lost during which he could be search-ing, you should go back to the case of the road to Alexandria. Sup-pose that a man sets out to start along that road when his age and occupation allow him to do so, and, as I described before, he dies before arriving at his destination, though he never leaves that
75   road. Surely you'll be greatly in error if this man seems to you to have been in error! Yet at every time he could, neither did he stop searching, nor was he able to find what he had set out to find.

"Consequently, if my account is true and according to it the man who is searching for the truth perfectly is not in error even though he doesn't find it, and he is happy because he lives accord-
80   ing to reason — whereas your definition has been shown to be useless and, even if it weren't useless, I wouldn't be obliged to care about it further, given that my position has been adequately upheld by my definition — why then, I ask you, has the question between us not yet been resolved?"

[1.5.13]   Trygetius said: "Don't you grant that wisdom is *the right way of life*?"[34]

33. Because the man forms his opinion "straightaway" (though "care-lessly"), he does no searching, and hence cannot be said to be searching but not finding the truth.

34. Cicero, *Tusculan Disputations* 1.1.1: "Since the study of wisdom,

"Yes," replied Licentius, "there's no doubt about it. Yet I still want you to define 'wisdom' for me, to know whether what it seems to be for me is the same for you."

"Does it seem to be defined inadequately by the question you 5 were just now asked? You've already conceded what I was after. If I'm not mistaken, the right way of life is called 'wisdom.'"

Then Licentius exclaimed: "Nothing seems more laughable to me than that definition!"

"Maybe," responded Trygetius, "but please be careful to think before you laugh! Nothing is more contemptible than laughter that itself deserves laughter."

"Well," said the other, "don't you admit that death is the con- 10 trary of life?"

"Yes."

"Then a 'way of life' seems to me no more than a way along which anyone sets forth to avoid death."[35]

Trygetius agreed.

"Therefore, if any traveler who avoids a byway he has heard is filled with bandits by setting out to go along the direct way, and 15 thereby avoids being killed — hasn't he then followed the way of life, and indeed the right way of life? Yet nobody calls this 'wisdom'! How, then, is every right way of life 'wisdom'?"

"I granted that wisdom was a right way of life, but not the only one."

"Well, a definition shouldn't include anything irrelevant. So, if 20 you please, define it again. What does wisdom seem to you to be?"

Trygetius was silent for a while, and then said: "Look, if you've [1.5.14] decided never to end this, I'll define it again. Wisdom is the right way that leads to the truth."

"This definition is refuted in a similar fashion," Licentius countered. "For instance, Aeneas was told by his mother:[36]

Now set forth and direct your step as the way leads you. 25

---

which is called 'philosophy,' contains the rationale and system of all the arts that pertain to the right way of life . . ."

35. Here and in the exchange that follows, Licentius is taking advantage of Trygetius's description of wisdom as a kind of 'way' or 'path' (or 'road'): *via*.

36. Vergil, *Aeneid* 1.401.

When Aeneas followed this way, he arrived at what he had been told about. That is to say, he arrived at the truth. Maintain, if you like, that where he placed his foot as he was walking can be called 'wisdom'!

"However," Licentius continued, "it's silly for me to try to get
30   rid of your account, since nothing helps my position more. You declared that wisdom isn't the truth itself, but the way that leads to it. Therefore, anyone using this way surely uses wisdom, and anyone using wisdom must be wise; hence the man who searches for the truth perfectly, even if he hasn't yet arrived at it, will be
35   wise. In my opinion, the way that leads to the truth is best understood as the diligent search for the truth. So, using this way alone, he'll already be wise. Now no wise man is unhappy. But every man is either unhappy or happy. Hence not only the finding of the truth but also the search for it will by itself make him a happy man."

[1.5.15]   Trygetius said wryly: "I deserved these things to happen to me
40   when I boldly agreed with my opponent on a side issue! — as though I were a great definer, or think anything more useless in arguments! What will be the end of it, if I again should like you to
45   define something, and then demand that all the words of this self-same definition be defined one by one, and likewise what follows upon them, pretending that I understood nothing? What is so plain that I'm not within my rights to insist that it be defined, if a definition of wisdom is rightfully demanded of me? Has nature marked out a more evident notion in our minds of any word than
50   it has of 'wisdom'? Yet — I don't know how — when this notion floats away from the harbor of our mind and unfurls its sails of words, so to speak, a thousand sophistries immediately threaten it with shipwreck. So let there be no demand for a definition of 'wisdom,' or let our referee be good enough to step down and come to its defense!"

I postponed the debate to another day at that point, since the
55   night was already interfering with the transcription, and I saw that a large topic had come up that needed to be gone through as though from the start. We had started to debate when the sun had already begun to set, since we were occupied for almost the whole day on the one hand with putting the affairs of the farm in order, and on the other hand in reviewing the first book of Vergil's *Aeneid*.

[12 November 386]

When it was daylight again — for matters had been arranged the day before so that there would be a good deal of free time — the business to be gone through was undertaken immediately. I said: "Trygetius, yesterday you asked me to step down from the role of referee and come to the defense of wisdom. As if wisdom faced any opponent in your conversation! Or, no matter who its defender, it were to be in such distress as to be forced to plead for greater support![37] The only issue that has arisen for you debaters to look into is what wisdom is. Neither of you is opposed to wisdom here, since you each desire it. Trygetius, if you think you've failed at defining 'wisdom,' you nevertheless shouldn't abandon the rest of the defense of your view for this reason. [1.6.16]

"Therefore, you'll get nothing from me but a definition of 'wisdom.' It's not mine, and it's not new. It was given by our worthy predecessors. I'm surprised you didn't remember it. You aren't hearing this for the first time now: *wisdom is the knowledge of human and divine matters.*"[38]

I thought that after this definition Licentius would need time to search for something to say. Yet he immediately replied: "Then why, I ask you, don't we call 'wise' that disreputable man who indulges himself with countless prostitutes, as we well know? I'm talking about Albicerius![39] For many years at Carthage he gave surprising yet reliable answers to those who consulted him. I could remind you of innumerable cases, but I'm talking to people who are already acquainted with him, and a few cases are sufficient for my purposes." [1.6.17]

Now, turning to me, Licentius continued: "When a spoon

37. A similar response is given by Cicero, *Academica* 2.11.36: "This is enough on the subject of perception; if someone wants to upset the things that have been said, truth will easily defend itself, even if we absent ourselves."

38. Cicero, *Tusculan Disputations* 4.26.57: "It may be said very briefly that wisdom is the knowledge of human and divine matters and acquaintance with the cause of each of them." The same definition is offered by Cicero in *On Moral Duties* 2.2.5: "Wisdom has been defined by the old philosophers as the knowledge of divine and human matters, and of the causes by which these matters are controlled."

39. Nothing else is known about Albicerius.

25   couldn't be found anywhere in the house and I contacted Albice-
      rius about it at your instructions, he not only told me promptly
      and accurately what was missing but also named its owner and
      where it was hidden, did he not?

          "Here's another case where I was present. We were going to see
      Albicerius, and the boy who was carrying our coins stole a certain
30   number of them. Before Albicerius had seen the selfsame coins or
      had heard from us how much had been brought for him, he com-
      manded the boy to count out the full sum, and before our eyes
      forced the boy to return what he had taken. I pass over the fact that
      his reply to what he was consulted about was completely true!

[1.6.18]   "What about the case you yourself told us about, the one that
      regularly caused Flaccianus, a man of distinction and learning, to
35   wonder?[40] When Flaccianus was talking about buying a farm, he
      brought the affair to that diviner for him to say, if he could, what
      he had been doing. Albicerius immediately not only described the
      nature of the business but also gave the name of the farm — at
      which Flaccianus gave a loud cry of surprise, since it was so pecu-
40   liar that he himself scarcely remembered it!

          "I can't recount the next case without amazement. A friend of
      ours, one of your disciples, wanted to annoy Albicerius by inso-
      lently demanding that Albicerius say what he was thinking to
      himself about. Albicerius replied to him that he was thinking of a
      line of Vergil. He was dumbfounded and couldn't deny it. He
45   went on to ask just which line of Vergil it was. Albicerius, who had
      scarcely ever seen a grammarian's school while passing by one,
      recited the line fluently and confidently without any hesitation.

          "Were they then *not* human matters about which he was con-
      sulted? Or did he give such reliable and true answers to those con-
      sulting him *without* knowledge of divine matters?

50   "Each supposition is ridiculous. 'Human matters' are nothing
      but the things that pertain to men — for example: silver, coins, a
      farm, and finally even a thought itself. And wouldn't anyone be
      correct in thinking matters 'divine' through which divination
      itself is possible for a man?

          "Therefore, Albicerius was wise, if we grant in accordance with

---

40. This is likely the same Flaccianus as the man mentioned in *The City
of God* 18.23, whom Augustine there describes as "a man of ready eloquence and profound learning," proconsul in Africa in 393.

the definition that wisdom is the knowledge of human and divine 55
matters."

I then replied:[41] "First, I don't call anything 'knowledge' where [1.7.19]
the person who professes it is sometimes mistaken. Knowledge
doesn't consist merely in the matters that are apprehended.
Instead, it consists in the fact that they are apprehended in such a
way that nobody should be in error about it or vacillate when
pressed by any opponents. Accordingly, some philosophers have 5
said most truly that knowledge can be found in no one save the
wise man: what the wise man maintains and follows he should
hold not only without qualification but also steadfastly.[42] We
know that Albicerius, whom you mentioned, often said many
falsehoods. I've found this out not only from the accounts of others, but, being present on one occasion, I perceived it for myself. 10
Shall I then say that he has knowledge, though he has often said
falsehoods? I wouldn't even say that he has knowledge if he had
said *truths* with hesitation!

"You may take what I've said as my opinion of haruspices,
augurs, astrologers, and oneiromancers[43] — or come up with a

41. See the textual notes for the ascription of this lengthy reply, extend-
ing to 1.8.22.16, to Augustine rather than Trygetius.

42. "What the wise man maintains and follows he should hold not only
without qualification but also steadfastly": *qui non modo perfectum habere
debet id, quod tuetur et sequitur, verum etiam inconcussum tenere.* Augustine
derives this idea from Cicero, *Academica* 2.9.27: "Hence it can't be doubted
that no decision by a wise man can be false. Nor is it sufficient that it not
be false. It must also be stable and fixed and established: no argument can
disturb it." To know something is to know *why* it is the case, to grasp an
account of it — the classical explication of the requirement that knowledge be justified true belief. The idea is ultimately Socratic in origin: see
Greco [1992], Ch. 1.

43. Haruspices tried to foretell the future by inspecting the internal
organs of sacrificial animals, among other methods. Augurs were pagans
who had the job of reading from signs (usually involving birds) whether
the gods approved or disapproved of a certain resolution or course of
action. Astrologers are still with us. Oneiromancers study dreams, using
them as guides to action and as means to foretell the future. Seers, mentioned in the next paragraph, all "speak from the mind of another" in acting as mediums, since they are thought to be possessed by a demon or
another spirit who speaks through them.

15   man of this type, if you can, who upon consultation never hesi-
      tated about his replies and in the end never gave false answers.
          "I don't think I need to spend any time on seers, who speak
      from the mind of another.

[1.7.20]   "Next, although I grant you that 'human matters' are things
20   that pertain to men, do you hold anything to be ours that chance
      can give to us or snatch away from us? Well, when we talk about
      the knowledge of human matters, are we talking about that by
      which anyone knows how many or what kind of farms we have,
      or how much gold or silver, or even what poem written by others
25   we're thinking about? Knowledge of human matters is that which
      knows the light of prudence, the splendor of moderation, the
      strength of courage, the sanctity of justice. These are the things we
      dare to call truly our own, without any fear of fortune.[44] Believe
      me: if that fellow Albicerius had learned these things, he wouldn't
      have lived so extravagantly and disgracefully!

          "Furthermore, I don't think the fact that Albicerius told the
30   man who consulted him what line of verse he was thinking to
      himself about should be counted among the things that are ours.
      I don't mean to deny that worthwhile studies are fit to be pos-
      sessed by our mind in some fashion. Yet we all admit that even
      ignorant people can recite and deliver other men's verses. When
35   such things come up in our memory, then, it's no surprise if they
      can be sensed by some vile animals of the air that are called
      'demons.'[45] I don't know in what mysterious way, far beyond the
      reach of our senses, this happens. I grant that demons can outstrip
      us in the keenness and subtlety of their senses, but I deny that they
40   outstrip us in reason. If we wonder at the little bee flying from
      someplace to where its honey is deposited, using some unknown
      sagacity that surpasses man's, are we thereby bound to put it
      ahead of us or at least on the same level?

[1.7.21]   "I would, therefore, think more of your Albicerius if, when he
      was questioned by someone who wanted to learn, he had taught
45   him versification — or, when invited by one of his clients, imme-
      diately composed his own verses on some subject that was pro-

---

44. See 1.1.1.1–6 and the discussion in 3.2.2–4 below.

45. Augustine's point is incomplete. He finishes it in the next paragraph:
these airborne demons, once they have sensed someone's thoughts, pass
them to another person.

posed to him. The selfsame Flaccianus often said this, as you usually remind us, because, with the great grandeur of his mind, he ridiculed and scorned that kind of divination and attributed it to some contemptible little demon or other — so he said — and Albicerius usually gave his replies once prompted and inspired by this 'spirit.'[46] Flaccianus, that learned man, used to ask those filled with wonder at such replies whether Albicerius could teach grammar or music or geometry. Well, didn't anyone who knew Albicerius admit that he was completely ignorant of all these? For this reason Flaccianus strongly encouraged those who had learned such things to prefer their own spirits to such divination without hesitation, and to take pains to instruct and support their own minds with these studies. In this way, they could fly past and go beyond the airy nature of these invisible demons.

"Now divine matters, as all agree, are much better and more elevated than human matters. How was Albicerius, not even knowing what he himself was, able to attain them? Perhaps he thought that the stars we observe every day are something great compared to the true and hidden God, to Whom the intellect perhaps reaches (but only rarely), and no sense does. Yet the stars are right before our eyes! So they aren't the divine things that wisdom professes itself alone to know. Furthermore, the other things exploited by these so-called diviners either to show off or for profit are surely of less account than the stars.

"Hence Albicerius had no share in the knowledge of human or divine matters, and your attack in this way on our definition has been in vain.

"Finally, since we ought to consider worthless and completely condemn anything apart from human and divine matters, I ask you: in what matters is your wise man to search for the truth?"

"In divine matters," replied Licentius. "Virtue is without a doubt divine, even in man."

---

46. There is some complicated wordplay here: *quo ille quasi spiritu admonitus vel inflatus. . . .* The term *'spiritus'* does double duty for 'spirit' and 'breath,' the latter sense being picked up in *'inflatus,'* which carries the primary meaning of 'inspired' but the secondary meaning 'pompous' (literally 'puffed up'). The "contemptible little animal" is a demon, as described previously. Therefore, Albicerius is inspired by this demonic spirit, and likewise made a pompous ass.

"Then did Albicerius already know these matters that your wise man is always searching for?"

"He knows divine matters," Licentius said, "but not those that
20   are to be sought by the wise man. Wouldn't anyone who grants divination to Albicerius, yet takes away from him divine matters (in virtue of which divination is so called), be twisting every linguistic convention? So that definition of yours, if I'm not mistaken, includes something or other that is irrelevant to wisdom."

[1.8.23]   Trygetius said: "The one who put forward that definition will
25   defend it, if he's willing. Now: answer me, so that we may finally come to the point at issue!"

"I'm ready!"

"Do you grant that Albicerius knew the truth?"

"Yes."

"Then he was better than your wise man!"

"Not at all," Licentius asserted, "because not only does that raving soothsayer not reach the kind of truth the wise man is
30   searching for, neither does the wise man himself while he's living in his body. This kind of truth is nevertheless so great that it's far preferable always to look for it than at any time to find the other kind."

Trygetius said, "The definition of 'wisdom' must come to my assistance in these difficulties. If it seemed defective to you
35   because it includes someone we can't call a wise man, I ask you: would you approve it if we were to say that wisdom is the knowledge of human and divine matters, but only of those that are relevant to the happy life?"

"Yes," Licentius replied, "that is wisdom, but not that alone. The former definition trespassed on the territory of others, whereas the present one abandons its own lands.[47] Accordingly,
40   the former is guilty of avarice, the latter of stupidity. In fact, now for me to explain by a definition what I mean, wisdom seems to me to be not only knowledge but also the diligent search for knowledge of the human and divine matters that are relevant to the happy life. If you want to split up this account, the first part,
45   which embraces knowledge, belongs to God, whereas the latter, which remains content with the search, belongs to man. God,

─────

47. That is, the former definition is too wide and the present one too narrow.

then, is happy in the former condition. Man is happy in the latter."

Trygetius said: "I'm surprised that your wise man spends his labor in vain, as you maintain."

"How is his investigation in vain," asked Licentius, "since there is such a great reward? By the very fact that he is searching, he is wise. He is happy in being wise, since he frees his mind as far as 50
he can from all the wrappings of the body and gathers himself within himself. He doesn't allow himself to be torn to pieces by his desires. Instead, he's always tranquil. He turns toward himself and toward God, so that even here[48] he makes full use of his reason, and we agreed above that this is happiness. On the final day 55
of his life, he is found to be ready to attain what he desired, and, having thoroughly enjoyed human happiness, he deservedly enjoys divine happiness."

[Summary]

I stepped in at that point, after Trygetius had sought for a long [1.9.24]
time for something to say in reply. I said: "Licentius! I don't think that arguments will forsake Trygetius if we permit him to search for them at his leisure. Was he ever at any point at a loss for a reply?

"First, when the question was raised about the happy life and 5
that of necessity only the wise man is happy (if foolishness is unhappiness even in the judgment of fools), Trygetius concluded that the wise man ought to be perfect, but that anyone still searching for what the truth is isn't perfect, and accordingly not even happy (1.3.7.4–6).

"At that point you countered with a weighty authority (1.3.7.15–27). While moderately disturbed by the name of Cicero, 10
Trygetius immediately recovered and, with some noble firmness, leaped to the pinnacle of freedom. He again seized what had been violently wrestled from his hands by asking whether it seemed to you that someone still searching was perfect (1.3.9.60–63). If you were to admit that he isn't perfect, he would return to 15
the beginning and prove, if he could, that according to the definition a man who rules his life by the law of his mind is perfect

---

48. By 'here' Augustine presumably means in this life, as contrasted with the afterlife (described in the next sentence).

and, from this, that he can't be happy unless perfect.

"Once you had extricated yourself from this trap —more clev-
20   erly than I expected! — by claiming that the perfect man searches
for the truth most diligently (1.3.9.78–89), while fighting for your
position you put too much confidence in the definition where we
said that the happy life is precisely the one that is led in accordance with reason (1.3.9.89–95). You left yourself open, and
Trygetius clearly set you back (1.4.10.1–18): he fell upon your
guards, and, driven back, you would have lost the whole issue
25   had not a truce revived you! Where have the Academicians,[49]
whose view you endorse, located their stronghold but in the definition of 'error'? If this definition hadn't come back to your mind
during the night, perhaps in a dream, then you wouldn't have had
anything to say in reply to Trygetius (1.4.11.31–37), though in
explaining Cicero's opinion you had yourself already called the
definition to mind previously.[50]

30   "Next we came to the definition of 'wisdom' (1.5.13.2–4). You
tried to undermine it with so much cunning that maybe not even
your helper Albicerius would himself have been wise to your
tricks. Trygetius resisted you with so much watchfulness and
strength! He had practically tied you up and kept you down. In
the end you saved yourself with your new definition, saying that
35   human wisdom is the search for the truth in virtue of which, due
to the mind's tranquility, the happy life would follow (1.9.23.40–
43). Trygetius won't make any reply to this view, especially if he
requests that the favor be returned to him of putting the debate off
for the day, or for what's left of it.

[1.9.25]   "Let's now end this discussion, please, so as not to go on at
40   length. I think it's also unnecessary to linger over it. The subject
has been treated adequately for the business we undertook. It
could be completely finished off after just a few words, were I not
to want to exercise both of you and explore your resources and
enthusiasms. This is of great interest to me. When I started to
45   encourage you strongly to search for the truth, I began by asking
you how much weight you attached to it. You were all so dedi-

49. This is the first time the Academicians have been mentioned by
name.

50. The reference is apparently to 1.3.7.19–27, but the definition of
'error' is not mentioned or alluded to there.

cated that I couldn't want more. Since we all want to be happy, we should carefully investigate whether that can happen only by finding the truth, or, putting all else aside if we want to be happy, by the diligent search for the truth.

"So now, as I said, let's end this debate and send a written 50
account of it especially to your father, Licentius. I'm already steering his spirit toward philosophy, but I'm still waiting for the turn of fortune that sends him to it. He can be more powerfully incited to these studies when he knows about them not only by hearing that you're now sharing this way of life with me, Licentius, but 55
also by reading our account. If, as I perceive, you favor the Academicians, prepare stronger means to defend them! I've resolved to prosecute them myself."

Once I had said this, our midday meal was announced, and we all got up.

[Book 2]

[Second Dedicatory Introduction]

If it were as inevitable to find wisdom when searching for it as it [2.1.1]
is to be unable to be wise without discipline and the knowledge of wisdom, then surely the trickery, obstinacy, and persistence[51] of the Academicians — or, as I sometimes think, their policy — which were suitable to the times would then have been interred 5
with those times, and interred with the bodies of Cicero and Carneades themselves. Yet it happens that knowledge is cultivated rarely and by only a few. This is due to either (*a*) the many different upheavals of this life, as you, Romanianus, have learned though experience; (*b*) some thickness or laziness or sluggishness of our dulled minds; (*c*) our despair at finding [wisdom], since the 10
star of wisdom doesn't appear to our minds as easily as the light does to our eyes; or (*d*) the common error that men, having found a false opinion, do not search diligently for the truth if they search at all, and even turn away from the desire for searching.

So it happens that the weapons of the Academicians, when 15
one joins issue with them, seem invincible. It is as if they were

---

51. Cicero disclaims the "trickery" and "obstinacy" thought to characterize the Academicians in *Academica* 2.20.65.

forged by Vulcan.[52] They seem this way not only to insignificant
men, but to learned and acute men. Accordingly, while one
should row against the winds and waves of fortune with the oars
of whatever virtues are available, one should first implore divine
20   assistance with all devotion and piety, so that the resolute application of oneself to good studies holds to its course and no chance
drives it astray from reaching the secure and pleasant harbor of
philosophy.

This is your first responsibility, and I fear for you on this score.
25   I want you to be set free from it. I don't stop praying for favorable
winds for you in my daily prayers. If only I were worthy enough
to bring it to pass! I pray to the power and wisdom itself of God
the Highest.[53] What else is He whom the mysteries[54] reveal to us
as the Son of God?

[2.1.2]   You'll help me a great deal while I'm praying for you if you
don't despair of our being able to be heard, and if you exert your-
30   self with us, not only with your prayers but also with your will
and the natural profundity of that mind of yours. It is on account
of your mind that I seek you out: it gives me exceptional delight
and I always admire it. But alas! Your mind is like a thunderbolt
that is wrapped up in clouds of domestic matters. It is hidden
from most people; indeed, almost from all. Yet it can't be hidden
35   from me, or from one or two of your intimate friends. We have
often listened attentively to your rumblings, and in addition we
have seen a few of the flashes that announce the thunderbolt. For
the time being I'll recall just a single case and keep quiet about the
rest. Who has ever suddenly thundered and shone the light of his
40   mind so greatly that, with a single thunderclap of his reason and
a brilliant flash of restraint, he killed off in a single day a passion
that had been most fierce the day before? Will that power of yours,
then, not burst forth at some point and turn the jeers of many who
had given up hope into consternation and bewilderment? Will it

52. See Vergil, *Aeneid* 8.535 for this simile.

53. I Corinthians 1:24: "[We preach] Christ, the power of God and the
wisdom of God, to the Jews and the Greeks." See *The Teacher* 11.38.48–49,
where Augustine alludes to "the unchangeable power and everlasting
wisdom of God." See also *The Happy Life* 4.34: "We have it on divine
authority that the Son of God is nothing other than God's wisdom."

54. That is, the Christian mysteries. See *On Order* 2.9.27.

not speak in this world some 'signs,' as it were, of future events, and then cast off the burden of the whole body and return again   45
to Heaven?[55] Has Augustine said these things about Romanianus in vain? No! He to Whom I have wholly given myself, He Whom I have now begun to know a little again, will not allow it!

Therefore, come with me to philosophy. In it there is every-   [2.2.3]
thing that is wont to move you wonderfully whenever you're anx-ious and thrown into doubt. I have no fears on the score of moral looseness or the dullness of your wit! When you were allowed to take a little time off [from work], who showed himself more alert than you in our conversations, or more penetrating? Shall I not   5
fully repay your favors to me? Do I perhaps owe you only a very little?

When I was an impoverished young man setting out on my studies away from home, you welcomed me into your house, into your munificence, and, what is much more, into your spirit.[56] You comforted me with your friendship when I lost my father, encour-aged me with your counsel, and helped me with your wealth. You   10
made me nearly as renowned and important in our own town as yourself by your patronage, familiarity, and reception of me in your home. You alone were the one, when I returned to Carthage to get a more advantageous position, to whom I confided my plan and my hopes, not anyone in my family.[57] Though you hesitated   15
for a little while out of love for your home town, since I was already teaching there, when you weren't able to overcome a young man's ambition for things that seemed better you turned your opposition into support, with admirable self-control and

55. "And then cast off the burden of the whole body and return again to Heaven": Augustine uses a similar phrase in 2.9.22.21, emended in *Revisions* 1.1.3.

56. *Confessions* 2.3.5: "When I was sixteen years old my studies were interrupted; I was brought back home from Madauros, the nearby town wherein I had already begun my residence in order to learn about litera-ture and oratory, while funds were gathered for a longer residence at Carthage, a venture for which my father had more enthusiasm than cash." Romanianus apparently began to subsidize Augustine's education at this point, making it possible for him to pursue his studies in Carthage.

57. *Confessions* 4.7.12: "I fled from my home town . . . and from the town of Thagaste I came to Carthage."

benevolence. You furnished all that was necessary for my venture.
You watched over the cradle and, so to speak, the nest of my stud-
20   ies, and you again now supported my first efforts in daring to fly.
When I sailed away in your absence and without your knowledge,[58] you weren't at all angry that I didn't communicate with
you, as I usually did. Suspecting anything but defiant behavior,
you remained unshaken in your friendship. You worried no more
25   about your children, who had been deserted by their teacher, than
you did about the purity and innermost depths of my mind.

[2.2.4]   Finally, you are the one who has inspired, advanced, and
brought about whatever I now enjoy in my retirement — that I've
escaped from the chains of superfluous desires; that in putting
down the burdens of mortal cares I breathe, come to my senses,
30   return to myself;[59] that I'm searching for the truth most eagerly;
that I'm now beginning to find it; that I'm confident about arriving at its highest degree.[60] Whose assistant you were, however, I
still conceive by faith rather than apprehend by reason. When we
35   were face to face, I set out the inner turmoils of my mind. I
declared earnestly many times that no fortune would seem good

58. Augustine describes his departure in *Confessions* 5.8.14, where he
relates how he tricked his mother and sailed away without telling her of
his departure.

59. "I breathe, come to my senses, return to myself": *respiro resipisco
redeo ad me*. There is an echo of this passage in *Confessions* 7.10.16: "I was
thereby counselled to return to my own self," *et inde admonitus redire ad
memet ipsum*. Augustine may be following Plotinus, *Enneads* 1.6.9, in the
notion of 'returning to oneself.'

60. The 'highest measure' of truth is God, as Augustine explains in *The
Happy Life* 4.34: "The fact that truth exists happens through some highest
measure, from which it proceeds and toward which it turns itself when
perfected. Furthermore, no other measure is imposed on this highest measure: if the highest measure is a measure through a highest measure, then
it is a measure through itself; the highest measure must be a true measure;
therefore, just as truth is begotten from measure, so too measure is known
by truth. Therefore, truth has never existed without measure, and measure has never existed without truth. Who is the Son of God? He has been
called 'Truth' [John 14:16]. Who is there who doesn't have a father? Who
else but the highest measure? Therefore, whoever comes to the highest
measure through the truth is happy. In the case of souls, this is the possession of God, *i.e.*, to enjoy God completely."

to me except what would provide leisure for doing philosophy, and that no life would seem happy except one in which I might live in philosophy. Yet I was held back by the heavy burden of my dependents whose life was supported by my job, and by many expenses, be they due to propriety or to the embarrassing circum-   40
stances of my dependents. You were elevated by so great a joy, so inflamed by a holy zeal for this kind of life, that you told me that if you could somehow extricate yourself from the chains of your troublesome lawsuits you would break all the chains holding me, even to the extent of sharing your patrimony with me.[61]

Therefore, when you departed after the tinder had been   [2.2.5]
sparked in us, we never stopped yearning for philosophy. Nor did   45
we think about anything except that way of life, a way of life both appropriate and suitable for us. We thought about it constantly. Yet we weren't as passionate as we might have been, despite our thinking we were passionate enough. We hadn't yet been touched by the greatest flame, the flame that was to consume us. We   50
thought that the flame with which we were burning slowly was really the greatest flame. But look! When certain books[62] *brimming*

61. In *Confessions* 6.14.24 Augustine describes a plan to retreat from the world for a life of contemplation, with communal living and communal resources, where the tranquility of all would be safeguarded by the appointment of two 'magistrates' each year to see to all necessary business: "Anything we could raise would be placed in common and we would create a single household treasury, so that in genuine friendship there wouldn't be any private property for one or another person, but what had become one from all the contributions would belong as a whole to each and every person: everything would belong to everyone. . . . Some among us were extremely wealthy, especially Romanianus from our home town, who had come to the [Imperial] court because of serious problems involving his property. He had been a close friend of mine from my youth. He lent great support to this project and carried great weight in it, since his financial resources far outstripped anyone else's." Augustine is likely referring to this plan when he speaks of Romanianus's "holy zeal for this kind of life" and his offer to share his patrimony.

62. These books were neoplatonist treatises: see *Confessions* 7.9.13 (*quosdam platonicorum libros*), where Augustine says that these books were translations from Greek into Latin; *Confessions* 7.20.26 (*lectis platonicorum illis libris*); and *Confessions* 8.2.3 (*quosdam libros platonicorum*), where Augustine says that the translations were made by Marius Victorinus. In

full (as Celsinus[63] says) wafted their exotic scents[64] to us, and when
a few drops of their precious perfume trickled onto that meager
55   flame, they burst into an unbelievable conflagration — unbelievable, Romanianus, unbelievable, and beyond what perhaps even
you believe of me — what more shall I say? — even beyond what
I believe of myself!

What honor attracted me then? What human pomp moved me?
What desire for empty fame? What comforts or chains that belong
60   to this mortal life? I was quickly returning to myself as a complete
whole. Now I confess that I looked back on the religion implanted
in us as boys, binding us from the marrow, as though from a long
journey's end. Yet it was actually drawing me to itself without my
realizing it. And so stumbling, hastening, hesitating I snatched up
the Apostle Paul.[65] Truly, I declared, the [apostles] would not

---

The Happy Life 1.4 (Appendix 1), Augustine identifies them as books written by Plotinus (*lectis autem Plotini paucissimis libris*). Plotinian authorship
would be consistent with Augustine's characterization of the books as
'platonist,' since Augustine says in *The City of God* 8.12 that the most note-
worthy of the modern platonists are Plotinus, Iamblichus, and Porphyry,
writing in Greek, and Apuleius, writing in Latin and Greek. In a similar
vein, Augustine says that Plato has come to life again in Plotinus:
3.18.41.45–46. Some scholars, however, have argued that Augustine did
not mean to exclude Porphyry, and the relative influence of Plotinus and
Porphyry on Augustine's thought is a debated topic, as indeed is the
question precisely which treatises by Plotinus (or Porphyry) Augustine is
referring to here. See O'Donnell [1992], Vol. 2, pp. 421–24 for a clear
account of the scholarly debates and the secondary literature on these
issues.

63. Most likely (Aulus) Cornelius Celsus, the first-century encyclopedist
who wrote a six-volume work collecting the opinions of famous philosophers: Augustine refers to him by name in his *Soliloquies* 1.12.21 and
describes his work in the prologue to his *Treatise on Heresies*.

64. "Wafted their exotic scents to us": *bonas res Arabicas ubi exhalarunt in
nos*, an echo of Plautus, *cepere urbem in Arabia / plenam bonarum rerum*
(*Persa* 4.3.36–37).

65. "And so stumbling, hastening, hesitating I snatched up the Apostle
Paul": *itaque titubans properans haesitans arripio apostolum Paulum,* a partial
echo of Cicero, *Tusculan Disputations* 1.30.73, *itaque dubitans circumspectans
haesitans multa adversa reverens.* For the events described here see *Confessions* 7.21.27 (*arripui . . . apostolum Paulum*) and 8.12.29 (*codicem apostoli*

have been able to do such great deeds, nor would they have lived   65
as they clearly did live, if their books and arguments were
opposed to so great a good. I read all of it with the greatest attention and the greatest care.

Then, no matter how little the light was that had already been   [2.2.6]
cast by the visage of philosophy, it now appeared so great to me
that if I could show it to — I don't say "to you," Romanianus, since
you always burned with the hunger for it, despite your not yet
knowing it, but instead I say "to your adversary" (I don't know   70
whether he's more of an annoyance than a hindrance to you) — if
I could show it to your adversary, he would rush to its beauty as
a passionate and holy lover, admiring and breathless and exhila-
rated. He would forsake and abandon his fashionable resorts, his
pleasant orchards, his luxurious and elegant banquets, his household performing troupe; and, in the end, he would shun whatever   75
strongly inclines him to all kinds of pleasures. We should admit
that even your adversary has a certain beauty of spirit — or rather
we should admit that he has a seed of beauty, so to speak. It's
straining to blossom forth into true beauty, but it sends forth only
twisted and misshapen shoots among the rough underbrush of
vices and the brambles of fallacious opinions.[66] Yet it continues to   80
bloom and to exhibit itself, as far as it is able, to those who peer
keenly and intently into the thicket. From this source comes his
hospitality; the civility that seasons his banquets; his elegance,
charm, sophisticated taste in all things; and his urbanity that   85
everywhere sprinkles all things with traces of loveliness.

This is commonly called 'philocaly.' Don't condemn the name   [2.3.7]
because it's common! Philocaly and Philosophy are nearly the
same names[67] and they want to be seen as members of the same
family, as in fact they are. What is Philosophy? The love of wis-

---

[*Pauli*] . . . *arripui, aperui, et legi*), and the discussion in O'Meara [1992],
Ch. 2.

66. "The brambles of fallacious opinions": *inter opinionum fallacium
dumeta*, an echo of Cicero, *Academica* 2.35.112, *Stoicorum dumeta*. Augustine uses the same image in *Letter* 1.1 (*umbrosa et spinosa dumeta*), translated
in Appendix 3.

67. Augustine writes *prope similiter cognominatae sunt*, which may be
read 'are near-perfect synonyms' and 'are closely similar in their
(sur)names.'

5   dom. What is Philocaly? The love of beauty. (Just ask the Greeks!)
What, then, is wisdom? Is it not true beauty itself? Hence they are
sisters born of the same father.[68] Although Philocaly was dragged
down from her heights by the birdlime[69] of lust and kept in an
ordinary cage, she retains the close resemblance in her name to
10 remind the birdcatcher not to despise her. Her sister, flying freely,
often sees her in a debased and needy condition with her wings
clipped. She rarely sets her free. Philocaly does not know from
what origin she springs; only Philosophy knows that.

(This whole fable — I've suddenly become an Aesop! — will be
recounted to you more pleasantly in a poem by Licentius. He's
15 close to being an accomplished poet.)[70]

If your adversary, then, who is a lover of false beauty, could
look upon true beauty through eyes that were open and healthy,
even for a moment, with what pleasure would he take refuge in
the bosom of philosophy! How he would embrace you there,
knowing you as his true brother!

You're surprised at these things. Maybe you're laughing at
20 them. What if I could explain them as I should like? What if you
could hear the voice of philosophy even without yet seeing its visage? You would surely be surprised, but you wouldn't laugh at or
despair of [your adversary]. Believe me, we should never despair
of anyone, and least of all of such men. There are many examples.
This kind of bird easily escapes and flies away again, while many
25 others are caged and look on in great astonishment.

[2.3.8]   Let's return to ourselves — let us, I say, devote our attention to
philosophy, Romanianus. I should like to thank you: your son is
beginning to do philosophy. I'm restraining him so that he may
proceed with more strength and vigor after first getting the necessary training. You yourself need not be afraid because you lack
30 this training. Knowing you so well, I only wish for you to have a

68. In *Revisions* 1.1.3 (Appendix 11) Augustine calls his allegory of Philosophy and Philocaly "completely inept and tasteless."

69. See *The Teacher* 10.32.82: birdlime and reeds were used to catch birds.

70. Writing to Licentius in 395 (*Letter* 26), Augustine quotes some poetry
Licentius had sent to him for his approval, the only sample of Licentius's
poetry we have — 154 hexameters of dreadful verse. Augustine spends
most of the letter castigating Licentius for not being a proper Christian,
taking less care for his soul than for the metrical accuracy of his verses.

favorable opportunity. What can I say about your natural abilities? If only they were not so uncommon among men as they are
constant in you!

There remain two defects and obstacles to finding truth. I don't
have much fear for you on their account. Still, I'm afraid that (*i*)
you may underrate yourself and despair of your ever finding the
truth; or (*ii*) you believe yourself to have found it.[71]

Now if you're hindered by the first of these obstacles, perhaps 35
our discussion will remove it for you. You have often been angry
at the Academicians: the more severely, in fact, the less knowl-
edgeable you were about them; the more gladly, because you were
led on by your love of the truth. Therefore, I'll now join battle with
Alypius, under your patronage, and easily persuade you of my
views — only as plausible views, however, since you won't see the 40
truth itself unless you give yourself over completely to philosophy.

As for the second obstacle, namely that you perhaps assume
that you have found some truth, despite the fact that you were
searching and doubting when you left us — if any superstition has
returned to your mind, it will surely be cast out once I've sent you
a discussion among ourselves concerning religion[72] or once I talk 45
many things over with you in person.

For my part, I'm doing nothing at present except purging [2.3.9]
myself of futile and harmful opinions, so I'm undoubtedly better
off than you are. There is only one matter in which I envy your
good fortune, namely that you alone are enjoying the company of 50
my Lucilianus.[73] Are you in turn jealous because I called him *my*

71. The difficulties given here as (*i*) and (*ii*) are the final two obstacles
mentioned in 2.1.1.9–14, namely (*c*) and (*d*): Augustine has already
acknowledged (*a*), and his remarks throughout 2.1.2 and in 2.2.3.3–5
address (*b*). In the present passage, in (*ii*), Augustine is referring to his
(correct) suspicion that Romanianus may yet be a Manichaean. See below,
where he refers to Manichaeanism as a 'superstition.'

72. Most likely *The True Religion*, dedicated to Romanianus but not completed until 390: see *Letter* 15.1 (Augustine to Romanianus) of that year: "I
have written something about the catholic religion, as far as the Lord
found it worthwhile to grant to me; I want to send it to you before my
arrival if I don't run out of paper in the meantime." The clear implication
is that he has only recently finished *The True Religion*.

73. Lucilianus — perhaps Lucianus or Lucinianus — is paired with

Lucilianus? What have I called him except *yours* and *everyone's*, since we're all one? What might I ask of you to ease my longing for him? Do I deserve you yourself? You know that you owe me
55   that much. I now declare to both of you: take care lest you think yourselves to know anything except only what you've learned in the manner in which you know that the sum of one and two and three and four is ten. Again, take care lest you think that in philosophy you will not know the truth or that it can't be known in this manner at all. Believe me — or rather, believe Him, for He says
60   *Search and you shall find*[74] — knowledge is not to be despaired of, and it will be clearer than those numbers are.

Let us now come to the matter at hand. Too late have I started to fear that this introduction exceeds its proper limit! This is no small matter, since measure is surely divine, but it's easy to make a mistake when it beckons so agreeably. I'll be more cautious when I'm wise.

[19 November 386]

[2.4.10]   After the initial discussion written up in Book 1, we took a break from our debate for nearly seven days, since we were reviewing the second, third, and fourth books of Vergil's *Aeneid* and talking about them. This seemed to be a suitable activity at the
5   time. Yet as a result Licentius was so inflamed with a passion for poetry that it seemed to me he should be restrained a bit, seeing that he was unwilling to be dragged away from this pursuit to any
10   other. When I had praised the light of philosophy as much as I could, he eventually agreed to discuss again the question about the Academicians we had put off. The day, by chance, had dawned so bright that it seemed precisely suitable to enlightening our minds.[75] We therefore got up earlier than usual and, because

---

Romanianus in a letter from Nebridius to Augustine written in 389 (*Letter* 5), and again mentioned by Augustine in a letter to Nebridius of the same year (*Letter* 10); in each case he is described as a close friend. He is otherwise unknown.

74. Matthew 7:7.

75. Note the wordplay: the day is bright (*serenus*), suitable for enlightening our minds (*serenandis animis nostris*). Augustine regularly uses metaphors involving light to describe intellectual activity, and especially the act of comprehension.

it was urgent, we did a little work with the farmhands.

Then Alypius began: "Before I hear you debating about the   15
Academicians, I want to have read to me that discussion of yours
which you told me was completed in my absence.[76] Otherwise,
since the occasion for this disputation arose from that one, I cannot help but make mistakes, or at least have some difficulty, while
listening to you."

When this had been done and we saw that almost the whole
morning had been taken up with it, we decided to return to the   20
house from the fields where we were walking about.

Then Licentius said: "If it's not too much trouble, please briefly
recount and explain the entire view of the Academicians before
our midday meal, so I don't miss anything in it that helps my
side."

"I'll do so," I said, "and all the more gladly because you'll eat   25
less while you're thinking about this subject!"

"Don't be too sure on that score!" he replied. "I've often noticed
that many people, and especially my father, eat the more heartily
the more burdened with cares they are. Furthermore, you also
know by experience that I didn't neglect the table when I was
thinking about poetic measures. I typically wonder about this
myself. Why do we eat with greater appetite when we're concen-   30
trating our minds on something else? Who is it that takes control
of our hands and teeth when our minds are occupied?"

"Listen instead," I said, "to what you've asked me about the
Academicians, so I don't have to put up with your pondering
those measures, not only in feasting without measure but also in   35
raising questions without measure! If I conceal anything that
favors my side, Alypius will make it good."

"We rely on your good faith," said Alypius. "If there were any
danger that you conceal anything, I think it difficult for me to
catch out the person from whom I learned these matters, as everyone who knows me is aware — especially because in putting the
truth forward, you'll be no more mindful of victory than you are   40
of your real purpose."

"I shall do so in good faith," I said, "as you rightfully prescribe.   [2.5.11]

"The Academicians held that man isn't able to have knowledge

76. See 1.3.8.45, where Alypius departed from the country-house for
Milan.

as far as matters that pertain to philosophy are concerned, and
Carneades asserted that he didn't care about other matters. Yet
5   man is able to be wise, and the whole duty of the wise man — as
you, Licentius, also maintained in our previous discussion — is
accomplished in seeking for the truth. It follows from this that the
wise man doesn't assent to anything.[77] If he were to assent to
something uncertain, he must be in error, which is shameful in the
wise man.[78]

"Not only did the Academicians say that everything is uncer-
10   tain; they also reinforced their view with a rich supply of arguments. They seem to have appropriated their claim that the truth
can't be apprehended from a definition given by Zeno the Stoic.
He said:

> The truth that can be apprehended is impressed on the mind by what
> it comes from in such a way that it couldn't be from something other
> than what it does come from.[79]

77. Cicero, *Academica* 1.12.45: "[Arcesilaus] held that all things were hidden in obscurity and that nothing could be discerned or understood: for
these reasons, nobody should either say anything positive, affirm anything, or give approval by assenting." See also 2.18.59: "If nothing can be
perceived that seemed to be so to both [Arcesilaus and Carneades], assent
should be withheld. What is so useless as giving approval to something
that is not known?" Augustine himself attributes this argument to Arcesilaus in 2.6.14.22–25.

78. Cicero, *Academica* 2.20.66: "Just as I judge it supremely attractive to
look upon truths, so it is supremely disgraceful to approve falsehoods as
truths."

79. Augustine takes this formulation practically verbatim from Cicero,
Academica 2.6.18: "[Philo] denied that there was anything that could be
'apprehended' (which is how we render καταληπτόν) if the 'appearance'
(we're now accustomed by yesterday's discussion to use this word for
φαντασία) was, as Zeno defined it, an appearance that has been
impressed and brought about by what it comes from in such a way that it
couldn't be from something other than what it does come from." This formulation includes the 'dual' form: the apprehension (*a*) accurately mir-
rors what it derives from, and (*b*) could not derive from anything other
than what it does derive from. It seems that (*b*) was a later addition, not
given by Zeno. See Sextus Empiricus, *Against the Mathematicians* 7.247–
252, who remarks that (*b*) was a later addition prompted by controversies
with the Academicians. See the discussion in Frede [1987]. This fits with

This can be more briefly and plainly expressed as follows: the   15
truth can be apprehended by means of these signs, and what is
false can't have these signs. The Academicians leaned heavily on
this definition to prove that the truth could not be found at all.
Accordingly, in defense of this contention they put great emphasis on disagreements among philosophers, errors of the senses,
dreams and madnesses, fallacies and sophisms.[80] Since they had   20
also taken from the selfsame Zeno the view that nothing is more
shameful than mere opinion, they cleverly drew the conclusion
that if nothing could be perceived and mere opinion was shameful, the wise man would never give his approval to anything.

"Much indignation arose against them on this score, for it   [2.5.12]
seemed to follow that the man who gives his approval to nothing
also would do nothing.[81] Accordingly, the Academicians seemed   25
to portray your wise man, who they believed gave approval to
nothing, as being always asleep and sloughing off all his duties.
At this point they introduced a kind of plausibility which they
even named 'truthlike,' and asserted that the wise man isn't at all
derelict in his duties since he has something to follow [as a guide
to action].[82] The truth lies hidden, however, since it is buried or   30

---

earlier reports that include only (*a*), which also attribute the definition
explicitly to Zeno. Kirwan [1989], pp. 26–28 briefly discusses Augustine's
treatment of Zeno's definition.

80. Augustine's list is compiled from Cicero's *Academica*. For "disagreements among philosophers" see 2.5.14, 2.17.55, 2.48.147; for "errors of the
senses" 2.25.81–2.26.82; "dreams and madnesses" 2.15.47–48, 2.16.51–
2.17.54; "fallacies and sophisms" (*pseudomenoe et soritae* — see 2.16.49 for
the latter translation) 2.14.45–2.15.46, 2.28.92, 2.29.94, 2.30.96, 2.48.147.

81. Cicero, *Academica* 2.12.39: "Accordingly, someone who takes away
presentation or assent also takes every action away from life." See also
Academica 2.19.62: "By doing away with assent, [the Academicians] have
done away with every mental movement and every physical action."
Cicero describes the objection in 2.33.108 and discusses it in 2.34.108.

82. "Since he has something to follow [as a guide to action]": *cum haberet
quid sequeretur*. That is, the plausible or the truthlike can guide and regu-
late the wise man's conduct, without knowledge of the truth. See Cicero,
Academica 2.10.32: "[The Academicians] hold that something is plausible
and in a way 'truthlike,' and that they employ this as a guide (*regula*) both
in the conduct of life and in [philosophical] investigation and discussion."
Again, Cicero, *Academica* 2.31.99: "The wise man will therefore employ

indistinct, either by reason of some natural obscurities or because of resemblances among things.[83] At the same time, they maintained that withholding or (so to speak) 'suspension' of assent is precisely the great action performed by the wise man.[84]

35 "I think I've explained the whole matter briefly, as you wanted, and I haven't departed from your injunction, Alypius. That is, I've acted in good faith, as noted (2.5.11.1). If I said anything that isn't so, or perhaps left something out, I did nothing of the sort deliberately. Good faith, then, stems from the mind's intention: it should be clear that a man who is in error ought to be taught and that a deceitful man should be guarded against. The former needs

40 a good teacher, the latter a wary student."

[2.5.13] Then Alypius said: "Thank you for having satisfied Licentius, and for relieving me of the burden that was put on me! You need not have feared that you should say something less to test me (for

45 how else could it happen?), any more than I, had it been necessary to catch you out on any point. Now if it isn't too tiresome, please explain something missing not so much in our investigation as in this investigator: the difference between the New Academy and the Old Academy."

"Well, it is very tiresome," I said, "but I can't deny that what you've mentioned is extremely relevant to the matter at hand.

50 You'll accordingly do me a service if you're willing to distinguish between these names and to expound the position of the New Academy, while I keep to myself for a bit."

Alypius replied: "I would believe that you also wanted to keep me away from our midday meal, if I didn't think instead that you

---

whatever is apparently plausible if nothing happens that is contrary to that plausibility, and his whole plan of life will be governed in this fashion."

83. The 'natural obscurities' are apparently the limitations and defects inherent in sense-perception. See Cicero, *Academica* 2.23.73: "[Democritus] says that the senses are not so much dim as they are 'full of darkness' (*tenbricosos* [= σκότιος]) — for so he calls them." Augustine says that the senses are 'shadowy' (*tenebras*). The 'resemblance among things' makes it difficult to distinguish one thing from another: see 3.1.1.13–14.

84. Cicero, *Academica* 2.34.108: "I for one think that the greatest action is to oppose presentations, to withstand opinions, and to suspend those slippery acts of assent."

were scared off by Licentius a little while ago, and if his demand required us to explain to him whatever complication there is in this question before we eat!"

While he was trying to finish his remarks, my mother — for we were now at the house — began to hustle us to our midday meal, so that there was no place for any more discussion. 55

Afterward, once we had eaten as much as was necessary to satisfy our hunger, we returned to the meadow, and Alypius said to me: "I'll go along with your plan. I wouldn't dare refuse! If I leave nothing out, the credit will be due to your teaching, and to my memory as well. If I perhaps make a mistake on any point, you'll make good the deficiency, so that from now on I need not fear this kind of assignment. [2.6.14]

5

"I think that the secession of the New Academy wasn't directed against the old conception as much as it was directed against the Stoics.[85] It shouldn't be considered a 'secession,' since the new question raised by Zeno had to be discussed and resolved. Although the point about nonperception[86] hadn't provoked any controversies, it can reasonably be held to have occupied the minds of the Old Academicians. This is also easily proved by the authority of Socrates himself, and Plato, and the rest of the Old Academicians, who believed that they were able to be shielded from error so long as they didn't entrust themselves recklessly to any assent,[87] even though they didn't introduce any special discussion of this topic into their schools, nor did they at any point straightforwardly address the question whether the truth can be perceived. Zeno raised this question as something new and untried. He contended that nothing can be perceived except what is true in such a way that it can be distinguished from the false by

10

15

20

85. See 3.18.41.29–32. Cicero remarks that the 'New' Academy seems to him to be the Old (*Academica* 1.12.46).

86. See the discussion in 2.5.11: Zeno claimed that 'perception' of the truth excluded any possibility of error; members of the New Academy maintained, in response, that truth was never perceived — which is "the point about nonperception."

87. Cicero, in *Academica* 1.4.15–16 and again in 1.12.44–46, associates Socrates and Plato (and their followers in the 'Old Academy') with skeptical views, though he doesn't say in so many words that they recommend the suspension of assent.

a dissimilarity in their marks,[88] and that opinion should not enter the mind of the wise man.[89] When Arcesilaus heard this, he denied that anything of the sort can be discovered by man, and further-more that the life of the wise man shouldn't be entrusted to the
25   dangerous waters of opinion. Accordingly, he then concluded that one should not assent to anything.

[2.6.15]   "As matters stood, the Old Academy seemed to be made stron-ger rather than beleaguered. But Philo's pupil Antiochus made his appearance and brought the views of the two Academies into con-flict. He seemed to many to be more interested in his reputation
30   than in the truth.[90] Antiochus declared that the New Academi-cians had tried to introduce a topic out of line with and far removed from the opinion of the Old Academicians. He urged us to put our trust in the old physicists and in other great philoso-phers on this topic. He also opposed the [New] Academicians who maintained that they were following something truthlike,
35   even though they admit not knowing the truth itself. He assem-bled many arguments, which I think should be passed over for now, defending before all else the claim that the wise man can per-ceive the truth.

"This, in my view, was the controversy between the New Aca-demicians and the Old Academicians. If the matter is otherwise, I would request you to give Licentius a complete account, for the
40   benefit of both of us. If it is as I've tried to say, proceed with the discussion you've undertaken."

[2.7.16]   I said: "Licentius, how long are you going to be idle in our con-versation (which is lengthier than I expected!)? Now do you understand just who your Academicians are?"

Smiling ruefully though a little upset by this rebuke, Licentius
5   replied: "I'm sorry to have maintained so emphatically against Trygetius that the happy life consists in the search for the truth.

88. See n. 79 above.

89. Cicero, *Academica* 2.18.59: "I'm not as certain that something can be apprehended (the point I've been arguing for too long already!) as I am that the wise man holds nothing as an opinion — that is to say, he never assents to anything false or unknown."

90. Cicero, *Academica* 2.22.70: "Some people said that [Antiochus] did this for the sake of glory, even hoping that those who followed him would be called 'the Antiochans.'"

This question so embarrasses me that I'm hardly anything but miserable. If you have any decency, surely I seem pitiable to you! Yet why do I foolishly torment myself? Why am I daunted when I'm supported by such a worthwhile cause? I won't give in to anything but the truth!" 10

"Do the New Academicians," I asked, "meet with your approval?"

"Very much so," he responded.

"Then do they seem to you to be speaking the truth?"

He was about to assent when, warned by Alypius's laughter, he hesitated for a moment and then said: "Repeat that little question."

I said: "Don't the Academicians seem to you to be speaking the truth?"

After he had been silent again for a while, he replied: "I don't 15 know whether it is the truth, but it is plausible, and I can't see anything else to follow."

"You do know," I said, "that they also name the plausible 'truthlike'?"

"So it seems," he answered.

"Therefore," I said, "the view of the Academicians is truthlike."
"Yes."

"Please pay the closest attention," I said. "If a man unac- 20 quainted with your father were to see your brother and assert that he is like your father, won't he seem to you crazy or simpleminded?"

He was silent for a long time. Then he said: "That doesn't seem absurd to me."

When I started to reply to him, he interrupted: "Please wait a [2.7.17] moment!" Then, with a smile, he said: "Tell me, are you now cer- 25 tain of your victory?"

"Suppose that I am certain," I replied. "You still shouldn't abandon your position on that account, especially since we have engaged in this discussion of ours to train you and to incite you to cultivate your mind."

"Have I ever read the Academicians?" he rejoined. "Have I 30 been instructed in the many branches of knowledge you're prepared to bring against me?"

I replied: "The philosophers who first defended this view of yours hadn't read the Academicians either! Moreover, if you lack

instruction or a supply of knowledge, your natural talents should
35   nevertheless not be so weak that, with no attack, you yield to a few
comments and questions of mine.[91] I'm already beginning to fear
that Alypius may take your place sooner than I wish. With him as
my opponent I won't feel as secure going along in this fashion."

"Well then," said Licentius, "if only I were already defeated!
Then I could at last hear the two of you argue — what's more, I
40   could watch you at it, and there can be no sight more satisfying
shown to me! Of course, since you prefer to disseminate your
words rather than squander them[92] — to catch them with a pen
rather than let them 'fall to the ground' (as they say) — it also will
be possible to read what the two of you say. Yet somehow when
the people bandying words about[93] are right before our eyes, a
45   good debate fills the mind with greater pleasure, though not with
greater practical value."

[2.7.18]   "We thank you," I replied, "but these unanticipated delights of
yours have pushed you into the thoughtless claim that no sight
more satisfying can be shown to you. Yet surely no one will drink
of philosophy more eagerly than your father, after so long a thirst.
50   What if you saw him investigating and arguing these matters with
us? I for one will never think myself more fortunate than at that
moment. What, then, is it proper for you to think and say?"

Licentius now cried for a little while. When he was able to
speak, he looked up to heaven with his hands outstretched and
55   said: "When, O God, shall I see this? Yet there is nothing we need
despair of obtaining from You!"

Here almost all of us were distracted from the debate and began

---

91. "... that, with no attack, you yield to a very few comments and questions of mine": *ut nullo facto impetu paucissimus verbis meis rogationibusque
succumbas*. The Latin is ambiguous. Either Licentius is being chastised for
not having made any (counter-) attack upon hearing Augustine's remarks
and questions, or else Augustine is pointing out that his remarks and
questions hardly amount to making an attack.

92. Note the wordplay: "... since you prefer to disseminate (*fundere*)
your words rather than squander (*effundere*) them ..."

93. "The people bandying words about": *ipsi quos inter sermo caeditur*, an
echo of Syrus in Terence's *The Self-Tormenter* 242: *Verum interea dum sermones caedimus*. Priscian asserts that this is a graecism: *caedere sermones* =
κόπτειν τὰ ῥήματα.

to cry. I struggled with myself and barely recovered my composure: "Come now," I exclaimed, "gather your forces again! I had
warned you some time ago to bring them together from whatever
quarter you could, since you were to be the protector of the Academy. I don't think that now *fear grips your limbs even before the trum-*   60
pet sounds.[94] Nor do I think you want to be captured so quickly
because you want to watch while someone else does the fighting!"

Then Trygetius, after observing that we had now sufficiently
regained our composure, said: "Why shouldn't such an upstand-
ing man want God to grant his prayer before he offers it? Have   65
faith now, Licentius! You who cannot find anything to say in reply
and still want to win seem to me to have little faith!"

We laughed. Then Licentius retorted: "Speak, you happy man!
Happy not in finding the truth, but certainly not in searching for
it!"

We were all cheered up by the good spirits of the young men. I   [2.7.19]
said to Licentius: "Pay attention to my question[95] and return to the   70
discussion with more determination and vigor, if you can."

"I'm as ready as I can be! What if the man who saw my brother
had known from hearsay that my brother is like my father? Can
he be taken to be crazy or simple-minded for believing it?"

"Can't he at least be called foolish?" I asked.   75

"Not necessarily," he responded, "unless he maintains that he
knows it. If he follows as plausible what rumor has repeatedly
spread about, he can't be accused of any rashness at all."

Then I said: "Let's consider this matter briefly — set it before our
eyes, so to speak. Suppose that this man we've been describing,   80
whoever he is, were present. Your brother arrives from somewhere.
·Then the man asks: 'Whose son is this boy?' He receives this
answer: 'The son of a certain Romanianus.' The man remarks: 'How
like his father he is! How accurately rumor has reported this to me!'
At this point you or someone else asks: 'Do you know Romanianus,
my good man?' 'I don't know him,' he replies, 'but the boy seems   85
like him to me.' Will anyone be able to keep from laughing?"

"Certainly not!" he replied.

94. Vergil, *Aeneid* 11.424.

95. That is, the question Augustine raised in 2.7.16.20–22: "If a man
unacquainted with your father were to see your brother and assert that he
is like your father, won't he seem to you crazy or simple-minded?"

"Therefore, you see what follows."

"I've seen it all along," Licentius asserted. "I still want to hear the conclusion from you. You should start to feed someone you've captured!"

90 "Why shouldn't I draw the conclusion? This example makes it obvious that your Academicians should likewise be laughed at, since they say that in this life they follow something truthlike, although they do not know what the truth is."

[2.8.20]   Then Trygetius said: "The caution exercised by the Academicians seems to me unlike the idiocy of the man you've described. The Academicians arrive at what they say to be truthlike through reasoning, whereas that fool of yours was guided by rumor, and there is no more worthless authority than that."

5 I replied: "As though he wouldn't be more foolish in saying: 'I don't know his father at all, nor have I ever heard from rumor how like his father he is, but he still seems like him to me!'"

"He certainly would be more foolish," Trygetius agreed. "What's the point of these remarks?"

"Because," I replied, "in the same class are people who say: 'We
10 don't *know* the truth, but what we see is *like* what we don't know.'"

"They call it 'plausible,'" Trygetius objected.

I replied: "Why do you say this? Do you deny that they call it 'truthlike'?"

Trygetius said: "I wanted to say it for this reason: to exclude the element of *likeness*.[96] It seemed to me that it was wrong for rumor to enter into your question, since the Academicians don't even
15 trust human eyes, much less the thousand unnatural eyes of rumor, as the poets depict it.[97] Yet who am I to be a defender of the Academy? Do you envy my unconcern on this question? Look — here's Alypius. His arrival will give *us* some peace, I hope![98] We
20 think that you've been afraid of him for some time now, and not without reason."

[2.8.21]   In the silence that followed, Trygetius and Licentius looked at Alypius, who then said: "As far as my abilities permit I should like

96. Carneades used the term τό πιθανόν (translated by Cicero as *probabile*), which includes no element of likeness.

97. For 'thousand-eyed rumor' see Vergil, *Aeneid* 4.173–83.

98. Trygetius seems to mean that he and Licentius will now be able to retire from the debate in favor of Alypius.

to give some measure of assistance to your positions, but your
omen frightens me. Unless my hope deceives me, however, I'll
easily banish that fear. At the same time it's encouraging to me 25
that the one who is presently attacking the Academicians almost
took over Trygetius's burden when he was defeated, and that
now, by your admission, it's plausible that he'll be the victor. I'm
more afraid that I not be able to avoid negligence in abandoning
my role and effrontery in taking over another one. I'm sure you
haven't forgotten that the referee's job had been assigned to me." 30

"That job is one thing," Trygetius asserted; "this is something
else. Accordingly, we request that you allow yourself to be free
from any official capacity for a while."

"Let me not refuse," Alypius declared, "so that in wanting to
avoid negligence and effrontery I not fall into the snares of pride
— which is the most heinous of all vices — should I hold on to an
honor you've granted to me longer than you allow." 35

Alypius turned to me and continued: "Well then, my good [2.9.22]
accuser of the Academicians, I should like you to explain your
position to me. That is, in whose defense are you attacking them?
I'm afraid that you may want to prove yourself an Academician in
refuting the Academicians!"

"I think you well know," I replied, "that there are two kinds of
accusers. Even if Cicero in his modesty said that he was an accuser 5
of Verres only insofar as he was a defender of the Sicilians,[99] it isn't
thereby necessary that anyone who accuses someone has another
person whom he is defending."

Alypius retorted: "Do you at least have something on which
your view is based that supports it?"

"It's easy for me to give an answer to that question," I said, 10
"especially since it isn't unexpected! I've already pursued the
whole issue for myself and pondered it for a long time. So, Alypius, listen to what I think you already know perfectly well: I don't
want this debate to be undertaken just for the sake of debating.
Let's end the preliminary exercises we engaged in with these
young men, where philosophy itself freely played along with us, 15
so to speak.[100] Accordingly, let childish tales be put beyond our

99. Cicero, *The Action Against Verres* 1.12.34.
100. "Let's end the preliminary exercises we engaged in with these
young men": see Plato, *Theaetetus* 168E. Note that philosophy 'plays

reach! The matter at hand concerns our life, morality, and spirit. The spirit will return more safely to Heaven since it supposes that it will (*a*) overcome the dangers of all fallacious arguments; (*b*) triumph over the passions in returning to the region of its origin,[101]

20   so to speak, once truth has been apprehended; and (*c*) exercise its rule once it has been wedded to moderation in this fashion.[102] You see what I mean. Let's now put aside all these trifles. *Weapons are to be made for a spirited warrior.*[103] There is nothing I ever wanted

25   less than that anything should occur from which a new conflict of some sort might arise among people who have lived and conversed together a great deal. I've chosen to commit to writing what we've often discussed at length among ourselves for two reasons: as an aid to the memory, which is an unreliable guardian of what has been thought out, and, at the same time, so that these young men learn to pay attention to these issues and try to approach and tackle them as well.

[2.9.23]   "Therefore," I continued, "don't you know that up to now there
30   is nothing I perceive to be certain? I'm prevented from searching for it by the arguments and debates of the Academicians. They somehow persuaded me of the plausibility — so as not to give up their word just yet — that man cannot find the truth. Accordingly,

35   I had become lazy and utterly inactive, not daring to search for what the most ingenious and learned men weren't permitted to find. Unless, therefore, I first become as convinced that the truth can be found as the Academicians are convinced that it cannot, I shall not dare to search for it. I don't have anything to defend. Thus please withdraw that question of yours.[104]

40   "Instead, let's discuss between ourselves, as carefully as possi-

---

along' (*iocare*), which picks up the preliminary exercises, the 'playing around' (*pro-ludere*), that Augustine and Alypius have engaged in with Trygetius and Licentius.

101. See *Revisions* 1.1.3 (Appendix 11). See also Augustine's report of Porphyry in *The City of God* 12.27.

102. See Plotinus, *Enneads* 4.8.3. Augustine may have derived these ideas from Cicero, *Hortensius* frag. 97 (Müller) [< *The Trinity* 14.19.26]; his phrase *rediturus in caelum* is certainly an echo of Cicero's *reditum in caelum fore*.

103. *Aeneid* 8.441.

104. Augustine is referring to Alypius's question (2.9.22.8–9): "Do you at least have something on which your view is based that supports it?"

ble, whether the truth can be found. I think I already have many arguments for my position, and I'm trying to rely on them in opposition to the reasoning of the Academicians. The only difference between my viewpoint and the viewpoint of the Academicians is that to them it seems plausible that the truth can't be found, whereas to me it seems plausible that the truth can be 45 found. If they are only pretending, then ignorance of the truth is peculiar to me alone; otherwise, it is common to both."

Alypius said: "Now I may proceed safely, for I see that you [2.10.24] won't be an accuser as much as a helper. Therefore, so as not to digress any further, let us please first see to it that in dealing with this question, where I seem to have replaced those who have yielded to you, we not fall into a controversy that is merely verbal. 5 In line with your suggestion and Cicero's authority,[105] we have often admitted that this is utterly disgraceful.

"Now unless I'm mistaken," Alypius went on, "when Licentius said that he was content with the view of the Academicians regarding plausibility, you immediately asked whether they also called this 'truthlikeness,' which he confirmed without any hesitation. I know well that the doctrines of the Academicians are not 10 unfamiliar to you, since it is from you that they are known to me. Since these doctrines are firmly entrenched in your mind, as I said, I don't understand why you're carping about words!"

"Believe me," I replied, "this isn't a controversy about words! Instead, it's a serious controversy about the issues themselves. I don't think the Academicians were the sort of men who didn't 15 know how to give names to things. On the contrary, these terms ['plausible' and 'truthlike'] seem to me to have been chosen to conceal their view from the unintelligent and to reveal it to the more penetrating. I'll explain why and how this seems so to me once I first discuss their arguments, which men think the Academicians have advanced as the enemies of human knowledge.[106]

105. Cicero, *The Orator* 1.11.47.

106. See 3.17.38.51–52. Cicero, *Academica* 2.18.60, suggests that the skeptical posture of the New Academy was merely a smokescreen to conceal their positive doctrines: "Who would adopt views so obviously and evidently perverse and false unless there had been a great supply of facts and precepts in Arcesilaus — and so much the more in Carneades?" See Augustine's *Letter* 1 (Appendix 3) for a similar point.

20   "I'm pleased that our discussion has come along this far today,
then, so that the question between us is clear and openly agreed
upon. The Academicians do seem to me to have been completely
serious and prudent men. If there is anything that we're going to
argue about, it will be against those who believe that the Acade-
25   micians are opposed to finding the truth. Don't think I'm afraid!
I'll also be willing to arm myself against the Academicians themselves if they sincerely maintain the things we read in their books
— that is, if they didn't maintain them merely to conceal their real
view, so that they don't unthinkingly divulge certain mysteries of
the truth to men of defiled and profane minds, so to speak.
30   "I would do this today, but the setting of the sun now compels
us to return home."
        Thus far did our discussion proceed on that day.

[20 November 386]

[2.11.25]   Now although the following day dawned no less pleasant and
peaceful, we couldn't extricate ourselves from domestic concerns.
We devoted a large part of the day especially to writing letters. We
5   went to the meadow when there were barely two hours left. The
weather was pleasant and inviting, and we decided not to permit
even the short time left to us to be wasted. Therefore, when we
arrived at our customary tree and had sat down, I began: "Since
no serious matter is to be taken up today, I should like you young
10   men to refresh my memory of how Alypius answered yesterday
the trivial question that had disturbed both of you."
        Licentius replied: "His answer is so short that it's no trouble to
remember it! As for how trivial it is — well, that's for you to see.
Since the matter was settled, it prevented you, I think, from raising a question about words."
15   I asked: "Have both of you paid sufficient attention to what this
point is and the force it has?"
        "I think I see what it is," Licentius responded, "but please
explain it a little. I've often heard from you that it's shameful for
disputants to linger on a question of words when no disagreement over the subject matter remains. However, this point[107] is

107. That is, the "point" mentioned in Augustine's preceding question,
namely the distinction between the plausible and the truthlike.

too subtle for me to be pressed to explain it." 20

"Then listen, both of you," I said, "to what the explanation is. [2.11.26]
The Academicians call what can incite us to act without assent
'plausible' or 'truthlike.' Now I say 'without assent' inasmuch as
we don't hold the opinion that what we do is true, or think that we
know it, and yet we do it nevertheless. For example, if someone 25
were to ask us whether, since last night was so bright and clear, an
equally cheerful sun would rise this morning, I believe we would
deny knowing it. Yet we would say that it seems so. The Academician says:[108]

> All the things I think ought to be called 'plausible' or 'truthlike' seem
> to me to be like this. I make no objection if you want to call them by 30
> another name. It's enough for me that you grasp what I mean, that is
> to say, the realities to which I'm giving these names. The wise man
> should be not a craftsman of words but an investigator of realities.

Now do you understand full well how those playthings I was stirring you up with have been dashed from my hands?"

When both of them had replied that they understood, and by 35
their expressions demanded some response from me, I said:
"Well, do you think Cicero — whose words I've just cited — was
so poor a Latinist that he gave unsuitable names to the realities he
was considering?"

Then Trygetius said: "Since the issue is clear now, we're happy [2.12.27]
not to provoke any controversies over words. Accordingly, think
instead what answer you might give to Alypius, who has relieved
us — we against whom you are once more aroused and trying to
attack!"

Licentius added: "Wait a moment, please. I'm catching a glim- 5
mer of something — a glimmer by which I see that so great an
argument shouldn't be snatched away from you so easily!" After
being silent for a while, absorbed in thought, he said: "Well, nothing seems more absurd than for someone who doesn't know the
truth to say that he's following something truthlike. Nor does
your example (2.11.26.25–28) cause me any difficulty. When the 10
question is put to me whether the mildness of this evening's sky
entails that there be no rain tomorrow, I correctly answer that this

108. Cicero, *Academica* frag. 19 (Müller).

is likely true (*veri simile*), since I don't deny that I myself know some truth. I know that this tree can't become silver in the next moment. There are many things of this sort I say that I truly know, without being overconfident, and I see that they're like those I
15   have called truthlike. But you, Carneades, or any other Greek pest, to say nothing of our compatriots — why should I hesitate to change sides and go over to him whose prisoner I am by right of victory? — you, then, Carneades: since you say that you don't know any truth, on what grounds do you follow something truth-like? 'I was unable to give another name to it!' [Carneades replies].
20   Why then should we argue with someone who doesn't know how to express himself?"

[2.12.28]   Alypius replied: "I'm not afraid of deserters, and so much the less is Carneades himself! You were stirred up by boyish or by childish levity, I don't know which, and thought it proper to attack him with invective rather than with some weapon. Yet in
25   support of his view, which was always grounded on something plausible, the following point will still be sufficient in his favor and against you: we're so far removed from the discovery of the truth that you can be a strong argument against yourself! You were so shaken in your position by one little question that you have no idea where you should stand.[109]

       "Let's put these matters aside for another time, along with your 'knowledge' of this tree, which you claimed a little while ago was
30   imprinted on you (2.12.27.12–13). Though you've now changed sides, you still ought to be carefully taught just what I said a little while ago. We hadn't yet gotten as far, I think, as the question ask-ing whether the truth can be found. Instead, I thought that an important point should be settled right at the doorstep of my
35   defense, where I saw you sprawled in exhaustion; namely, whether one should not search for the truthlike, or the plausible, or whatever else it may be called, which the Academicians hold to be enough for them. It's of no interest to me if you now seem to yourself to be the best discoverer of the truth! Perhaps you'll teach
40   me these things later, if you're thankful for my protection."

109. According to Cicero, *Academica* 2.22.71, the argument Alypius offers in the last sentence here — namely, that Licentius's vacillation supports the Academicians' contention that nothing is securely known — was employed (and perhaps invented) by Antiochus.

Since Licentius was dismayed and chagrined by Alypius's [2.13.29] onslaught, I intervened: "Alypius, you've preferred to speak of everything but the manner in which we are to argue with persons who don't know how to express themselves."[110]

Alypius replied: "Since I as well as everyone else have known for a long time that you're an expert in speaking, a fact you now 5 make generally known by your profession, I would like you first to explain the point of your inquiry. Either it is pointless (which is my view), and so much the more is it pointless to reply to it; or, if it seems that it is to the point and that I can't explain it, let me prevail upon you with my earnest plea that you not weary of the role of teacher."

"You remember," I said, "that yesterday I promised to deal 10 with these terms ['plausible' and 'truthlike'] later (2.10.24.12–19). Now the sun reminds me to put away in their boxes the playthings I was showing to the young men — especially since I was showing them as display ornaments rather than as items for sale. Right now, before the darkness (which is the traditional protector of the Academicians!) prevents our transcription, I want us to be 15 in full agreement today on what question is to be taken up in the morning.

"Accordingly, please tell me whether it seems to you that the Academicians held a definite view about the truth and didn't want to relate it recklessly to ignorant or unpurified minds, or 20 whether they understood matters to be as their disputations relate."

Alypius said: "I won't recklessly assert what they had in mind! [2.13.30] You're better informed how they customarily relate their view in words, insofar as it can be gathered from their books. If you're asking me about my view, well, I think that the truth hasn't yet been found. In addition, as for the point you were pressing about 25 the Academicians, I think that the truth can't be found — not only because of my ingrained opinion, which you've noticed practically from the start, but also because of the authority of great and outstanding philosophers to whom we are somehow compelled to

110. This was the challenge Licentius raised at 2.12.27.19–20. Augustine's point is that Alypius hasn't answered the question (despite intimidating Licentius). Notice that Alypius again dodges the question by asking about the purpose of the whole undertaking.

30   submit, either through our mental inadequacy or through their
     sagacity; and we must believe that nothing further can be found."

     "This is what I wanted," I said. "I was afraid that if matters
     seemed to you as they do to me, our debate would remain incom-
     plete, there being nobody on the other side to force us to come to
     grips with the issue so that we thrash it out as carefully as we can.
35   So, if this had happened, I was prepared to ask you to defend the
     position of the Academicians as though they seemed to you not
     only to have called into question whether the truth can be appre-
     hended, but also to have held that it can't be apprehended.

     "Therefore, the question between us is whether their argu-
     ments make it plausible that nothing can be perceived and that
     one should not assent to anything. Now if you prevail, I'll gladly
40   yield. Yet if I can demonstrate that it's much more plausible that
     the wise man be able to attain the truth and that assent need not
     always be withheld, then you'll have no reason, I think, for refus-
     ing to come over to my view."

     Alypius and the others present agreed to this. Since the shad-
     ows of the evening were now covering us, we returned to the
     house.

[Book 3]

[21 November 386]

[3.1.1]   On the day after the discussion recorded in Book 2, when we had
          taken our places in the bathing hall — the weather was too dis-
          agreeable for us go down to the meadow — I began as follows: "I
5   think all of you have been properly attentive, and so the question
          about the matter we are to discuss has been settled.[111]

          "Before I do my part, which is to explain the issue, please be
          willing to listen to a few remarks about our hopes, lives, and prin-
          ciples of conduct not unrelated to this matter.

          "I believe that our business is neither trivial nor superfluous,
          but necessary and of supreme importance: to search wholeheart-
10   edly for the truth. Alypius and I agree on this point. Philosophers
          other than the Academicians thought that their wise man had

---

111. "The question about the matter we are to discuss has been settled":
the question is posed in 2.13.29.15–17 and resolved in 2.13.30.37–43.

found the truth. The Academicians declared that the wise man should exert himself to the utmost in his search for the truth, and that he does this conscientiously. Yet since the truth is either buried away in hiding or is so indistinct it doesn't stand out,[112] in living his life the wise man follows what strikes him as plausible or truthlike.

"This was also the conclusion of your previous disputation. Despite the fact that one of you maintained that man becomes happy through finding the truth, whereas the other that he becomes happy merely by carefully searching for the truth, none of us has any doubt that we should put this business before anything else. Accordingly, what kind of day do we seem to have spent yesterday [before our evening discussion], I ask you? You were both free to follow your interests, of course. You, Trygetius, entertained yourself with Vergil's poems. Licentius devoted himself to fashioning verses, and he is so overcome with love for this occupation that it was especially on his account that I thought this discussion should be brought up. It's high time that philosophy take and retain a greater part in his mind than poetry or any other branch of learning.

"Tell me: didn't you both feel sorry for us all? The night before last, we had gone to bed intending to address that postponed question and practically nothing else upon rising.[113] Yet there were so many domestic affairs to be seen to that we were completely occupied with them. We had barely the last two hours of the day for ourselves in which we could breathe freely. It has accordingly always been my view that nothing is necessary for a man who is already wise, whereas fortune is necessary for a man to become wise.[114] Does it seem otherwise to you, Alypius?"

Alypius replied: "I don't yet know how much jurisdiction you attribute to fortune. If you hold that fortune is needed to condemn fortune, then I join you in this view. If, on the other hand, you grant to fortune nothing except goods that can't provide for bodily necessities unless fortune is favorable, then I don't agree.

112. These points were mentioned at 2.5.12.29–31, there given as a reason to withhold assent.

113. At the end of 2.10.24 Augustine describes the question to be discussed the next day.

114. Cicero argues for this view in *Tusculan Disputations* 5.9.25.

15   Either the man who is not yet wise but still desirous of wisdom
      can procure the goods we deem necessary for life, even if fortune
      is adverse or unfavorable; or it should be granted that fortune also
      dominates the entire life of the wise man, since even the wise man
      can't dispense with the need for goods that are bodily necessities."

[3.2.3]   "You're saying, then," I responded, "that fortune is necessary
20   for the man striving after wisdom, but you deny this to be so for
      the wise man."

      "It's not out of place to repeat the same thing!" he rejoined.
      "Thus, I now also ask you: do you hold that fortune is of any assis-
      tance in condemning itself? If you think so, I say that the man who
      is desirous of being wise is in great need of fortune."

      "I do think so," I answered, "if by fortune he'll be the sort of
25   person who can condemn it. This isn't absurd. [Maternal] breasts
      are necessary for us when we are infants, and, thanks to them, it
      happens that later we can live and flourish without them."

      Alypius replied: "It's clear to me that if the conception in our
      minds isn't different, then our views agree — unless perhaps any-
30   one thinks he should argue that it's not breasts or fortune but
      something else that makes us condemn fortune or breasts."

      "It's not difficult to use another analogy," I said. "For example,
      nobody crosses the Aegean Sea without a ship or another means
      of transport, or, not to fear the example of Daedalus[115] himself,
35   even without any equipment suitable for this purpose or some
      secret power. If he proposes to do nothing save get to the other
      side, then once he has made the crossing he's ready to throw away
      and condemn whatever carried him there.[116] Thus it seems to me
      that anyone who wants to get to the harbor of wisdom (as though
      it were a safe and tranquil country) must have fortune to attain
      what he desires. For example, to pass over other cases, if someone
40   is blind or deaf he can't [become wise]. This is in the power of for-
      tune. Once he has attained wisdom, then, although he is thought
      to require certain goods pertaining to his physical well-being, he

115. Daedalus is said to have fled from the Labyrinth of the Minotaur on
Crete by fashioning wings from wax and feathers, enabling him to fly
across the sea to Sicily.

116. O'Meara [1950], pp. 185–86, n. 3 argues that this passage should be
compared to *Confessions* 1.18.28 and *The City of God* 9.17, all reflecting the
influence of Plotinus, *Enneads* 1.6.8.

clearly needs these things not to be wise but merely to live among   45
men."

"Well," said Alypius, "if he be blind and deaf, he will, in my
view, rightly condemn the acquisition of wisdom, and life itself,
for which wisdom is sought."

I replied: "Yet since our life while we're living on this Earth is   [3.2.4]
in the power of fortune, and only someone alive can become wise,
shouldn't it be admitted that we need its favor to be brought to   50
wisdom?"

"Since only those who are alive require wisdom," he replied,
"and there isn't any need of wisdom if life be taken away, I don't
have any fear of fortune concerning the continuation of life. I want
wisdom because I'm alive. It's not that I want to live because I
desire wisdom! Accordingly, if fortune takes my life away, it   55
deprives me of the reason for searching for wisdom. Hence there
is no reason why, to become wise, I should either hope for the
favor of fortune or fear its interference — unless, perhaps, you put
forward other reasons."

Then I said: "So you don't hold that someone who is a devotee
of wisdom can be prevented from attaining wisdom by fortune,   60
even if it doesn't deprive him of life?"

"I don't think so," Alypius replied.

I said: "I want you to tell me briefly what seems to you to be the   [3.3.5]
difference between the wise man and the philosopher."

"I don't think the wise man differs from the devotee [of wis-
dom] in any way," he replied, "except this: the wise man defi-
nitely has the possession[117] of some things that the devotee is only
eager to have."

"What are these things?" I asked. "To me, nothing seems to dif-   5
ferentiate them except that one knows wisdom and the other
desires to know it."

"If you define 'knowledge' within reasonable limits, you've
expressed the matter clearly."

"However I define it," I replied, "all agree on this point: there   10
can't be knowledge of falsehoods."[118]

---

117. This translates *habitus* (itself a translation of ἕξις) following Cicero,
Treatise on Invention in Rhetoric 1.25.36 (see also 2.9.30). The 'devotee [of
wisdom]' is literally the philosopher, the "lover of wisdom."

118. That is: $Kp \rightarrow p$; 'what you know must be so.'

"In this regard," Alypius said, "it seemed to me that a limitation should be proposed, so that your eloquence doesn't prance unrestrained over the grounds of the principal question because of my thoughtless agreement!"[119]

I replied: "You clearly haven't left me anywhere to prance at
15   all! If I'm not mistaken, we have now arrived at our objective. I've been striving for this all along. If, as you stated so subtly and truly, [the following conditions hold]: (*i*) there is no difference between the devotee of wisdom and the wise man except that the former loves, whereas the latter possesses, the learning that is wisdom (and you accordingly didn't hesitate to use the name 'possession'); (*ii*) nobody can possess this learning in his spirit if he hasn't
20   learned anything; (*iii*) anyone who knows nothing has learned nothing; (*iv*) nobody can know a falsehood — well, then, the wise man knows the truth! You've already granted that he possesses the learning that is wisdom in his spirit; that is, he has it as his possession."

"I don't know how impertinent I may be," Alypius said, "if I wish to deny that I granted there to be in the wise man the 'pos-
25   session' of inquiring into human and divine matters. I don't see why it seems to you that he doesn't have the 'possession' of plausibilities that have been found."

"Do you grant me that nobody knows falsehoods?"

"Yes, of course."

"Now say, if you can, that the wise man doesn't know wisdom!"

"Why do you draw this conclusion, with everything restricted
30   so that it can't *seem* to him that he apprehends wisdom?"

"Let's shake hands!" I said. "If you recall, this is what I said yesterday I was going to establish (2.13.30.37–39). I'm delighted now that the conclusion wasn't drawn by me but offered by you on your own accord. I said that the difference between me and the Academicians was that to them it seemed plausible that the truth
35   can't be apprehended, whereas to me, though I hadn't yet found it, it seemed that it can be apprehended by the wise man. Now, when you were being pressed by my question whether the wise man fails to know wisdom, you declared 'It seems to him that he knows.'"

119. Augustine's imagery is derived from Cicero, *Academica* 2.35.112: "There is a large field in which our discourse can range about."

"What follows from that?" he asked.

"If it seems to him that he knows wisdom," I replied, "then it does *not* seem to him that the wise man can know nothing! Or, if   40
wisdom is nothing, I want you to say so!"

"I would believe that we had come to our final objective,"   [3.3.6]
Alypius stated, "but suddenly, as we were clasping hands, I see
that we're far apart and separated by a long distance. It seemed to
us yesterday that the only question before us was whether the   45
wise man can arrive at an apprehension of the truth. You affirmed
it. I denied it. I don't think I've conceded anything to you now
except that it can seem to the wise man that he has acquired wisdom concerning plausibilities (3.3.5.25–26). Yet I think there isn't
any doubt among us that I determined this kind of wisdom to be
in the investigation of divine and human matters."   50

"You won't disentangle yourself by tangling things up," I said.
"Right now you seem to me to be arguing for the sake of exercise!
You abuse the ignorance of our judges, since you well know that
these young men can hardly make out subtle and acute reasoning.
As a result, you're free to say whatever you like without anyone   55
protesting. Now a little while ago, when I asked whether the wise
man knows wisdom, you replied that it seemed to him that he
knows it. Therefore, if it seems to someone that the wise man
knows wisdom, it surely doesn't seem that the wise man knows
nothing! This can only be in dispute if someone were to dare to say   60
that wisdom is nothing. It follows from this that what seems so to
you does to me too. It seems to me that the wise man doesn't know
nothing — and to you too, I believe, since you agree that it seems
to the wise man that he knows wisdom."

Then Alypius replied: "I don't think I want to exercise my talents any more than you do. I'm surprised at that, since you don't   65
need any exercise in this matter! Now perhaps I'm blind, but it
still seems to me that there is a difference between 'It seems to him
that he knows' and 'He knows.'[120] Likewise, there is a difference
between 'wisdom,' which is bound up with investigation, and
'truth.' I don't find any way for the things each of us says to be
squared with one another."

Since we were called to our midday meal at that point, I said:
"I'm not at all displeased that you're opposing me so vigorously.   70

120. See the remarks on this discussion in the Introduction.

Either both of us don't know what we're talking about and we should take pains not to be such a disgrace, or just one of us doesn't, and again it's no less of a disgrace to leave that one behind in neglect. We'll meet again in the afternoon. Although it

75 seemed to me that we had reached our objective, you were still trading blows with me!"

At this *they all laughed, and we departed.*[121]

[3.4.7]   When we returned, we found Licentius, whose thirst Helicon never quenched, longing to engage in the composition of poetry.[122] Although our meal ended almost as soon as it had begun, he arose quietly in the middle of our meal and drank noth-

5 ing. I said to him: "I hope that someday you will gain mastery of poetics as you desire. Not that this accomplishment pleases me very much! I see that you're so infatuated that you can't escape this love except through tiring of it, however, and it's customary for this to happen readily after one becomes accomplished. More-

10 over, since you're quite musical, I would prefer you to press your verses on our ears rather than singing words you don't understand from Greek tragedies, like the little birds we see shut up in cages. I suggest that you go drink something, if you wish, and then return to our school, if philosophy and the *Hortensius* still mean something to you. You've already tasted the first and sweet-

15 est fruits of philosophy in the discussion between the two of you, which inflamed you more powerfully than does poetics for the knowledge of important and genuinely worthwhile things. While I want to call you both back within the circle of those branches of learning that cultivate the mind, I fear that it has become a labyrinth to both of you, and I almost regret having checked your natural inclination."

20   Licentius blushed and went off to drink. He was thirsty, and besides it was an opportunity to escape from me, for perhaps I was going to say more, and more pointed, things to him.

[3.4.8]   Once he had returned and everyone was paying attention, I began as follows: "Is it really the case, Alypius, that we disagree

121. Tacitus, *Dialogue on Oratory* §42 (the final line).

122. Mount Helicon was sacred to Apollo and the Muses; two streams flowed down from its summit, Aganippe and Hippocrene, the latter welling up when the tip of the mountain was struck by the hoof of Pegasus.

on this matter that seems so evident to me?"

"It isn't surprising," he replied, "if what you say is obvious to   25
you be obscure to me. After all, many evident matters can be more
evident to some people. Likewise, some obscure matters can be
more obscure to not a few. Well, if this matter is genuinely evident
to you, believe me: there is someone to whom what is evident to
you is even more evident, and again there is someone to whom   30
what is obscure to me is even more obscure. Let me entreat you to
explain this evident matter more evidently, so that you no longer
think me so contentious."

"Please pay careful attention," I said, "as though the trouble of
making a reply were put aside for the time being. Since I know
myself and you well, taking a few pains will readily clarify what   35
I'm saying, and one of us will quickly persuade the other. Did you
say — or perhaps I didn't hear you properly at that moment —
that it seems to the wise man that he knows wisdom?"

He nodded in agreement.

"Let's put that wise man aside for the moment," I said. "Are
you a wise man yourself, or are you not?"

"By no means!" he replied.

"Yet I want you to give me an answer about the wise man of the   40
Academicians. Does he seem to you to know wisdom?"

"Does it seem to him that he knows, or does he know? Do you
think these are the same or different? I'm afraid this confusion
might afford a refuge for one or the other of us."

"This is what's usually called a 'Tuscan dispute,'" I remarked,   [3.4.9]
"where what seems to be good for the question (which remains   45
unresolved) is not an answer to it but the proposal of another
question instead! Our poet Vergil — to get Licentius's attention
for a moment — rightly judged this to be something rustic and
countrified. When one shepherd asks the other where "the
expanse of the heavens is no more than three ells wide," the latter   50
replies (*Eclogues* [3.106–7]):

In what lands do flowers grow inscribed with the names of kings?

Please, Alypius, don't think that we're permitted to engage in such
Tuscan disputes at this country-house! At least, let these small
baths make you mindful of the decorum proper to places of high

learning.[123] Please answer the question I'm asking. Does it seem to
55   you that the wise man of the Academicians knows wisdom?"

"Not to keep bandying words back and forth — it seems to him
that he knows [wisdom]."

"Does he therefore seem to you *not* to know it?" I asked. "I'm
not asking what it seems to you that *seems* to the wise man, but
instead whether it seems to you that the wise man *knows* wisdom.
You can, I take it, either affirm or deny it here and now."

60   Alypius replied: "I wish it were either as easy for me as it is for
you, or as hard for you as it is for me! Then you would neither be
so insistent nor have any expectations for anything in these matters. When you asked me what seemed to me about the wise man
of the Academicians, I replied that it seemed to me that it seems to
him that he knows wisdom — so as not to assert rashly that I
65   know, or to say no less rashly that he knows."

"Please do me a great service," I said. "First, deign to answer
the question I put to you, rather than the one you put to yourself.
Next, put aside for a while now my expectations, which I know
are of no less concern to you than your expectations. To be sure, if
70   I'm deceiving myself with this line of questioning, I'll go over to
your side immediately and we'll end this controversy. Finally,
banish whatever anxiety I see has you in its grips, and pay close
attention, so that you may readily understand what answer I want
you to give me.

"Now you said that you haven't given a strict 'yes' or 'no' to my
75   question, as it surely calls for, in order not to say rashly that you
knew what you didn't know. As though I were to ask about what
you know and not about what seems to you! Thus, I now ask you
the same thing more plainly, if it can be stated more plainly. Does
it seem to you that the wise man knows wisdom, or doesn't it?"

Alypius replied: "If a wise man of the sort that reason describes
80   can be found, it seems to me he can know wisdom."

"Reason, then," I said, "shows you that a wise man is the kind
of person who is not ignorant of wisdom. You're correct on that
score. It was fitting that it seem to you to be so.

123. Philosophical debates were often held in baths, and so the "small
baths" of Augustine's country-house should make everyone aware of the
"decorum proper to places of high learning" and not to engage in "Tuscan
disputes."

"Therefore, I now ask you whether the wise man can be found. [3.4.10]
If he can, then he can know wisdom, and every question between 85
us has been settled. If you say he can't be found, then the question
isn't whether the wise man knows anything, but instead whether
anyone can be a wise man. If this is established,[124] then we'll have
to part company with the Academicians, and we should examine
that question with you, carefully and cautiously, as far as we are
able. The Academicians held — or, better, it *seemed* to them — that 90
the wise man can exist, but that man can't attain knowledge.
Accordingly, they maintained that the wise man knows nothing.
Yet it seems to you that he knows wisdom, which is surely not to
know nothing. We're also united in agreement, as are all the
Ancients and even the Academicians themselves, that nobody can 95
know falsehoods.[125] Consequently, you're left with either maintaining that wisdom is nothing, or admitting that reason doesn't
countenance the sort of wise man described by the Academicians
and, once these matters are put aside, agreeing to investigate
whether man can achieve wisdom of the sort reason describes. We
shouldn't — we can't — correctly call anything else 'wisdom'!" 100

"Even if I were to grant what I see you're so eagerly striving [3.5.11]
for," Alypius said, "namely that wisdom is known by the wise
man and that we have thereby uncovered something that the wise
man can perceive, it still doesn't strike me that the whole design
of the Academicians has been weakened in any way. I foresee that
there is a strong defensive position reserved for them: the suspen- 5
sion of assent hasn't been cut off. They are helped in their cause by
the very argument you think has refuted them! They'll say that it's
so true that nothing is apprehended and assent shouldn't be given
to anything, that even this [first] claim about not perceiving anything has now been wrestled away from them by the conclusion
you've reached. (They made a case for this claim as plausible 10
almost since the beginning, until you came along.) As a result,
whether the force of your argument is invincible by virtue of its
own genuine strength, or just because of my stupidity, it can't dis-
lodge the Academicians from their position. They can still boldly

124. "If this is established": if it is established that it is possible for someone to be a wise man. See the end of the paragraph.
125. Cicero, *Academica* 2.13.40: "Some things that seem to be so are true
and others are false; what is false cannot be perceived."

assert that even now consent shouldn't be given to anything, since
15   perhaps someday they themselves, or someone else, can find
something against this [argument of yours][126] that can be pro-
pounded with accuracy and plausibility.

"The likeness and 'image' (so to speak) of the Academicians
should be seen in Proteus. It's said that Proteus was typically captured by some means that barely captured him, and his pursuers
20   never were sure they really had him except by the indication of
some divine spirit.[127] May that divine spirit be present, and may
he deign to show us the truth that is of such importance to us!
Then I'll also admit that the Academicians have been overcome,
even if they don't agree, although I think they will."

[3.5.12]   "Good!" I responded; "I didn't want anything more at all.
Please look at how many great benefits have come to me!

25   "First, the Academicians are now declared to be so beaten that
no defensive position remains for them except the impossible.
Who can in any way understand or believe that a beaten man
boasts himself to be the victor by the very fact that he has been
beaten?

"Next, if there remains any point of contention with the Acade-
30   micians, it isn't due to the fact that they say that nothing can be
known. It's due to the fact that they maintain that one shouldn't
assent to anything. Thus we're now in agreement. It seems to the
Academicians, as it does to me, that the wise man knows wisdom.
Yet they still warn us to refrain from assenting to this. They say
that it only seems so to them and they don't in any way know it.[128]

126. That is, the Academicians might someday find a plausible objection
to Augustine's argument — given in the preceding sections and culmi-
nating in the dilemma stated in 3.4.10 — against their first claim (namely
that nothing can be known). Alypius's argument here is restated at
3.14.30.3–12.

127. See Vergil, *Georgics* 4.388–414. Proteus was a sea-god, a shapeshifter,
who transforms himself into "the appearance of wild beasts" when captured, so that his captors are unsure whether what they hold really is Proteus. Only a "divine spirit" can tell them whether they have caught
Proteus.

128. That is, the Academicians say that it *seems* to them that the wise man
knows wisdom; they don't assert that the wise man does know wisdom
(or that they know this to be so).

As though I professed to know it! I also say that it seems to me to   35
be so. If they don't know wisdom, then I'm foolish, and they are
too. Yet I think we ought to give approval to something, namely
to the truth. I ask the Academicians whether they deny this, that
is, whether they hold that one should *not* assent to the truth.
They'll never say this, maintaining instead that the truth hasn't
been found. Therefore, they keep me as an ally on this score too,   40
namely that we don't disagree (and so necessarily agree) that one
ought to consent to the truth. 'Who will show us the truth?' they
ask. I shall decline to get into a fight with them. It's enough for me
that it is no longer plausible that the wise man knows nothing.
Otherwise, they would be forced to make the absurd claim that
either wisdom is nothing or the wise man doesn't know wisdom.   45

"Furthermore, you yourself, Alypius, have said who can show   [3.6.13]
the truth to us. I should make an effort to disagree with you as little as possible! You remarked briefly as well as piously that only
some [divine] spirit can show man what the truth is (3.5.11.19–21).
For this reason, there has been nothing I've heard in our discus-   5
sion with more pleasure, nothing more important, nothing more
plausible — and, if that spirit, as I firmly believe, be present to us,
nothing is more true. You reminded us of Proteus, aiming with
profound understanding at the best kind of philosophy. Now so
that you young men see that poets shouldn't be completely con-   10
demned by philosophy, Proteus is himself introduced as an image
of the truth.[129] Proteus in poetry plays the role of truth, which no
one can obtain if, deceived by false images, he loosen or release
the bonds of understanding. These images, in the customary manner of corporeal things, try to fool and deceive us through our   15
senses (which we use for the necessities of our life), even when we
apprehend the truth and hold it, so to speak, within our hands.

129. Augustine derives this claim, and his interpretation of the legend of
Proteus as a whole, from his unusual reading of Vergil, *Georgics* 4.405:

verum ubi correptum manibus vinclisque tenebis

Augustine takes *verum* not as an adversative particle ("But when you
shall grasp [Proteus] who is held fast by your hands and your chains . . .")
in line with the *tum* in 4.406, but as a noun ("When you shall grasp the
truth that is held fast by your hands and your chains . . ."). Augustine
paraphrases this reading at the end of the paragraph, in 3.6.13.16–17.

"Therefore, this is a third benefit that has come to me, and I find it invaluable. My closest friend agrees with me not only
20   about the issue of plausibility in human life, but also about religion itself. This agreement is the clearest indication of a true friend, if friendship has been correctly and properly defined as *agreement on human and divine matters combined with charity and good will.*[130]

[3.7.14]   "Nevertheless, so that the arguments of the Academicians not seem to cloud the issue, and so that we ourselves not seem to anyone to be so insolent as to contest the authority of highly learned men, among whom Cicero above all must carry weight with us,
5   with your permission I'll first offer a few remarks against those to whom it seems that these contentions are opposed to the truth. Then I'll show you the reason, in my opinion, the Academicians concealed their view.[131]

"Thus even though I see that you're completely on my side, Alypius, defend them a little on these points and respond to me."
10   Alypius replied: "Since you got off on the right foot today, as they say, let me not get in the way of your complete victory! I'll undertake to defend their side with more confidence since you've given me this assignment. Yet if you prefer to turn what you mean to do by cross-examination into an uninterrupted discourse, should this be convenient for you,[132] then, although I'm now your prisoner, don't torture me with your barbed questions, as though
15   I were an unyielding adversary! This cruelty is far removed from your humane nature!"

[3.7.15]   I noticed that the others also wanted me to do this, and so I

130. Cicero, *On Friendship* 6.20.

131. Augustine's "few remarks" have a highly articulated structure. He first tries to clarify Cicero's actual position *vis-à-vis* the Academicians (3.7.15–3.8.17), and then turns to the arguments for skepticism. Augustine takes up the claim that nothing can be known (3.9.18–3.13.29) by first examining Zeno's definition, and then by arguing that we do have genuine knowledge. He then turns to the claim that assent should always be withheld and that the Academician follows the plausible/truthlike (3.14.30–3.16.36). He concludes his monologue with an explanation of the secret views of the Academicians (3.17.37–3.19.42).

132. Cicero, *On Good and Evil Goals* 1.8.29: "I prefer to use an uninterrupted discourse rather than to ask and answer questions."

made a new beginning, as it were.[133] "I'll go along with your wishes," I said, "although I had expected that after my hard work in the rhetoric school I should find some rest in light armor![134] 20
That is to say, to find some rest by doing these things through cross-examination rather than through a disquisition. Yet since we are so few that it isn't necessary for me to raise my voice beyond what is good for my health, and since I wanted the pen to guide and manage my discourse[135] for the sake of my well-being, so that my mind not be carried along more rapidly than is good 25
for my body, listen to what I hold — set forth, as you wish, in an uninterrupted discourse.

"Now first let's examine a point that the enthusiastic supporters of the Academicians typically emphasize a great deal. In the books that Cicero wrote in support of their position, there is a certain passage that seems to me to have a remarkably witty flavor; it seems to not a few people to be strong and forceful as well. It's 30
difficult for anyone not to be impressed by what is said there:[136]

> All the adherents of other schools, who seem to themselves to be wise, award second place to the wise man of the Academicians — since each inevitably claims first place for himself! From this it can be plausibly inferred that the Academician correctly judges himself to hold first 35
> place, since he is second in the judgment of all the others.
>
> Suppose, for example, that the wise man of the Stoics is present (for [3.7.16] the Academicians pitted their wits against the Stoics above all). Then if Zeno or Chrysippus were asked who the wise man is, he'll reply that 40
> the wise man is the one whom he himself has described. In return, Epicurus or another adversary will deny this and maintain instead that the wise man is the one most skilled at catching pleasures. And so the fight is on!

133. The remainder of the work, apart from a summary and brief conclusion, is a monologue by Augustine.

134. See the note on 1.1.3.71–72 above.

135. By "the pen" Augustine is presumably referring to the transcription being made of the discussion: he must speak slowly and carefully for the amanuensis to transcribe his discourse.

136. Cicero, *Academica* frag. 20 (Müller). Some scholars deny that 3.7.16.37–65 is authentic Cicero, but most take it as genuine, primarily on the basis of Augustine's remark at 3.7.16.66 that this "bit of theater" was provided by Cicero.

The whole Porch is in an uproar! Zeno is shouting that man is naturally apt for nothing but virtue, which attracts minds to itself by its
45   own grandeur without offering any extrinsic advantage and reward as
a kind of enticement; Epicurus's 'pleasure' is common only among
brute animals, and to push man — and the wise man! — into an asso-
ciation with them is abominable.

Epicurus, like Bacchus, has called together a drunken mob from his
Gardens to aid him against this onslaught! The mob is searching for
50   someone to tear to pieces with their long fingernails and savage fangs
in their Bacchic fury. Elevating the name of pleasure as agreeableness
and calm, with popular support Epicurus passionately insists that
without pleasure nobody could seem happy.

If an Academician should stumble into their quarrel, he'll listen to
55   both parties urging him to take up their side. If he gives in to one side
or the other, those whom he has left behind will declare him to be foolish, ignorant, and reckless. Consequently, if asked what he thinks after
listening attentively to the one side and the other side, he'll say that he
is in doubt.

Now ask the Stoic who is the better: Epicurus, who proclaims that
the Stoic is out of his mind, or the Academician, who states that he
must deliberate further about such an important issue? Nobody
60   doubts that the Academician is going to be preferred.

Next turn to Epicurus and ask him whom he likes the better: Zeno,
who names him a brute animal, or Arcesilaus, from whom he hears:
'Perhaps you're speaking the truth, but I'll look into it more carefully.'
Isn't it clear that to Epicurus the whole of the Stoic school seems foolish, whereas the Academicians, in comparison with them, are unas-
suming and cautious men?

65   In this way, Cicero presents his readers with an enjoyable bit of
theater, as it were, regarding almost all the sects [of philosophy].
He shows that although each inevitably gives first place to itself,
all of them give second place to the one whom it sees as not
opposed to but in doubt about its position. I won't raise any objec-
70   tion on this score, nor deprive them[137] of any glory.

[3.8.17]   "Cicero may seem to some people not to be speaking in jest but,
because he was appalled by the frivolity of these piddling Greeks,
to have held that certain inanities and trivialities do follow as logical consequences.

137. The 'them' are either the Academicians or those who are impressed
by this line of argument.

"If I should wish to oppose this travesty . . . Well, what prevents me from easily showing how much less evil it is to be untaught 5 than unteachable? It turns out that once this braggart of an Academician has offered himself as a student to each sect, and none of them could persuade him of what each respectively thinks it knows, then afterward he'll be laughed at by them all in grand agreement. Now each sect will judge that none of its adversaries has learned anything, whereas the Academician is incapable of 10 learning anything. As a result he'll be thrown out of all the schools — not with the rod, which would be more disgraceful than injurious, but with the clubs and cudgels of the men of the mantle.[138] There won't be any trouble in getting the help of the Cynics, as a herculean aid against the common nuisance!

"If it were appropriate to compete with the Academicians for 15 these petty triumphs of theirs — I ought to be allowed to do so the more readily since I apply myself to philosophy but I'm not yet wise — what do they have to refute me with? Look, suppose an Academician and I push our way into those controversies among the philosophers. Let them all be present; let them expound their views briefly in the time allotted; let the question be put to Car- 20 neades what he holds. He'll reply that he is in doubt. Thus each will prefer him to the others, and therefore all prefer him to all: an exceptionally great and remarkable triumph!

"Who wouldn't want to imitate him? I'll therefore give the same reply when asked my opinion. My praise shall equal his. Hence the wise man rejoices in a triumph wherein a fool is his 25 equal!

"What if the fool also overcomes him readily? Has he no shame? I'll seize the Academician just as he is leaving the courtroom. Foolishness is greedy for a victory of this sort. Therefore, holding him tight, I'll reveal to the judges what they don't know by saying: 'Gentlemen, I have it in common with this man to be in 30 doubt about who among you is following the truth. We also have

138. Philosophers wore a distinctive cloak or mantle: the *pallium* = ἱμάτιον. (Augustine's contemporary Ammianus Marcellinus also calls philosophers 'men of the mantle,' *palliati*, at 15.8.1, for instance.) The Cynics wore the mantle and in addition carried a staff; Augustine mocks them for this on the score of their pretension to imitate Hercules, the ideal of self-sufficiency, in *The City of God* 14.20.

our own views, and I ask you to render a verdict on them. On the
one hand, I'm uncertain where the truth lies, despite having heard
your doctrines, for the reason that I don't know who among you
is wise. On the other hand, the Academician denies that even the
35   wise man himself knows anything, not even the very wisdom by
reason of which he's called wise in the first place!' Does anyone
fail to see who gets the palm of victory? If my opponent admits my
charge, I'll surpass him in triumph. Yet if he blushingly admits
that the wise man knows wisdom, I'll win the judgment.

[3.9.18]   "Let's now withdraw from this now litigious tribunal to
another place, one where there is no crowd to disturb us. If only it
were Plato's school itself, which is said to have been given its
name from the fact that it was remote from the people![139] Here let
5   us no longer speak of 'triumph,' which is trifling and childish, but,
as far as we can, let us speak of life itself and any hope there is for
a happy mind.

"The Academicians deny that anything can be known. On what
grounds did you accept this claim, you scholarly and learned gentlemen? 'Zeno's definition has taught us this,' they reply. Tell me
how! If his definition is true, anyone who knows it knows some-
10   thing true. If it's false, it shouldn't disturb men of such steadfast
character.

"But let's look at what Zeno says. That is,[140]

> The appearance that can be apprehended and perceived is such that it
> does not have signs in common with what is false.

Did this definition move you, my dear platonist, to try to draw

139. Plato's school is the Academy (Ἀκαδήμεια). Diogenes Laertius, in
Lives of the Eminent Philosophers 3.7–8, asserts that the Academy was
named after a man called 'Hecademus' and hence was originally known
as Ἑκαδήμεια. (Suidas also asserts that this was the original form of its
name.) Augustine takes this to be a version of ἑκάς + δῆμος = 'remote
from the people.'
140. See 2.5.11.12–14 for a different version of Zeno's definition, and
2.5.11.14–16 for Augustine's paraphrase, from which this version seems
to be derived (in particular the mention of internal 'signs' in the appearance). See also 3.9.21.50–51. Cicero, *Academica* 2.11.34: "There won't be
any judgment in the case of a [presentation] if it has anything in common
with what is false, since a distinguishing property (*proprium*) cannot be
indicated by a common sign."

those interested away from the hope of learning, so that they
abandon the whole business of doing philosophy, helped along 15
by their deplorable mental laziness?

"Why didn't it upset Zeno greatly that nothing of the kind can [3.9.19]
be found, given that only something of that kind can be perceived? If this is the case, one should say that man can't possess
wisdom, rather than saying that the wise man doesn't know why 20
he lives, doesn't know how he lives, doesn't know whether he
lives, and finally — nothing more perverse and more crazy and
foolish can be said than this — that he be simultaneously wise and
ignorant of wisdom! Which is harder to take: that man can't be
wise, or that the wise man doesn't know wisdom? If the matter 25
itself doesn't offer sufficient grounds for making a judgment
when laid out in this way, then there is no use in discussing it any
further.

"If the claim [that man cannot be wise] were made, however,
perhaps men would be completely driven away from philosophy.
They are lured to it now by the seductive and holy name 'wisdom,' so that once they are old and have learned nothing they will
pursue you with their greatest curses: after forsaking at least the 30
pleasures of the flesh they followed you into the torments of the
mind!

"Let's see who it is that deters men the most from philosophy. [3.9.20]
Is it the one who says: 'Listen, my friend, philosophy is not called
wisdom itself but the zeal for wisdom. If you devote yourself to it
you won't be wise while you're living here on Earth, for wisdom 35
is in God's province and can't come to man. Once you've sufficiently exercised and purified yourself in this kind of pursuit,
your spirit will rejoice in it completely after this life — that is,
when you cease to be a man.' Or is it the one who says: 'Come,
mortal men, to philosophy! There is great advantage here. What is 40
more dear to man than wisdom? Come, therefore, so that you may
be wise and not know wisdom!' 'I won't put it that way,' says the
Academician. This is deception, then, for nothing else is found in
your sect. So it turns out that if you say this they will shun you as
though you were a madman, and if you bring them to your position in another way you make madmen out of them.

"Well, let's suppose that men on either view equally don't want 45
to do philosophy. If Zeno's definition compelled the saying of
something damaging to philosophy, my friend, which should a

man be told: something that makes him unhappy or something that makes him laugh at you?

[3.9.21]   "Still, let's discuss Zeno's definition as best we simple people
50   can. Zeno says that an appearance can be apprehended if it appears in such a way that it couldn't appear as a falsehood.[141] Clearly nothing else enters into perception.

"'I also recognize this point,' says Arcesilaus, 'and for this reason I teach that nothing is perceived. Nothing of the sort can be found.'

"Perhaps not by you, Arcesilaus, or by other simple people, but
55   why can't it be found by the wise man? Yet I think nothing can be said in reply to the simple person who tells you, Arcesilaus, to use your remarkable acumen to refute Zeno's definition and show that it too can be false. If you're unable to do so, you then have something you perceive, whereas if you refute it you have no grounds that prevent you from perceiving.[142]

60   "For my part, I don't see that Zeno's definition can be refuted, and I judge it to be completely truthful. Thus when I know it, I know something, despite being simple.

"Suppose it gives way to your cleverness, Arcesilaus. In that case I'll use the soundest kind of inference. Zeno's definition is either true or false. If it's true, I am correct to grasp it. If it's false,
65   something can be perceived though it has signs in common with what is false. 'How can that be?' Arcesilaus asks. Well, then, Zeno's definition is entirely true, and anyone who has even agreed with him on this score isn't in error. Are we going to think his definition of little worth or merit? While indicating the kind of thing that could be perceived (contrary to those who will say
70   many things against perception), it also shows itself to be that very kind of thing! In this way, it's both a definition and an example of things that can be apprehended.

"'I don't know whether Zeno's definition is itself even true,' says Arcesilaus. 'I follow it because it's plausible, and thereby show that there isn't anything of the sort it proclaims to be apprehensible!'

"Perhaps you show that there isn't anything apart from the def-

---

141. See the earlier formulations at 2.5.11.12–14.

142. This paragraph contains Augustine's argument that the skeptical challenge based on Zeno's definition is self-defeating.

inition itself. You see, I think, the implications.

"Knowledge still doesn't abandon us, even if we're uncertain   75
about it. We know that Zeno's definition is either true or false.
Hence we do not know nothing.

"Yet it will never happen that I fail to appreciate it! I for one
judge his definition to be entirely truthful. Either falsehoods can
also be perceived (of which the Academicians have a great dread
and which is in fact absurd), or neither can those things that are   80
similar to falsehoods. Accordingly, Zeno's definition is true. Now
let's look at what remains.

"Although these remarks, unless I'm mistaken, are sufficient   [3.10.22]
to gain my victory, they perhaps aren't enough for the fullness
of my victory. There are two statements made by the Academicians which we decided to argue against to the best of our ability:[143] (*a*) nothing can be perceived; (*b*) one should not assent to
anything. We'll talk about assenting shortly, but right now a few   5
other remarks about perception are in order.

"Have all of you said that nothing whatsoever can be apprehended? At this point, Carneades woke up — for none of the Academicians slept more lightly than he did — and looked about at
the evidentness of things. So while talking to himself, as sometimes happens, I believe he said: 'Well then, Carneades, are you
going to say that you don't know whether you're a man or a bug?   10
Will Chrysippus triumph over you? Let's say that we don't know
the things philosophers ask about, and that the rest is of no concern to us. Thus if I stumble in plain ordinary daylight, I'll appeal
to matters that are obscure to the ignorant, wherein only a certain
few who have godlike vision may see. Even if they see me tottering   15
and falling, they can't betray me to the blind, and especially not to
those who are arrogant and too proud to be taught anything.'

"You're doing well, you Greek subtlety, prepared and
equipped as you are! Yet you don't take into account the fact that
Zeno's definition is the invention of a philosopher. It is set and
placed firmly at the entrance to philosophy. If you try to cut it   20
down, your double-edged axe will bounce back onto your shins!
Once it is weakened, not only can something be perceived, but
unless you dare to get rid of the definition altogether, even what

143. See 3.7.14.4–6, where "these contentions" refers to (*a*) and (*b*) below,
mentioned previously at 3.5.11.8–9.

is very like the false can be perceived. Zeno's definition is your
hiding place from which you rush forth furiously and pounce
upon the unwary who want to pass along their way; some Her-
25   cules will strangle you in your cavern as though you were half-
human and crush you under its walls,[144] teaching that there is
something in philosophy that you can't make uncertain even
though it is like what is false.

"I was in a hurry to get to other points, of course. Anyone who
urges me to do so is hurling a great insult at you, Carneades, since
he thinks you're no better than a dead man and can be overcome
30   by me anywhere and from any angle. If someone doesn't think
that this is so, however, then he's merciless in forcing me to abandon my fortifications everywhere and to do battle with him on the
open plain. Although I began to come down to the plain, I was
frightened by your mere name and drew back and threw some
kind of missile from my high position. Whether it reached you, or
what it did — well, let those who are watching our struggle see for
themselves.

-35   "What am I foolishly afraid of? If I remember correctly, you are
dead, Carneades. Alypius is no longer fighting righteously before
your tomb. God will readily give me assistance against your
ghφst!

[3.10.23]   "You say that nothing can be perceived in philosophy, and, to
40   spread your claim far and wide, you seize upon the quarrels and
disagreements among philosophers and think them to furnish
you with weapons against philosophers themselves.[145]

"How shall we decide the controversy between Democritus
and earlier physicists about whether there is one world or innumerable worlds,[146] when Democritus and his heir Epicurus were

144. In *Aeneid* 8.184–279, Evander tells the story of Cacus, a half-human
monster who lived in a well-hidden cave and attacked men and livestock.
Hercules threw down the mountains concealing his cave, pinning Cacus
in the rubble, and strangled him.

145. See Cicero, *Academica* 2.41.127–28. Augustine's discussion proceeds
through the traditional Stoic division of philosophy into physics (3.10.23–
11.26), ethics (3.12.27–28), and dialectic or logic (3.13.29). See the specific
reference in 3.13.29.6–7.

146. Cicero describes Democritus's claim that there are innumerable
worlds in *Academica* 2.17.55.

unable to remain in agreement? Once that voluptuary Epicurus 45
allows atoms, as though they were his little handmaids — that is,
the little bodies he gladly embraces in the dark — not to stay on
their courses but to swerve freely here and there into the paths of
others, he has also dissipated his entire patrimony through such
quarrels.[147]

"This is all irrelevant to me. If it pertains to wisdom to know
something of these matters, it can't escape the notice of the wise 50
man. If wisdom is something else, then the wise man knows those
other matters to be wisdom, and he'll scorn these matters.

"However, although I'm still far from being anywhere close to
a wise man, I do know some things in physics. I'm certain that the
world is either one [in number] or not — and, if there isn't just one
world, the number of worlds is either finite or infinite. Let Car- 55
neades teach that this view is 'like' something false!

"Similarly, I know that this world of ours has been arranged as
it is either by the nature of bodies or by some providence; that it
always was and will be, or began to be and is never going to end,
or did not have a beginning in time but is going to have an end, or
it began to exist in time and is not going to exist forever. 60

"I know countless things about physics in this fashion. These
disjunctions are true, and nobody can confound them with any
likeness to what is false.

"'Choose one of the disjuncts!' says the Academician. I refuse
to do so, for this is to say: pass over what you know and assert
what you don't know. 'Your view is dangling in the air!' It's defi- 65
nitely better for it to dangle than to fall to the ground. It is of
course in plain view; it can now of course be named either true or
false. I say that I know it.

"You who don't deny that these matters are pertinent to philosophy and assert that none of them can be known — show me that
I don't know them! Tell me either that these disjunctions are false
or that they have something in common with what is false, so that 70
they are completely indistinguishable from what is false!

147. "He has also dissipated his entire patrimony through such quarrels": Augustine's point is that Epicurus has given up Democritus's atomism (his 'patrimony') by introducing theoretical changes (the 'quarrels')
such as the atomic swerve. For the latter, see Cicero, *On Good and Evil
Goals* 1.6.19.

[3.11.24]   "'How do you know that the world exists,' replies the Academician, 'if the senses are deceptive?'[148] Your arguments were
never able to disown the power of our senses to the extent of
clearly establishing that nothing seems to be so to us.[149] Nor have
you ever ventured to try to do so. However, you've energetically
committed yourself to persuading us that something seems so and
5   yet can be otherwise.

        "Therefore, I call the whole that contains and sustains us, what-
ever it is, the 'world' — the whole, I say, that appears before my
eyes, which I perceive to include the heavens and the earth (or the
quasi-heavens and quasi-earth).

        "If you say nothing seems to be so to me, I'll never be in error.
10   It is the man who recklessly approves what seems so to him
who is in error. You do say that a falsehood can seem to be so
to sentient beings. You don't say that nothing seems to be so.
Every ground for disputation, where you Academicians enjoy
being the master, is completely taken away if it is true not only
that we know nothing, but also that nothing seems to be so to
us. However, if you deny that what seems so to me is the world,
15   then you're making a fuss about a name, since I said I call this
'world.'

[3.11.25]   "You'll ask me: 'Is what you see the world even if you're
asleep?' It has already been said that I call 'world' whatever seems
to me to be such. If it pleases the Academician to call 'world' only
what seems so to those who are awake, or even better to those
who are sane, then maintain this if you can: that those who are
20   asleep or insane aren't asleep and insane in the world! For this reason, I state that this whole mass of bodies and the contrivance in
which we exist — whether we be asleep, insane, awake, or sane —
either is one or is not one. Explain how this view can be false! Now
25   if I'm asleep, it might be that I don't say anything. Or, if the words
escape from my mouth while I'm sleeping, as sometimes happens,

148. The Academician's reply is that Augustine's disjunctions are dubious because each disjunct assumes something dubious, namely that the
world exists in the first place.

149. "That nothing seems to be so to us": *nobis nihil videri*, literally 'nothing seems to us,' which might be paraphrased "that we don't perceive
anything." The reference is to the doctrine of nonperception, not to the
reality of the external world.

it might be that I don't say them here, sitting as I am, to this audience. Yet the claim itself can't be false.

"Nor do I say that I've perceived this because I'm awake. You can say that this also could seem so to me while I was sleeping, and thus it can be very like what is false. Yet if there is one world and six worlds, then, whatever condition I may be in, it's clear that there are seven worlds, and it isn't presumptuous for me to affirm that I know this.   30

"Accordingly, prove that either this inference or those disjunctions given above can be false because of sleep, madness, or the unreliability of the senses! If I remember them when I wake up, I'll   35
admit that I've been beaten. I think it's now sufficiently clear what falsehoods seem to be so through sleep and madness, namely, those that pertain to the bodily senses. For that three times three is nine and the square of rational numbers must be true, even if the human race be snoring away!

"I see that many things can also be said on behalf of the senses,   40
things we don't find censured by the Academicians. I think the senses aren't blamed when false imaginations befall madmen or when we see false things in dreams. If the senses report truths to those who are awake and sane, it's irrelevant to them[150] what the mind of a sleeping or insane person invents for itself.   45

"There remains the question whether, when the senses do   [3.11.26]
report, they are reporting the truth. Well, suppose that some Epicurean were to say: 'I have no complaint about the senses; it's unjust to require more from them than they can do. Whatever the eyes can see, they see to be the truth.' Then is what they see of an   50
oar in the water the truth?[151] Surely it's the truth! There is a cause intervening so that the oar should seem bent. If it were to appear straight while dipped in the water, then with good reason I would blame my eyes for giving a false report. They wouldn't be seeing what should have been seen, given the existence of such an intervening cause.

"What do we need many examples for? The same thing can be said about the [apparent] motion of towers, of the [changing   55

150. "It's irrelevant to them": *nihil ad eos*, presumably irrelevant to people who are awake and sane, although the natural reference here would be to the senses themselves.

151. An oar partially submerged in the water looks bent but is straight.

color] of bird feathers, and countless other cases.[152]

"'I'm in error if I assent!' someone objects.

"Don't assent to more than that you're convinced it appears so to you, and then there isn't any deception. I don't see how even an Academician can refute someone who says: 'I know that this
60   seems white to me; I know that this sound is pleasant to me; I know that this smells good to me; I know that this tastes sweet to me; I know that this seems cold to me.

"'Tell me instead whether the leaves of the wild olive-tree, which the goat so stubbornly desires, are bitter in themselves.'

"You shameless man! The goat itself has more modesty! I don't know how they are to brute animals, but they are bitter to me.
65   What more do you ask?

"'Perhaps there is some man to whom they aren't bitter.'

"You're trying to be annoying, aren't you? Have I ever said that they are bitter for all men? I said that they are bitter for me — and I don't affirm that this is always so: what if at different times and for different reasons something tastes now sweet and now bitter
70   in someone's mouth? I state that a man is able, when he tastes something, to swear in good faith that he knows whether it is sweet to his palate or the contrary, and no Greek trickery can beguile him from this knowledge. Who is so impudent as to say to me while I'm relishing the flavor of something: 'Perhaps you're not tasting this, since it may be a dream!'? Do I stop relishing it?
75   On the contrary, it would please me even in a dream! Thus no likeness of falsehoods confounds what I've said that I know.

"Perhaps an Epicurean or the Cyrenaics would say many other things on behalf of the senses. I'm not aware of anything said by the Academicians to refute them. What is that to me? If they want to, and if they can, let them refute these claims — even with my assistance.

80   "Whatever the Academicians maintain against the senses doesn't hold against all philosophers. There are philosophers who grant that everything the mind takes from the bodily senses can

152. A stationary tower in the midrange of the field of vision appears to be moving in the same direction as an observer on a passing ship; Augustine refers to this case in *The Trinity* 15.12.21 (Appendix 6). Some bird feathers appear to have different colors when seen from different angles: see the note to 3.12.27.3–4.

generate opinion. They deny that this is knowledge, however. They hold that knowledge is contained in the intelligence and abides in the mind, far removed from the senses.[153] Maybe the wise man we're searching for is found among their number.

    "We'll discuss this at some other time. Right now let's move on to the remaining parts [of philosophy]. Unless I'm mistaken, in view of what has been said we'll be able to explain them in a few words.

    "What help or hindrance do the bodily senses give to the man searching for ethics? Nothing prevents those who put the highest good of man in pleasure — neither the dove's neck, nor the uncertain cry, nor the weight that is heavy for a man but light for a camel, nor a thousand other things[154] — from saying that they know themselves to take pleasure in what they take pleasure in, and to be displeased by what displeases them. I don't see how this can be refuted. Will these things influence the man who places the final good in the mind?

    "'Which of these do you choose?'

    "If you're asking what *seems* so to me, I think that the highest good of man is in the mind.[155] Right now, though, we're asking about knowledge. Therefore, put your question to the wise man, who can't be ignorant of wisdom. Although I'm a dullard and a fool, meanwhile I'm permitted to know that the ultimate human good, wherein the happy life dwells, either is nothing, or is in the mind or in the body, or in both. Prove, if you can, that I don't know this! Your best-known arguments can do nothing. If you can't do this — for you won't uncover any falsehood it is like — shall I hesitate to draw the correct conclusion, namely that it seems to me the wise man knows whatever in philosophy is true,

85

[3.12.27]

5

10

15

153. These philosophers are the Platonists: see Cicero, *Academica* 1.8.31–32.

154. Cicero refers to "the case of the bent oar and the dove's neck" in *Academica* 2.7.19. He explains the latter by saying that "in the case of the dove there seem to be many colors but really there is no more than one" (*Academica* 2.25.79). See the note to 3.11.26.55. The "uncertain cry" is the sound that might be made by an animal or by a human — perhaps Augustine is thinking of the cries of cats and of human infants. The weight that is heavy for a man and light for a camel is a standard example meant to show the relativity of judgment.

155. See *Revisions* 1.1.4 (Appendix 11).

since I myself know so many truths in philosophy?

[3.12.28]
20   "'Perhaps [the wise man] is afraid of choosing the highest good while he's sleeping!'

"*There isn't any danger.*[156] If it displeases him when he awakens, he'll reject it. If it pleases him, he'll retain it.[157] Who will justly censure him for having seen something false in a dream?

"Well, maybe you're afraid that he'll lose his wisdom if he
25 approves falsehoods as truths while he's sleeping. However, not even a sleeping man would dare to dream that he call a man wise while he's awake but deny him to be so if he were to be sleeping!

"The same points can be made for the case of madness. Although our discussion is moving along to other matters, I won't leave this topic without drawing a solid conclusion: either wisdom is lost through madness, and then the person you declare to
30 be ignorant of the truth will not be the wise man, or his knowledge remains in his intellect even if the other part of his mind imagines, as if in a dream, what it receives from the senses.

[3.13.29]   "There remains dialectic, which the wise man certainly knows well. Nor can anyone know what is false. Now if the wise man doesn't know dialectic, the knowledge of dialectic is irrelevant to wisdom, since he was able to be wise without it, and it's superfluous for us to ask whether dialectic is true or whether it can be perceived.

5   "At this point someone may say to me: 'You fool, you usually tell us whatever you know. Weren't you able to know anything about dialectic?'

"I know more about dialectic than about any other part of philosophy. First, it was dialectic that taught me that all the propositions we used above are true. Furthermore, I know many other truths through dialectic.

10   "'Well, count how many there are, if you can.'

"If there are four elements in the world, there are not five. If there is only one Sun, there are not two. The same soul can't both die and be immortal. A man can't be simultaneously happy and miserable. It isn't the case here that the Sun is shining and that it

---

156. Terence, *The Lady of Andros* 350.

157. See Cicero, *Academica* 2.16.51, who argues that just as nobody is fooled by his own imagination once he is called back to himself, so too for dreams.

is night. We are now either asleep or awake. What I seem to see is   15
either a body or not a body. . . .

"These and many other things, which would take too long to
mention, I've learned to be true through dialectic. They are true in
themselves regardless of what condition our senses are in. If the
antecedent part of any of the conditional statements I've just put
forward is assumed, then dialectic has taught me to deduce necessarily what is connected to it.[158] The statements I've enunciated   20
that involve incompatibility or disjunction have this nature: when
the other parts are taken away (whether they be one or many),
something remains that is confirmed by their removal.[159]

"Dialectic has also taught me that there shouldn't be any dispute over words when there is agreement on the matter for the
sake of which the words are spoken. Anyone who disputes in this   25
way should be instructed if he does so through inexperience; he
should be ignored if he does so through malice; he should be
advised to do something other than waste our time and effort on
trivialities if he can't be instructed; and he should be disregarded
if he doesn't comply.

"Now there is a concise precept dealing with captious and fallacious petty arguments: *if the conclusion is inferred by means of a*   30
mistaken concession, one should return to what has been conceded.[160] If
truth and falsity are in conflict in one and the same conclusion, we
should take from it what we understand and leave behind what
can't be explained. If the criterion of certain matters is completely
hidden from man, the knowledge of that criterion isn't to be
looked for.

"I've learned all these things, and many others we need not   35
mention, from dialectic. Nor should I be unappreciative. Yet the
wise man disregards these matters — or, if perfect dialectic is itself
the knowledge of truth, he knows dialectic in such a way that he
demolishes the most captious sophism [of the Academicians],
namely 'If it is true it is false and if it is false it is true,' by spurning   40
it with pitiless contempt.[161]

158. That is: if $p \rightarrow q$ and p, then necessarily q. (*Modus ponens.*) The deduc-
tion is necessary, not the conclusion.

159. That is: if $p \lor q$ and $\neg p$, then q. (Disjunction-elimination.)

160. This precept is mentioned in 1.3.8.29–34.

161. The "captious sophism" Augustine is referring to is the Liar Paradox

"I think these remarks about perception are enough, especially since the whole topic will be dealt with again once I start to talk about assenting.

[3.14.30]   "Now, then, let's come to a point on which Alypius seems to be still in doubt, and first examine what it is that impels you, Alypius, to be so exacting and careful. This is what you've said:[162] 'If your discovery, [Augustine], namely that we're forced to admit that it's more plausible for the wise man to know wisdom,

5   destroys the Academicians' view that the wise man knows nothing — a view supported by many powerful arguments — then so much the more ought we to withhold assent! This very fact shows that no position can be advocated, no matter how keen and copi-

10   ous the arguments, that can't also be controverted with equal and perhaps greater acuity, given sufficient ingenuity. So it happens that the Academician wins even when he's beaten.'

"If only he were beaten! He'll never bring it to pass by any Greek trickery[163] that he is beaten by me and at the same time also goes away victorious. Of course, if nothing else be found that can be said against his arguments, then I freely confess that I have

15   been beaten. We aren't discussing these matters to attain glory but to find the truth. It's enough for me to get over, by any means, the mountain that gets in the way of those who are beginners at philosophy.[164] Casting shadows from unknown sources, it threatens

———
— the paradox generated by the sentence "I am lying" (or "This sentence is false"), which if true must be false and if false is thereby true. The Academicians used it to support their contention that dialectic is untrustworthy. ("Pitiless contempt," unfortunately, is not enough to deal with the Liar Paradox, which continues to inspire philosophical work today.) Augustine may derive his knowledge of the Liar Paradox from Cicero, *Academica* 2.29.95, who calls it "inexplicable."

162. See 3.5.11.6–14 for Alypius's statement of this argument.

163. "By any Greek trickery": *arte Pelasga*. Vergil uses this expression in *Aeneid* 2.106 and *Aeneid* 2.152. Augustine is referring to the argument summarized in the preceding paragraph.

164. See Augustine, *The Happy Life* 1.3: "Confronting all those who travel in any way to the region of the happy life there is a huge mountain, which is set in front of the harbor [of wisdom]. . . . What other mountain does reason maintain should be feared by those who are approaching and entering upon philosophy than the proud enthusiasm for empty glory?"

that the whole of philosophy is likewise obscure, and it doesn't
permit one to hope that any light is going to be found in it. 20

"There's nothing more I desire if it's now plausible that the
wise man knows something. *He should withhold his assent* seemed
truthlike precisely because *Nothing can be apprehended* was truthlike. Once this reason has been taken away — for the wise man
perceives at least wisdom itself, as has already been granted
(3.4.9.78–80) — then there won't be any reason left why the wise 25
man shouldn't assent at least to wisdom itself. It's undoubtedly
more monstrous that the wise man not give his approval to wisdom than it is for him not to know wisdom!

"For instance, let's envision for a moment the spectacle of some [3.14.31]
kind of conflict between the wise man and wisdom, if we can. 20
What else does wisdom say but that it is wisdom? However, he
replies: 'I don't believe you.' Who is saying to wisdom, 'I don't
believe that you are wisdom'? Who but the one to whom wisdom
can speak and with whom wisdom has deigned to dwell — that
is, the wise man?

"Now go and fetch me to fight with the Academicians. Now 35
you have a new contest! The wise man and wisdom are fighting
with one another! The wise man doesn't want to consent to wisdom! I'm waiting with you calmly, for who doesn't believe that
wisdom is invincible? Nevertheless, let's fortify our position with
some argumentation. In this contest either the Academician over- 40
comes wisdom (in which case he is overcome by me since he
won't be the wise man), or he'll be conquered by wisdom (in
which case we shall teach that the wise man consents to wisdom).
Hence either the Academician is not the wise man, or the wise
man will assent to something — unless the one[165] who was
ashamed to say that the wise man doesn't know wisdom perhaps
won't be ashamed to say that the wise man doesn't consent to wis- 45
dom! If it's now truthlike that at least the perception of wisdom
comes to the wise man, and there isn't any reason he not assent to
what he perceives, I see that what I wanted is truthlike, namely
that the wise man is going to assent to wisdom.

"If you ask me where he finds wisdom itself, I'll reply that he 50
finds it in himself. If you say that he doesn't know what he pos-

165. That is, Alypius. This claim is the crux of the argument between
Augustine and Alypius in 3.3.5–3.4.9.

sesses, you're returning to the absurdity that the wise man doesn't know wisdom. If you deny that the wise man himself can be found, then we'll argue about this in another discussion — not one with the Academicians, but a discussion with you, whoever you are, who hold this view. When the Academicians debate these
55   matters, they are certainly debating about the wise man! Cicero proclaims that he himself is a great one to hold opinions,[166] but that he's dealing with the wise man. If you young men were unaware of this, you've surely read in the *Hortensius*:[167]

> If, then, nothing is certain and the wise man doesn't hold mere opinions, the wise man will never give his approval to anything.

The Academicians are clearly dealing with the wise man in the
60   disputations of theirs we're wrestling with.
[3.14.32]   "Therefore, I think that the wise man surely possesses wisdom. That is to say, the wise man has perceived wisdom, and so he isn't holding a mere opinion when he assents to wisdom. If he didn't perceive the thing to which he assents, he wouldn't be wise. The
65   Academicians only assert that a person shouldn't assent to things that can't be perceived. Wisdom isn't nothing. Thus when the wise man knows wisdom and assents to wisdom, it isn't the case that he knows nothing and assents to nothing.

"What more do you want? Are we dealing with error, which the Academicians say is completely avoided if assent doesn't
70   incline the mind to anything? Someone is in error, they claim, not only if he gives his approval to a false thing, but even if he gives his approval to a doubtful one though it be in fact true. Well, for my part I find nothing that isn't doubtful. Yet the wise man, as we were saying, finds wisdom itself.
[3.15.33]   "Perhaps you want me to leave all this behind now. The soundest points shouldn't be abandoned lightly, since we're dealing with crafty people. Nevertheless, I'll comply with your request.

"What shall I say now? What? What indeed?
5   "A hoary old objection should be made, one where the Academicians also have a reply to offer. Well, what else shall I do?

166. Cicero, *Academica* 2.21.66: "I am indeed a great one to hold opinions, for I'm not a wise man."
167. Cicero, *Hortensius* frag. 100 (Müller).

You're pushing me out of my strongholds! Shall I plead for assistance from the learned, with whom, if I'm unable to win, it will be perhaps less shameful to lose? So I shall hurl with all my might a weapon that is now rusty and musty but, unless I'm mistaken, is still effective: *someone who gives his approval to nothing does nothing.*[168] 10

"'You simple fellow! What about the plausible? What about the truthlike?'

"This reply is what you expected. Don't you hear the clanging of Grecian shields? My strongest weapon has been withstood, though we hurled it with great force! So far as I see, we didn't inflict any wound, and my supporters provide me with nothing more potent. I'll turn to whatever assistance the country-house 15 and farm offer. The bigger weapons are burdensome rather than helpful to me.

"When in my retirement in the country I had been pondering [3.15.34] for a long time just how the plausible or the truthlike can defend our actions from error, at first the matter seemed to me nicely pro- 20 tected and fortified, as it usually seemed when I was peddling it.[169] Later, when I inspected the whole issue more carefully, I seemed to see an entrance through which error would rush in upon those who felt safe. I think that a man is in error not only when he follows the false path, but also when he's not following the true one.

"For example, suppose there are two men traveling to one place. One of them has decided not to believe anyone, whereas the 25 other is exceptionally credulous. They come to a fork in the road. The credulous traveler addresses a shepherd or other peasant who is there: 'Hello, my good man! Please tell me which is the best road to that place.' He receives this answer: 'If you take this road

---

168. See 2.5.12.23–27 for this objection.

169. Augustine often disparages his former career as a rhetorician by describing himself as no more than a "salesman of words" (*venditor verborum*: *Confessions* 9.5.13). See for example *Confessions* 4.2.2 ("I used to sell the loquacity that would overcome an opponent") and *Confessions* 8.6.13 ("I was selling my abilities at public speaking"). Here Augustine says he himself held that "the plausible or the truthlike can defend our actions from error" while he was a rhetorician, alluding to his period as a skeptic: see the Introduction n. 5.

you won't be in error.' To his companion he says: 'He's telling the
30   truth; let's go this way.' The careful traveler laughs and ridicules
the other for having assented so rapidly. While the other departs,
he stands still at the fork in the road. Well, he's starting to feel foolish for stopping there, when look! From the other branch of the
road, coming closer, there appears a well-dressed townsman
riding on a horse. The traveler is relieved, and after greeting the
man as he approaches, he describes his situation and asks him the
35   way. He even tells him the reason for his remaining there, prefer-
ring him to the shepherd, to make the townsman well disposed to
himself. Now the townsman happened to be a trickster, one of
those who are now commonly called 'double-dealers.'[170] The ras-
cal followed his usual practice (and did so gratuitously): 'Go this
way,' he said. 'I've just come from there.' He deceived him and
40   went along his way. Yet our traveler would not be deceived! 'I
don't give my approval to his information as true,' he said, 'but
since his information is truthlike, and remaining idle here is neither appropriate nor advantageous, I'll take this road.' Meanwhile
the traveler who was in error because of his assent, judging so rapidly that the shepherd's words were true, was already relaxing in
45   the place to which they were heading. The one 'not in error as long
as he followed the plausible' is wandering around in some woods
and still hasn't found anyone who knows his destination!

   "To tell the truth, I couldn't help laughing while I was thinking
about these things. According to the words of the Academicians,
it somehow happens that the one who keeps to the true road, even
50   by chance, is in error, whereas the one following plausibility was
led over out-of-the-way mountains, not finding the region he was
searching for, and yet doesn't seem to be in error! So that I may
rightly censure reckless consent: it's easier to hold that both trav-
elers are in error than that the latter is not in error.

   "As a result I was now more watchful against the words of the
Academicians, and I began to reflect on human deeds and cus-
55   toms. Then so many important considerations against them came
to mind that I wasn't laughing at them any longer. I was partly
angered and partly saddened that men so learned and ingenious
had fallen into such criminal and shameful views.

170. "Double-dealers": *samardoci* (or *samardaci*), a word most likely African in origin.

"To be sure, maybe not everyone who is in error is sinning. [3.16.35]
Everyone who is sinning, however, is granted to be either in error
or something worse. Then what if some young man, after he has
heard the Academicians saying: 'It's shameful to be in error, and
hence we ought not to consent to anything; but when someone 5
does what seems plausible to him he's neither remiss nor in error:
he'll only have to remember that no matter what comes to his
mind or his senses, it shouldn't be approved as a truth' — what if
the young man hearing this mounts an assault on the chastity of
another man's wife?

"I'm asking you, Cicero, for your advice! We're discussing the
life and morals of young men, and all your writings have been 10
concerned with their education and instruction. What else are you
going to say except that it isn't plausible to you for the young man
to do this? Yet it's plausible to him. If we are to live according to
what is plausible to another, then you shouldn't have governed
the Roman Republic, since it seemed to Epicurus that one ought
not do this.

"The young man, then, will commit adultery with another
man's wife. If he gets caught, where will he find you to defend 15
him? Even if he finds you, though, what are you going to say [in
his defense]? Surely you'll deny it. What if it's so clear that gain-
saying it is pointless? You'll certainly convince everyone, as
though you were in school at Cumae or even Naples, that he 20
hadn't committed any sin — or rather, that he hadn't even been in
error. He didn't convince himself that *Adultery should be committed*
is a truth. It struck him as plausible; he followed it up; he committed adultery. Or maybe he didn't commit adultery, but it merely
seemed to him that he had done so! Moreover, the husband, a silly
man, is throwing everything into turmoil by his lawsuits and
shouting about his wife's chastity. Perhaps he's now asleep with 25
her and he doesn't know it!

"If the judges understand this, they will either (*a*) ignore the
Academicians and punish him as though it really were a true
crime, or (*b*) go along with the selfsame Academicians and find the
[young] man guilty in a plausible and truthlike way, so that now
his lawyer is completely at a loss what to do. He won't have any
reason to be angry with anyone, since they all say that they did 30
nothing in error when they did what seemed plausible while not
assenting to it. So he'll put aside the role of lawyer and take up

that of the philosopher offering consolation. He'll thus easily convince the young man, who has already made such progress in the Academy, to think that he has been found guilty only in a dream.

35   "You think I'm joking! I'm ready to swear by everything holy[171] that I'm utterly at a loss to know how that young man sinned, if anyone who does what seems plausible doesn't sin — unless perhaps the Academicians say that to be in error is one thing and to sin is a completely different thing, and that they formulated their teachings so that we not fall into error, whereas they thought sinning to be of no great consequence.

[3.16.36]   "I say nothing about cases of homicide, parricide, sacrilege, and
40   in general all the crimes and misdeeds that can be perpetrated or thought up — they are all justified by a few words and, what is more serious, before the wisest judges: 'I consented to nothing and so was not in error, but how could I not do what seemed plausible?'

45   "Well, let those who don't think that such claims can be plausibly convincing read Catiline's speech![172] There he defends 'parricide' of the Fatherland, and in this crime all others are included.

"The Academicians say that in their actions they follow only the plausible, and they are searching mightily for the truth, although it's plausible to them that it can't be found. Now doesn't
50   everyone laugh at this? What a wonderful monstrosity!

"Let's set this point aside, since it doesn't concern us or endanger our lives or belongings. The earlier point is fundamental, appalling, and abhorrent to every upright person. If the reasoning of the Academicians is plausible, a person may commit any atroc-
55   ity whenever it seems plausible to him that it ought to be done, as long as he doesn't assent to anything as a truth, and he may do so not only without being blamed for a crime but also without being blamed for an error.

"What then? Didn't the Academicians see this?

"They did see it, with great cleverness and sagacity. I wouldn't lay claim in any way to follow in Cicero's footsteps on the score of

171. Augustine regrets having sworn this oath in *Revisions* 1.1.4 (Appendix 11). The oath derives from Terence, *The Eunuch* 331 (*illum liquet mihi deierare . . .*).

172. Catiline's speech is 'reported' in Sallust, *The War Against Catiline* 20.2–17.

subtlety, alertness, ingenuity, or learning. Yet when he declares 60
that man can't know anything, if someone were to say only this: 'I
know that it seems to me that he can,' Cicero wouldn't have any
grounds on which to refute it.

"Why, then, did such great men enter into endless and dogged [3.17.37]
disputes against anyone's seeming to have knowledge of the
truth?

"Listen now a bit more carefully: not to what I know, but to
what I think. I've saved this to the last to explain, if I could, what 5
seems to me to be the whole policy of the Academicians.

"Plato, the wisest and most learned man of his day, spoke in
such a way that anything he said became important, and he said
things that, regardless of how he might say them, were not unim-
portant. After the death of his teacher Socrates, whom he had 10
loved so deeply, Plato is said to have also learned many things
from the Pythagoreans. Now Pythagoras himself had been dissat-
isfied with Greek philosophy (which hardly existed then or was at
least well hidden); after being influenced to believe in the immortality of the soul by the arguments of a certain Pherecydes of
Syros, he also traveled far and wide to hear many wise men.[173] 15
Plato added the knowledge of natural and divine matters, which
he had diligently acquired from those I've mentioned, to
Socrates's ethics with its wit and subtlety. He brought these com-
ponents together under dialectic as their organizer and judge,
since dialectic either is wisdom itself or that without which there 20
can't be wisdom. Plato is thereby said to have constructed a complete system of philosophy.

"There isn't time to discuss this now. For my purposes, it's
enough that Plato perceived that there are two worlds: an intelligible world where truth itself resides, and this sensible world that 25
we obviously sense by sight and touch. The former is the true
world, the latter only truthlike and made to its image. Consequently, truth about the former world is refined and brightened
(so to speak) in the soul that knows itself,[174] whereas only opinion,
and not knowledge, can be engendered about the latter world in
the souls of those who are unwise. Furthermore, whatever was

173. This account is derived from Cicero, *Tusculan Disputations* 1.16.38.
See also Plotinus, *Enneads* 1.2.1.
174. See *The Teacher* 12.40.30–33.

30   done in this world as the result of the virtues Plato called 'civic' —
        virtues that are like the other true virtues, which are known to
        only a few wise men — can only be called 'truthlike.'

[3.17.38]   "These and other matters of this kind seem to me to have been
        preserved, as far as possible, by Plato's successors and guarded as
35   'mysteries.' On the one hand, they are easily perceived only by
        those who purify themselves of all vices and adopt a different way
        of life, one that is more than human. On the other hand, someone
        who knows them and wanted to teach them to men of any kind at
        all commits a serious sin.

        "Consequently, I suspect that Zeno, the first of the Stoics, was
40   held in suspicion when he came to the school founded by Plato
        (presided over by Polemo then) after having heard and believed
        some of these doctrines. He didn't seem to be the kind of man to
        whom the Platonic teachings, sacrosanct as they were, should be
        disclosed and entrusted before he had unlearned the doctrines he
        had received from others and brought with him to the Platonic
        school.

45   "Polemo dies and Arcesilaus succeeds him. Arcesilaus was one
        of Zeno's fellow-students under the tutelage of Polemo. There-
        fore, when Zeno became enamored of a certain theory of his own
        regarding the world and especially the soul (on behalf of which
        true philosophy is ever vigilant), saying that the soul is mortal,
        that there is nothing beyond this sensible world,[175] and that noth-
50   ing transpires in the world except by means of a body — for he
        thought that God Himself was fire[176] — since this evil was spread-
        ing far and wide, Arcesilaus, it seems to me, prudently and with
        great advantage completely concealed the view of the Academy.
        He buried it as a golden treasure to be found someday by poster-
        ity. Since most people are rather prone to rush into false opinions
55   and, through their familiarity with bodies, are easily but injuri-
        ously led to believe that all things are bodies, Arcesilaus — the
        most clever and humane of men — decided, therefore, to disabuse
        those he found to have been wrongly taught rather than to bear
        the burden of teaching those he didn't consider teachable. All the
        teachings attributed to the New Academy arose from these cir-

175. See Epiphanius, *Against Heresies* 3.2.9 and 3.2.26 for another report
of Zeno's doctrine.

176. Aëtius 1.7.23 confirms that Zeno made this claim.

cumstances, since their predecessors had no need for them.

"Now if Zeno had only come to his senses at some point and [3.17.39] seen that nothing could be apprehended unless it were such as he 60 himself defined it to be, and that nothing of the sort could be found in bodies, to which he attributed everything, then surely this kind of controversy, which unavoidably flared up, would have been extinguished long ago.

"To the Academicians, and to me as well, it seemed that Zeno 65 was led astray by the mere appearance of consistency.[177] He held firmly to his view, and his pernicious doctrine of bodies[178] survived as best it could until the time of Chrysippus, who strengthened it, as he was well able to do, to spread it more widely. Yet Carneades was on the other side, and he was more keen and careful than the others mentioned above. He fought against this view 70 so well that I'm surprised it had any influence later. Carneades straightaway discarded all shameless quibbling — he saw that Arcesilaus had fallen into serious disrepute because of this practice — so that he not seem to want to speak against everything as though for the sake of showing off. Instead, he set out to over- 75 whelm and destroy Chrysippus and the Stoics themselves.

"Carneades was then attacked on all sides with the objection [3.18.40] that if the wise man were to assent to nothing he'll do nothing.

"Carneades — what an extraordinary man! and yet not so extraordinary, for he was a stream flowing out of Plato's springs — Carneades wisely examined the characteristics of the actions of which his opponents approved. Seeing them to be like some 5 truths or other, he called what he followed while acting in this world 'truthlike.' What they are like he knew well and prudently concealed. He also called it 'the plausible.' Someone who gazes upon an exemplar does, indeed, rightly approve an image of it. How then does the wise man give his approval to nothing, or fol- 10 low the truthlike, if he doesn't know what the truth itself is? Therefore, the Academicians knew the truth, and gave approval to falsehoods in which they recognized a commendable imitation

177. Presumably Augustine means that Zeno thought his views were consistent, although the argument given in the preceding paragraph shows that they were in fact inconsistent. Hence Zeno was deceived by the mere appearance of consistency (*imagine constantiae*).
178. That is, Zeno's materialism (his "doctrine of bodies").

of true things.[179] Since it was neither right nor convenient to reveal this to the uninitiated, as it were, they left some indication of their view to posterity (and to any of their contemporaries they were able to). They rightly prevented dialecticians from raising questions about words, insulting and deriding them.

"For these reasons, Carneades is also said to have been the founder and leader of a third Academy.

[3.18.41]   "The conflict has lasted down to the time of our own Cicero,
20   and, though plainly weakened now, with its last breath it is about to fill Latin literature with hot air. Nothing seems more full of hot air to me than that [Cicero][180] say so many things at length and eloquently for a view he doesn't hold! Yet these windy blasts were enough, it seems to me, to dissipate and blow away that Platonic
25   straw man, Antiochus. (The Epicurean herds built their sunny stables in the souls of voluptuaries.)[181] Antiochus was actually a student of Philo. . . . I think that Philo was a cautious man. He began at that time to open the gates, so to speak, since the enemy was giving up the fight, and to call the Academy and its laws back to the authority of Plato. Metrodorus had previously attempted to
30   do this, and he is said to have been the first to admit that the Academicians didn't endorse the principle that nothing can be apprehended but had to take up weapons of this kind against the Stoics.

"Antiochus, as I had started to say, had been a student of Philo the Academician and of Mnesarchus the Stoic. So in the guise of a helpful citizen Antiochus infiltrated the Old Academy, which was undefended and not safe from any enemy, bringing with him some kind of evil out of the ashes of Stoicism to desecrate Plato's
35   innermost sanctuary. Philo resisted him by taking up the old weapons again. After Philo's death, our Cicero buried all Antiochus's remains, for he didn't tolerate anything he loved to be weakened or undermined while he was alive.

40   "Shortly afterward, all the obstinacy and stubbornness died down. Plato's visage, which is the most pure and bright in philosophy, shone forth once the clouds of error had been dispelled — and above all in Plotinus. This Platonic philosopher is considered

179. See *Revisions* 1.1.4 (Appendix 11).

180. See 3.18.41.38 for confirmation that Cicero is being referred to here.

181. Horace calls himself "a swine belonging to the herd of Epicurus" (*Letters* 1.4.16).

to be so like Plato that they seem to have lived at the same time. The interval of time between them is so great, however, that Plato 45 should be thought of as coming to life again in Plotinus.

"Thus we rarely see philosophers today unless they are either [3.19.42] Cynics or Peripatetics or Platonists. We have the Cynics because some people delight in a certain freedom and license in their manner of living. Yet regarding erudition, doctrine, and morals — all 5 of which care for the soul — there is, in my opinion, one system of really true philosophy. It has finally emerged after many centuries and many controversies, because there have been acute and clever men who taught in their disputations that Aristotle and Plato agree with each other, although they did so in such a way that to the unskilled and inattentive they seemed to disagree.[182]

"This philosophy is not of this world — the philosophy that our 10 Holy Writ rightly abhors[183] — but of the other world, the intelligible world. Yet the most subtle chain of reasoning would never call back to this intelligible world souls that have been blinded by the manifold shadows of error and rendered forgetful[184] by the deepest filth from the body, had not God the Highest, moved by a certain compassion for the multitude, humbled and submitted the 15 authority of the Divine Intellect even to the human body itself.[185] Our souls, awakened not only by its precepts but also by its deeds, could return to themselves and regain their homeland without the strife of disputation.

182. Cicero, *Academica* 1.4.17: "A single system of philosophy, although it went under two labels, was established under Plato's authority: the Platonic and Peripatetic schools, which differ in name but not in substance." Cicero repeats this claim in very similar words in *Academica* 2.5.15.

183. See, for example, *Colossians* 2:8: "Be careful, so that nobody deceives you through philosophy and trivial fallacy, after the tradition of men, according to the elements of the world and not according to Christ."

184. Other translators read this passage by taking *oblitus* as 'stained' [< *oblino*] rather than as 'made forgetful' [< *obliviscor*], going along with the sense of *altissimis a corpore sordibus*. However, this ignores the parallel with *caecatus* and the sense of the passage as a whole: the soul has to 'unforget' what it knows within itself, a central theme of *The Teacher*.

185. Augustine is referring to the Incarnation, the nonrecognition of which was the principal philosophical defect of platonism: see the Introduction.

[3.20.43]   "I've convinced myself at times, as far as I could, that this view
of the Academicians is plausible. Yet it doesn't matter to me if it's
false. It's enough for me that I no longer think that the truth can't
be found by man.

"Furthermore, if anyone thinks that the Academicians also held
5   this view, let him hear Cicero himself. He says that the Academicians customarily concealed their doctrine and did not reveal it to
anyone unless he had lived with them up to his old age.[186] God
knows what that doctrine was! For my part, I think it was that of
Plato.

[Summary and Conclusion]

10   "So you have all my theme in brief: whatever human wisdom
may be, I see that I haven't yet gotten hold of it. Although I'm
thirty-three years old, I don't think I should despair of someday
reaching it. I've renounced all the other things that mortal men
think to be good and proposed to devote myself to searching for
15   wisdom. The arguments of the Academicians seriously deterred
me from this undertaking. Now, however, I'm sufficiently pro-
tected against them by this discussion of ours. Furthermore, no
one doubts that we're prompted to learn by the twin forces of
authority and reason. Therefore, I'm resolved not to depart from
the authority of Christ on any score whatsoever: I find no more
20   powerful [authority]. As for what is to be sought out by the most
subtle reasoning — for my character is such that I'm impatient in
my desire to apprehend what the truth is not only by belief but
also by understanding — I'm still confident that I'm going to find
it with the Platonists, and that it won't be opposed to our Holy
Writ."

[3.20.44]   At this point they saw that I had finished my discourse.
25   Although it was already nighttime and some of the transcription
had been written after a lantern was brought in, the young men
were eagerly waiting to see whether Alypius would promise to
make a reply to it — at least on another day.

"I'm ready to assert," Alypius said, "that nothing has ever been
30   as surprisingly pleasant to me as the fact that I leave today's dispute a beaten man! Nor do I think that this joy ought to be mine

186. Cicero, *Academica* frag. 21 (Müller). See also *Academica* 2.18.60.

alone. Therefore, I'll share it with all of you, my partners in disputation — or, if you will, the judges of our battle. Perhaps even the
Academicians themselves hoped in this way to be vanquished by
their descendants! Could we see or have shown to us anything   35
more delightful than the charm of this discourse, more carefully
considered than the seriousness of its views, more evident than its
good will, more expert in its teaching? I'm completely unable to
express properly my admiration for the fact that difficult matters
were treated so elegantly, challenging matters so courageously,
conclusive arguments so modestly, and obscure matters so
clearly. Accordingly, my friends, exchange now the longing by   40
which you were inciting me to make a reply for a more certain
hope: to learn with me. We now have a leader who, with God's
guidance, will bring us to the sanctuaries of the truth."

The young men childishly showed their disappointment on   [3.20.45]
their faces, as though they had been cheated because Alypius was
not going to make a reply.   45

"Do you envy the praise given to me?" I asked with a smile.
"Well, since now I am sure of Alypius's support and have nothing
to fear from him, so that all of you may thank me as well, I'll arm
you against him, since he has foiled your fond expectations. Read
the *Academica*! When you find there that Cicero has overcome all   50
my trifling arguments — for what is easier? — then let Alypius be
forced by you to defend my discourse against those invincible
objections![187] This is the hard payment I make to you, Alypius, for
the undeserved praise you bestowed upon me."

They all laughed then, and so to this great debate we put an end
— whether permanent or not, I don't know — more rapidly and   55
calmly than I had expected.

---

187. At the end of *Revisions* 1.1.4, Augustine says: "even though I said this
in jest and above all with irony, I still ought not to have said it."

The Teacher [1]

[The Purpose of Language]

[1.1]   AUGUSTINE: When we speak, what does it seem to you we want to accomplish?

5   ADEODATUS: So far as it now strikes me, either to teach or to learn.

AUGUSTINE: I see one of these points and I agree with it, for it's clear that by speaking we want to teach. But to learn? How?

ADEODATUS: How do you suppose we learn, after all, if not when we ask questions?

10   AUGUSTINE: Even then I think that we want only to teach. I ask you: do you question someone for any reason other than to teach him what you want [to hear]? [2]

ADEODATUS: You're right.

AUGUSTINE: So now you see that we seek nothing by speaking except to teach.

15   ADEODATUS: I don't see it clearly. If speaking is nothing but uttering words, I see that we do this when we're singing. Given that we often sing while we're alone, without anyone present who might learn, I don't think we want to teach anything.

---

1. Augustine, *Revisions* 1.12: "I wrote a work entitled *The Teacher* [in 389]. There it is debated, sought, and found that there is no teacher giving knowledge to man other than God. This is also in accordance with what is written by the Evangelist: *Your teacher, Christ, is unique* (Matthew 23:10)." The brevity of Augustine's entry is remarkable. In *Confessions* 9.6.14 he writes: "In our book entitled *The Teacher*, [Adeodatus] there speaks with me. You, Lord, know that all the thoughts put in there in the person of my interlocutor were his, though he was only sixteen years old. I have experienced many more wonderful things in him at other times: I was in awe of his talents." This suggests that Augustine's love for his dead son may have prevented him from making any revisions to *The Teacher*.

2. The addition 'to hear' is taken from Adeodatus's summary below (7.9.7).

AUGUSTINE: Well, for my part I think there is a certain kind of 20
teaching through reminding — a very important kind, as our discussion will itself bring out. Yet if you don't hold that we learn
when we remember or that the person who reminds us is teaching, I won't oppose you. I now stipulate two reasons for speaking:
to teach or to remind either others or ourselves. We do this even 25
when we're singing. Doesn't it seem so to you?

ADEODATUS: Not exactly. I would seldom sing to remind
myself; I do it only to please myself.

AUGUSTINE: I see what you mean. But aren't you aware that
what pleases you in a song is its melody?[3] Since this melody can 30
be either added to or taken away from the words, speaking is one
thing and singing is another. There are [musical] songs on flutes
or on the guitar, and birds sing, and we occasionally make some
musical sound without words. This sound can be called 'singing'
but can't be called 'speaking.' Is there anything here you would 35
object to?

ADEODATUS: Nothing at all.

AUGUSTINE: Then doesn't it seem to you that speaking is [1.2]
undertaken only for the sake of teaching or reminding?

ADEODATUS: It would seem so were I not troubled by the fact
that we certainly speak while we're praying, and yet it isn't right 40
to believe that we teach God or remind Him of anything.

AUGUSTINE: I dare say you don't know that we are instructed
to pray "in closed chambers"[4] — a phrase that signifies the inner
recesses of the mind[5] — precisely because God does not seek to be
taught or reminded by our speaking in order to provide us what
we want. Anyone who speaks gives an external sign of his will by 45
means of an articulated sound.[6] Yet God is to be sought and

---

3. "Is its melody": *modulatio soni.*

4. Matthew 6:6.

5. In his *Commentary on the Sermon on the Mount* 2.3.11, Augustine says
that the 'chambers' are the hearts themselves mentioned in Psalms 4:5–6
(Vulgate) = 4:4–5 (RSV) cited below, and that they are 'closed' to the external distractions and temptations that come via the senses.

6. As a technical definition of speaking, a necessary condition is that an
utterance be produced which is literally 'articulated' — expelled air inten-
tionally modulated by the muscles of the larynx, palate, tongue, and the
like. This sets speaking apart from involuntary sounds, such as snoring or

entreated in the hidden parts of the rational soul, which is called the 'inner man'; for He wanted those parts to be His temples. Have you not read in the Apostle:[7]

50   Do you not know that you are the temple of God and that the Spirit of God dwells within you?

and:[8]

Christ dwells in the inner man.

Didn't you notice in the Prophet:[9]

Speak in your hearts and be stricken in your bedchambers; offer up the sacrifice of justice, and hope in the Lord.

55   Where do you think the "sacrifice of justice" is offered up but in the temple of the mind and in the bedchambers of the heart? What is more, one should pray where one should sacrifice. There is accordingly no need for speaking when we pray. That is, there is no need for spoken words — except perhaps to speak as priests do, for the sake of signifying what is in their minds: not that God
60   might hear, but that men might do so and by remembering might, with one accord, be raised to God.[10] Do you hold otherwise?

---

cries of pain; see *On Christian Doctrine* 2.1.2 (Appendix 10). Articulated sounds are 'external signs' of something internal, namely the will. Much of the rest of *The Teacher* is devoted to exploring how a given sound can be a sign.

7. I Corinthians 3:16.

8. Ephesians 3:16–17.

9. Psalms 4:5–6 (Vulgate) = 4:4–5 (RSV). The beginning of Augustine's text, *Dicite in cordibus vestris* ("Speak in your hearts . . ."), differs from the Gallican version incorporated in the Vulgate: *Quae dicitis in cordibus vestris* ("What you have spoken in your hearts . . .").

10. Madec [1976], p. 46, n. 9 suggests that this is related to the liturgical text *Sursum cor — Habemus ad Dominum*. The sense of the passage is that collective recitation, whether sung or not, effects a unity among the participants and simultaneously exalts them. See *Confessions* 10.33.49: "I feel that when the holy words are recited in this fashion [*i.e.*, collectively], our spirits are moved more religiously and more ardently to the flame of piety than if they were not so recited."

ADEODATUS: I agree completely.

AUGUSTINE: Then doesn't it trouble you that when the supreme Teacher was teaching His disciples to pray, He taught them certain words?[11] In so doing, what He seems to have done is   65
precisely to have taught them how we ought to speak when we pray.[12]

ADEODATUS: Nothing at all troubles me on that score. He taught them not the words but the things themselves by means of the words. With these words they remind themselves of Whom they should pray to and of what they should pray for, since they   70
would be praying in the inner recesses of the mind, as mentioned (1.2.43–44).

AUGUSTINE: You understand this correctly. Someone might object that, although we don't produce any sound, nonetheless we do 'speak' internally in the mind, since we think these very words. Yet I believe you're also aware that in 'speaking' in this way we do nothing but remind ourselves, since by repeating the words   75
our memory, in which the words inhere, makes the very things of which the words are signs come to mind.

ADEODATUS: I understand, and I go along with this.

[The Nature of Signs]

AUGUSTINE: Then we are in agreement: words are signs.   [2.3]
ADEODATUS: Yes.

AUGUSTINE: Well, can a sign be a sign if it doesn't signify anything?

ADEODATUS: It can't.   5

AUGUSTINE: Consider this line of verse:[13]

If nothing from so great a city it pleases the gods be left . . .

How many words are there?

11. The Lord's Prayer: Matthew 6:9 and Luke 11:2–4.

12. Augustine discusses this extensively in his *Commentary on the Sermon on the Mount* 2.3.10–14.

13. Vergil, *Aeneid* 2.659: *Si nihil ex tanta superis placet urbe relinqui*, spoken by Aeneas to his father Anchises, in reference to the imminent destruction of Troy. Adeodatus takes up the first three words in order, namely *si* ('if'), *nihil* ('nothing'), and *ex* ('from').

ADEODATUS: Thirteen.

AUGUSTINE: Then there are thirteen signs?

10   ADEODATUS: Yes.

AUGUSTINE: I believe you understand this line of verse.

ADEODATUS: Quite well, I think.

AUGUSTINE: Tell me what each word signifies.

ADEODATUS: Well, I do see what 'if' signifies, but I don't know
15   any other word by which it can be explained.

AUGUSTINE: At least you know where anything signified by
this word would be.

ADEODATUS: It seems to me that 'if' signifies doubt. Now
where is doubt but in the mind?

20   AUGUSTINE: I accept that for now. Continue with the other
words.

ADEODATUS: What else does 'nothing' signify except that
which doesn't exist?

AUGUSTINE: Perhaps you're right, but I'm hesitant to agree
with you, because you granted above that there is no sign unless
it signifies something (2.3.4–5). Yet what does not exist can't in
25   any way be something. Accordingly, the second word in this line
of verse isn't a sign, because it doesn't signify anything. So we
were wrong to agree either that all words are signs or that every
sign signifies something.

ADEODATUS: You're really pushing too hard. It's stupid to
30   utter a word when we don't have anything to signify. Yet in
speaking with me now I believe you yourself aren't making a
sound pointlessly. Instead, you're giving a sign to me with everything that comes out of your mouth, so that I may understand
something. Thus you shouldn't enunciate those two syllables ['nothing'] when you speak if you don't signify anything with them! If
35   you see that they are necessary for producing an enunciation, and
that we are taught or reminded when they strike the ears, then
surely you also see what I want to say but can't explain.

AUGUSTINE: What then are we to do? Given that one doesn't
see a thing and furthermore finds (or thinks oneself to have found)
40   that it doesn't exist, shall we not say that this word ['nothing'] signifies a certain state of mind rather than the very thing that is
nothing?

ADEODATUS: Perhaps this is the very point I was trying to
explain.

AUGUSTINE: Then be the matter as it may, let us move on from here so that the most absurd thing of all doesn't happen to us.

ADEODATUS: Which is?   45

AUGUSTINE: If *nothing* holds us back, and we suffer delays!

ADEODATUS: This is ridiculous, and yet somehow I see that it can happen — or rather, I clearly see that it has happened.

AUGUSTINE: We shall understand this kind of difficulty more   [2.4]
clearly in due order, God willing.[14] Now return to that line of   50
verse and try to explain, as best you can, what the other words in it signify.

ADEODATUS: The third word is the preposition 'from,' for which I think we can say 'out of.'

AUGUSTINE: I'm not looking for this, that in place of one familiar word you say another equally familiar word that signifies the   55
same thing — if really it does signify the same thing; but for now let us grant that this is so. Surely if the poet had said 'out of so great a city' instead of 'from so great a city' and I were to ask you what 'out of' signifies, you would say 'from,' since these words ['from' and 'out of'] — that is, these signs — do signify some one thing, as you think. I'm asking for that one thing itself, whatever   60
it is, that is signified by these two signs.

ADEODATUS: It seems to me that they signify some kind of sep-
aration with regard to a thing in which something had been. This ['something'] is said to be "from" that thing, whether that thing (*a*) does not continue to exist, as for example in this line of verse some Trojans were able to be "from" the city when it no longer existed; or it (*b*) continues to exist, as we say that there are traders   65
in Africa "from" the city of Rome.

AUGUSTINE: Even supposing that I grant you these claims and do not enumerate how many exceptions to your rule may perhaps be discovered, surely it's easy for you to notice that you have explained words by means of words. That is to say, you have   70
explained signs by means of signs and familiar things by the same familiar things. I would like you to show me the very things of which these words are the signs, if you can.

ADEODATUS: I'm surprised that you don't know, or that you're   [3.5]
pretending not to know, that what you want can't be done in my

---

14. See 8.22–8.24 below, where Augustine discusses the autonymous and referential use of signs.

answer while we're engaged in discussion, where we can only answer with words. Furthermore, you're asking about things that,
5   whatever they may be, surely aren't words — and yet you're also asking me about them with words! First raise the question without words, so that I may then answer under that stipulation of yours.[15]

AUGUSTINE: You're within your rights, I admit. But if when one says *'wall'* I were to ask what this one-syllable[16] word signifies, couldn't you show me with your finger? Then when you
10   pointed it out I would straightaway see the very thing of which this one-syllable word is a sign, although you used no words.

ADEODATUS: I grant that this can happen only in the case of names that signify bodies, so long as the bodies themselves are present.

AUGUSTINE: Do we call color a body? Don't we instead call it a
15   quality of a body?

ADEODATUS: That's true.

AUGUSTINE: Then why can this too be pointed out with a finger? Are you also adding the qualities of bodies to bodies [in your proposal], so that those qualities too, when they are present, may nonetheless be taught without words?
20   ADEODATUS: Well, although I said 'bodies,' I wanted all corporeal things — that is, all the things sensed in bodies — to be understood [in my proposal].

AUGUSTINE: Consider whether you should make some exceptions even to this claim.

ADEODATUS: Your warning is a good one! I should have said
25   'all *visible* things' rather than 'all *corporeal* things.' I admit that sound, smell, flavor, weight, heat, and other things that pertain to the rest of the senses, despite the fact that they can't be sensed without bodies and consequently are corporeal, nevertheless can't be exhibited through [pointing] a finger.

AUGUSTINE: Haven't you ever seen that men "converse" with
30   deaf people by gesturing? That deaf people themselves, no less by

15. Augustine's 'stipulation' is that Adeodatus point out "the very things of which these words are the signs" without using signs.

16. Literally, 'these three syllables,' referring to the syllables *par-i-es* of *paries* ('wall'). Here and elsewhere the number of syllables of Latin terms has been altered to fit the English translation.

gesturing, raise and answer questions, teach, and indicate all the things they want, or at least most of them? When this happens, they show us without words not only visible things, but also sounds and flavors and other things of this sort. Even actors in the theaters unfold and set forth entire stories without words — for 35 the most part, by pantomime.[17]

ADEODATUS: I have nothing to say against this, except that neither I nor even that pantomiming actor could show you without words what 'from' signifies.

AUGUSTINE: Perhaps you're right, but let's imagine that he can. [3.6] You do not doubt, I suppose, that any bodily movement he uses 40 to try to point out to me the thing signified by the word ['from'] isn't going to be the thing itself but a sign [of the thing]. Accordingly, he too won't indicate a word with a word. He'll nonetheless still indicate a sign with a sign. The result is that this syllable *'from'* and his gesture signify some one thing, which I should like to be 45 exhibited for me without signifying.

ADEODATUS: Who can do what you're asking, pray tell?

AUGUSTINE: In the way in which the wall could [be exhibited].

ADEODATUS: Not even [the wall] can be shown without a sign, 50 as our developing argument has taught us. Aiming a finger is certainly not the wall. Instead, through aiming a finger a sign is given by means of which the wall may be seen. I see nothing, therefore, that can be shown without signs.

AUGUSTINE: What if I should ask you what walking is, and you were then to get up and do it? Wouldn't you be using the thing itself to teach me, rather than using words or any other signs? 55

ADEODATUS: I admit that this is the case. I'm embarrassed not to have seen a point so obvious. On this basis, too, thousands of things now occur to me that can be exhibited through themselves rather than through signs: for example, eating, drinking, sitting, standing, shouting, and countless others.

AUGUSTINE: Now do this: tell me — if I were completely igno- 60 rant of the meaning of the word ['walking'] and were to ask you what walking is while you were walking, how would you teach me?

17. Augustine says in *On Christian Doctrine* 2.3.4 that the gestures of pantomimists "are, in a manner of speaking, visible words" (*quasi verba visibilia*).

ADEODATUS: I would do it a little bit more quickly, so that after your question you would be prompted by something novel [in my
65   behavior], and yet nothing would take place other than what was to be shown.

AUGUSTINE: Don't you know that *walking* is one thing and *hurrying* another? A person who is walking doesn't necessarily hurry, and a person who is hurrying doesn't necessarily walk. We speak of 'hurrying' in writing and in reading and in countless other mat-
70   ters. Hence given that after my question you kept on doing what you were doing, [only] faster, I might have thought walking was precisely hurrying — for you added that as something new — and for that reason I would have been misled.

ADEODATUS: I admit that we can't exhibit a thing without a sign if we should be questioned while we are doing it. If we add nothing [to our behavior], the person who raises the question
75   will think that we don't want to show him and that we are persisting in what we were doing while paying no heed to him. Yet if he should ask about things we can do, but when we aren't doing them, after his question we can point out what he's asking about by doing the action itself rather than by a sign. (That
80   is, unless he should happen to ask me what speaking is while I'm speaking, namely because no matter what I say I must be speaking to teach him.) In this way I'll confidently teach him, until I make clear to him what he wants, neither getting away from the thing itself that he wanted to be pointed out nor casting about beyond the thing itself for signs with which I might show it.

[4.7]   AUGUSTINE: Very acute. See then whether we're now in agreement that the following things can be pointed out without signs: (*a*) things we aren't doing when we are asked [about them] and yet can do on the spot; (*b*) the very signs we happen to be 'doing'
5   [when asked about them], just as when we speak we are making signs (and [the word] 'signifying' is derived from this [activity]).[18]

ADEODATUS: Agreed.

18. "And [the word] 'signifying' is derived from this [activity]": *de quo dictum est significare,* literally "from which signifying is so called." That is, the word 'signifying' (*significare*) is derived from the activity of making signs (*signa facere*).

[Fundamental Division of Signs][19]

AUGUSTINE: Thus [1] when a question is raised about certain signs, these signs can be exhibited by means of signs. Yet [2] when a question is raised about things that aren't signs, [these things can be exhibited] either [(*a*)] by doing them after the query [has been made], if they can be done, or [(*b*)] by giving signs with which they may be brought to one's attention.

ADEODATUS: That's right.

10

[Discussion of Division [1]]

AUGUSTINE: Then in this threefold classification let us consider first, if you don't mind, the case in which signs are exhibited by

19. Augustine's fundamental division of signs is motivated by semantic and epistemological concerns. On the one hand, we might ask what conditions have to be satisfied for us to have knowledge of significates that are themselves signs. This is Division [1]. On the other hand, we might be concerned with knowledge of significates that are non-signs. This is Division [2]. Nevertheless, although we are interested in non-sign significates, signs might be relevant in two ways. First, the non-sign significates could be the sort of self-exhibiting items Augustine and Adeodatus have been discussing; this possibility is covered under Division [2(*a*)]. But even when the significates are not self-exhibiting items, signs might function instrumentally in somehow prompting us to gain knowledge of the significates, and this is covered in Division [2(*b*)].

Augustine and Adeodatus discuss each part of the fundamental division in turn. The discussion of Division [1] occupies 4.7–6.18, concluding with Adeodatus's summary in 7.19–20 and Augustine's apology in 8.21. The discussion of Division [2] begins in 8.22 and occupies the remainder of *The Teacher*. This division requires us to move beyond the knowledge of signs to the knowledge of significates that are not themselves signs. First, however, an intermediate case has to be ruled out, namely where signs are used to signify themselves as sounds, rather than either signifying themselves as signs or signifying their normal significates. This takes place in 8.22–24. Once this case has been put aside, the general issue of knowledge in relation to both signs and things may be raised, and the comparative value of the knowledge of things and the knowledge of signs can be spelled out. This takes place in 9.25–28. After these preliminaries are out of the way, Augustine and Adeodatus discuss Division [2(*a*)] in 10.29–32, and Augustine delivers a monologue about Division [2(*b*)] in 10.33–13.46.

means of signs. Are words the only signs?

15   ADEODATUS: No.

AUGUSTINE: Then it seems to me that in speaking we designate with words either (*a*) words themselves or other signs, such as when we say '*gesture*' or '*letter*,' for what these two words signify are nonetheless signs; or (*b*) something else that isn't a sign, such

20   as when we say '*stone*' — this word is a sign because it signifies something, but what it signifies isn't necessarily a sign. Yet the latter kind of case, namely when words signify things that aren't signs, isn't relevant to the part [of the threefold classification] we proposed to discuss. We have undertaken to consider the case in

25   which signs are exhibited by means of signs, and in it we have discovered two subdivisions, since with signs we teach or remind someone of either the same signs or other signs.[20] Doesn't it seem so to you?

ADEODATUS: That's obvious.

[4.8]   AUGUSTINE: Then tell me to which sense the signs that are
30   words are relevant.[21]

ADEODATUS: Hearing.

AUGUSTINE: What about gestures?

ADEODATUS: Sight.

AUGUSTINE: Well, when we come upon written words, aren't they understood more accurately as *signs* of words than as words?

35   After all, a word is that which is uttered by means of an articulated sound accompanied by some significate.[22] A sound, however, can be perceived by no sense other than hearing. Thus it is that when a word is written, a sign is produced for the eyes, and by means of

20. The two subdivisions of (*i*) are: (*i-a*) we teach or remind someone of the same signs; (*i-b*) we teach or remind someone of other signs.

21. See *On Christian Doctrine* 2.3.4 (Appendix 10).

22. "That which is uttered by means of an articulated sound accompanied by some significate": *quod cum aliquo significatu articulata voce profertur*, an extension of the technical definition of speaking given at 1.2.45 and slightly different from the definition given at the beginning of *On Dialectic* 5.7 (Appendix 4). To be 'accompanied by some significate' is just to say that the articulated sound in question signifies something. A looser translation might be 'a significant articulated sound.' Looser still, 'a meaningful utterance.' Augustine's point is that a *written* word is, strictly speaking, not a sound at all, and hence technically cannot be a word.

this [inscription] something that strictly pertains to the ears comes into the mind.

ADEODATUS: I agree completely.   40

AUGUSTINE: I think you also agree that when we say 'name' we signify something.

ADEODATUS: That's true.

AUGUSTINE: What then?

ADEODATUS: Obviously, what each thing is called; for exam-   45
ple, 'Romulus,' 'Rome,' 'virtue,' 'river,' and countless others.

AUGUSTINE: Do these four names signify nothing?

ADEODATUS: No, they each signify something.

AUGUSTINE: Is there any difference between these names and the things signified by them?   50

ADEODATUS: There is a great difference.

AUGUSTINE: I should like to hear from you what it is.

ADEODATUS: Well, in the first place, the fact that the former are signs whereas the latter are not.

AUGUSTINE: Do you mind if we call things that can be signified by signs and yet aren't signs 'signifiable,' as we call things that can   55
be seen 'visible,' so that we may discuss these things more easily from now on?

ADEODATUS: Not at all.

AUGUSTINE: Well, those four signs you cited a little earlier (4.8.45–46) — ['Romulus,' 'Rome,' 'virtue,' 'river'] — aren't they   60
signified by any other signs?

ADEODATUS: I'm surprised you think I have already forgotten that we found written [inscriptions] to be signs of spoken signs (4.8.34–40).

AUGUSTINE: Tell me what the difference between them is.

ADEODATUS: That the former are visible whereas the latter are   65
'audible' — why don't you also allow this name, given that we allowed 'signifiable'?[23]

AUGUSTINE: I do allow it, and I'm grateful [for the suggestion]. Yet I ask again: can't these four signs be signified by another audible sign, just as the visible signs you remembered?

ADEODATUS: I remember that this too was mentioned recently.   70

---

23. Adeodatus proposes coining the term 'audible' (*audibile*), on a par with Augustine's earlier coinage 'signifiable.' See Ambrose, *Noah* 15.52: "Sight sees the visible and the listener hears the audible."

I had answered that 'name' signifies something and put these four names under its signification (4.8.41–46). Furthermore, I know that both the former and the latter, if they are actually uttered by a sound, are audible.

75 AUGUSTINE: Then what's the difference between an audible sign and audible significates that in turn are signs?

ADEODATUS: I see this difference between what we call a 'name' and these four names that we put under its signification. The former is an audible sign of audible signs. The latter are audi-
80 ble signs, but not of signs: some are audible signs of visible things (such as Romulus, Rome, and a river) and others are audible signs of intelligible things (such as virtue).

[4.9]   AUGUSTINE: I accept and approve [your distinction]. Yet do you know that all things that are uttered by an articulated sound accompanied by some significate are called 'words'?[24]

ADEODATUS: I do.

85 AUGUSTINE: Then a name is also a word whenever we see that it is uttered by an articulated sound accompanied by some signif-icate. When we say that an eloquent man employs 'good words,' he surely is also employing names; when the slave in Terence replied to his aged master:[25]

Good words, if you please!

the latter had also spoken many names.
90 ADEODATUS: I agree.

AUGUSTINE: Then you grant that with the one syllable we utter when we say *'word'* a name is signified as well, and so the former (['word']) is a sign of the latter (['name']).

ADEODATUS: I do grant this.
95 AUGUSTINE: I would like your answer on this point as well. 'Word' is a sign of 'name,' and 'name' is a sign of 'river,' and 'river' is a sign of a thing that can be seen. You have already said what the difference is between this thing ([the river]) and 'river' (the sign of [the river]). [You have also said what the difference is] between the sign ['river'] and 'name,' which is the sign of the sign

24. This is the definition of 'word' given at 4.8.35–36.

25. Terence, *The Lady of Andros* 204. Davos uses the formula *bona verba quaeso* ironically to his master Simo, who is angrily threatening him with dire punishments and calling him names.

['river']. Now what do you suppose is the difference between the sign of a name — which we found to be 'word' — and 'name' 100 itself, of which ['word'] is the sign?[26]

ADEODATUS: I understand this to be the difference [between words and names]. On the one hand, things signified by 'name' are also signified by 'word.' A name is a word, and thus [the name] 'river' is a word. On the other hand, not all the things sig- 105 nified by 'word' are also signified by 'name.' The 'if' at the very beginning of the line of verse you mentioned, and the 'from' — we've come upon these matters after our lengthy discussion of the ['from'], guided by the argument — [the 'if' and 'from'] are both words, but they aren't names. Many such cases are found. Conse- quently, since all names are words but not all words are names, I 110 think it's obvious what the difference between 'word' and 'name' is — namely, [the difference] between the sign of a sign that signi- fies no other signs, and the sign of a sign that in turn signifies other signs.

AUGUSTINE: Don't you grant that every horse is an animal, but that not every animal is a horse?

ADEODATUS: Who will doubt it?   115

AUGUSTINE: Then the difference between a name and a word is the same as the difference between a horse and an animal. Yet per- haps you're kept from agreeing by the fact that we also say 'word' (*verbum*)[27] in another way, one in which it signifies things inflected by tenses, as for example 'I write, I have written' and 'I read, I have read': these are clearly not names.   120

ADEODATUS: You have said precisely what was making me doubtful.

26. This paragraph involves several ambiguities, including some (delib- erate?) confusion of use and mention, that are difficult to preserve in translation. Augustine considers three cases: (*i*) 'word' signifies names, perhaps among other things; (*ii*) 'name' signifies the particular name 'river,' among other things; (*iii*) the particular name 'river' signifies this very river; *e.g.*, the Nile, among other rivers. Now Adeodatus has already explained (*iii*) and (*ii*): names are not to be confused with what they name, and a particular name is picked out by the general term 'name.' Therefore Augustine is asking Adeodatus about (*i*), that is, about the difference between words and names.

27. The single Latin term *verbum* does duty for both English terms 'word' and 'verb.'

AUGUSTINE: Don't be troubled on that score. We do generally call 'signs' all those things that signify something — the condition we also found words to be in. Again, we speak of 'military banners' (*signa militaria*)[28] that are then named 'signs' in the strict
125   sense, a condition to which words do not pertain. Yet if I were to say to you that just as every horse is an animal but not every animal is a horse, so too every word is a sign but not every sign is a word, I think you wouldn't hesitate to agree.

ADEODATUS: Now I understand. I agree completely that the
130   difference between *word* in general and *name* is the same as the difference between *animal* and *horse*.

[4.10]   AUGUSTINE: Do you also know that when we say '*an-i-mal*,' this three-syllable name uttered by the voice is one thing and what it signifies is another?

ADEODATUS: I have already granted this point for all signs and all things that are signifiable (4.8.76–81).

135   AUGUSTINE: Now it doesn't seem to you that all signs signify something other than what they are, does it? For example, when we say '*an-i-mal*,' this three-syllable word in no way signifies the very thing that it itself is.

ADEODATUS: Not exactly. When we say '*sign*,' not only does it
140   signify the other signs, whatever they are, it also signifies itself, for it is a word, and certainly all words are signs.

AUGUSTINE: Well, when we say '*word*,' doesn't something of the sort happen in the case of this monosyllable? If everything that is uttered by an articulated sound accompanied by some signifi-
145   cate is signified by this monosyllable ['*word*'], then ['word'] itself is included in this class.

ADEODATUS: That's true.

AUGUSTINE: Well, isn't it likewise for 'name'? For ['name'] signifies names of all classes, and 'name' itself is a name of neuter
150   gender.[29] Alternatively, if I should ask you what part of speech a

28. The Latin term *signum* may refer to a banner or standard, as well as having the more general sense 'sign.' See *On Christian Doctrine* 2.3.4 (Appendix 10).

29. This translation depends on taking *genus* in two distinct ways: as 'kind' or 'class,' and as the gender of the name. If we insist on a uniform reading, the latter part of the sentence might be translated: "and 'name' is a name of neither class [*i.e.*, neither *word* nor *sign*]."

name is, could you answer anything but 'name' correctly?

ADEODATUS: You're right.

AUGUSTINE: Then there are signs that also signify themselves with the other things they signify.

ADEODATUS: Yes.

AUGUSTINE: Surely you don't think that when we say *'con-junc-* 155 *tion'* this three-syllable sign is this kind of sign, do you?

ADEODATUS: Not at all, because while ['conjunction'] is a name, the things it signifies aren't names.

AUGUSTINE: You have been properly attentive. Now see [5.11] whether we find [two] signs that signify each other mutually, such that the former signifies the latter, while at the same time the latter signifies the former. This three-syllable word (when we say *'con-junc-tion'*) and the words signified by ['conjunction'] (when we 5 say *'if,' 'or,' 'for,' 'surely,' 'unless,' 'therefore,' 'since,'* and similar words) are not related to one another in this way.[30] The reason for this is that these words are signified by that one three-syllable word ['*con-junc-tion'*], although it isn't signified by any of them.

ADEODATUS: I see, but I want to know which signs do signify each other mutually.

AUGUSTINE: Then don't you know that when we say *'name'* 10 and *'word'* we are saying two words?

ADEODATUS: I know that.

AUGUSTINE: Well, don't you know that when we say *'name'* and *'word'* we are saying two names?   15

ADEODATUS: I know that too.

AUGUSTINE: Then you know that 'name' is signified by 'word' as well as 'word' by 'name.'

ADEODATUS: I agree.

AUGUSTINE: Can you say what the difference between them is, 20 apart from the fact that they are written and pronounced differently?

ADEODATUS: Perhaps I can, for I see that it's what I said a little while ago (4.8.35–36). When we say *'words,'* we signify everything

30. That is, they are not related in the way described at the beginning of the paragraph — mutual signification. 'Conjunction' signifies *if*, but 'if' does not signify *conjunction*. The part of speech called 'conjunction' was used to cover most cases of 'linking' words, including logical particles: and, or, but, when, while, if, because, since, therefore, for, and the like.

that is uttered by an articulated sound accompanied by some sig-
25   nificate. Accordingly, every name — and when we say *'name,'* that
too — is a word. Yet not every word is a name, although when we
say *'word'* it is a name.

[5.12]   AUGUSTINE: Well, if anyone should say to you and prove that
just as every name is a word, so too every word is a name, will you
be able to discover in what respect they differ, apart from the dif-
30   fering sound of the letters?

ADEODATUS: No. I don't think they differ in any respect at all.

AUGUSTINE: Well, if all things uttered by an articulated sound
accompanied by some significate are both words and names, but
35   are words for one reason and names for another reason, will a
name and a word differ at all?

ADEODATUS: I don't understand how that could be.

AUGUSTINE: At least you understand this: everything colored
is visible and everything visible is colored, even though these two
words ['colored' and 'visible'] signify distinctly and differently.

40   ADEODATUS: I do understand this.

AUGUSTINE: Then what if every word is a name and every
name is a word in this fashion, even though these two names or
two words themselves — 'name' and 'word' — have a different
signification?

45   ADEODATUS: Now I see that this can happen. I'm waiting for
you to show me how it happens.

AUGUSTINE: You observe, I think, that everything expressed by
an articulated sound accompanied by some significate (*i*) strikes
the ear so that it can be perceived, and (*ii*) is committed to memory
so that it can be known.

50   ADEODATUS: I do.

AUGUSTINE: Then these two things happen when we utter
something by such a sound.

ADEODATUS: Yes.

AUGUSTINE: What if words are so called because of one of these
55   and names are so called because of the other — 'words' from striking [the ear] and 'names' from knowing[31] — so that the former

31. The false etymological connection proposed here may seem more
plausible in Latin: words (*verba*) are so called from striking the ear (*verbe-
rando*), and names (*nomina*) are so called from knowing (*noscendo*). See
Augustine, *On Dialectic* 6.9.7–8 and Collaert [1971], pp. 290–91.

deserve to be called after the ears, whereas the latter deserve to be called after the mind?

ADEODATUS: I'll grant this once you have shown me how we can correctly call all words 'names.' [5.13]

AUGUSTINE: That's easy. I believe you have accepted and do maintain that what can take the place of a name is called a 'pronoun,'[32] although it marks out a thing with a less complete signification than a name does. The person whom you paid to be your grammar teacher, I believe, defined it as follows: a pronoun is that part of speech which, when put in place of a name, signifies the same object but less completely. 60

ADEODATUS: I remember this, and approve of it. 65

AUGUSTINE: Then you see that according to this definition pronouns can only serve in place of names and can be put only in the place of names.[33] For example, we say "this man," "the king himself," "the same woman," "this gold," "that silver." Now 'this,' 'himself,' 'the same,' and 'that' are pronouns;[34] 'man,' 'king,' 'woman,' 'gold,' and 'silver' are names. Things are signified more completely by these [names] than by the pronouns. 70

ADEODATUS: I see and agree with you.

AUGUSTINE: Now then: enunciate a few conjunctions for me — whichever you like. 75

ADEODATUS: 'And,' 'too,' 'but,' 'also.'

AUGUSTINE: Doesn't it seem to you that all these you have mentioned are names?

ADEODATUS: Not at all.

AUGUSTINE: Doesn't it seem to you that I spoke correctly when I said, "*all these* you have mentioned"? 80

ADEODATUS: Quite correctly. Now I understand how surprisingly you have shown me to have enunciated names, for other-

32. A pronoun (*pronomen*) is what can take the place of a name (*nomen*), which is why it is so called (*pro-nomen*).

33. "Pronouns can only serve in place of names, and can be put only in the place of names": *nullis nisi nominibus servire et pro his solis poni posse pronomina*. This phrase could also be translated "pronouns serve only in place of names, and can be put only in the place of names." See Collaert [1971], p. 282, n. 9.

34. That is, they are pronouns when used by themselves. In "this man," 'this' is an adjective.

wise 'all these' could not have been said of them correctly.[35]

85　　Yet I still suspect that the reason it seems to me that you spoke correctly is as follows. I don't deny that these four conjunctions are also words. Hence 'all these' may be correctly said of them, because 'all these words' is correctly said of them. Now if you should ask me what part of speech 'words' is, I'll answer that it's

90　only a name. Thus perhaps the pronoun ['these'] was [implicitly] attached to this name ['words'], so that your locution ['all these (words)'] was correct.

[5.14]　　AUGUSTINE: Your mistake is subtle. Pay closer attention to what I say so that you may stop being mistaken — at least, if I should be able to say it as I wish; for discussing words with words

95　is as entangled as interlocking one's fingers and rubbing them together, where hardly anyone but the person doing it can distinguish the fingers that itch from the fingers scratching the itch.

　　ADEODATUS: Well, I'm paying close attention, for your analogy has aroused my interest.

100　AUGUSTINE: Words surely consist of sound and letters.
　　ADEODATUS: Yes.
　　AUGUSTINE: Then, to employ in the best way the authority most dear to us, when the Apostle Paul says:[36]

In Christ there was not Yea and Nay, but in Him was Yea,

105　I don't suppose it should be thought that when we say 'Yea' these three letters [y-e-a] we enunciate were in Christ, but what is signified by them.

35. The argument: pronouns only take the place of names; 'these' is a pronoun that takes the place of the four conjunctions; hence the four conjunctions must also be names. Adeodatus's objection, given in the following paragraph, is that the pronoun 'these' may be understood as 'these words,' which would block the preceding inference.

36. II Corinthians 1:19. The Septuagint has: Ναὶ καὶ οὔ, which means "Yea or Nay." Yet there is no straightforward way to say "yes" in Latin; locutions saying that something is the case were typically used instead — *sic, est, ita*. Various translators used the standard substitute, "It is so" (*est*), which can also simply be translated "is." Thus the Latin text reads "There was not in Christ *is* and *is not*, but in Him was *is* only." That is why Augustine argues later that it has the dual force of both verb (as 'is') and name (as 'yes').

ADEODATUS: You're right.

AUGUSTINE: Then you understand that a person who says "in Him was Yea" only said that what we call 'Yea' was in Him. In the same way, if he had said "in Him was virtue," he certainly would   110
be taken to have only said that what we call 'virtue' was in Him, nor should we think that these two syllables we enunciate when we say '*vir-tue*' were in Him rather than what is signified by these two syllables.

ADEODATUS: I understand, and I follow you.   115

AUGUSTINE: Don't you also understand that it makes no difference whether anyone says "it is called 'virtue'" and "it is named 'virtue'"?

ADEODATUS: That's obvious.

AUGUSTINE: Then it's obvious that it makes no difference whether one says "what is called 'Yea' was in Him" and "what is   120
named 'Yea' was in Him."

ADEODATUS: I see that this too makes no difference.

AUGUSTINE: Now do you see what I want to show you?

ADEODATUS: Not quite yet.

AUGUSTINE: Really? Don't you see that a name is that by which a thing is named?   125

ADEODATUS: I see clearly that nothing is more certain than this!

AUGUSTINE: Then you see that 'Yea' is a name, given that what was in Christ is named 'Yea.'

ADEODATUS: I can't deny it.

AUGUSTINE: Well, if I should ask you what part of speech 'Yea'   130
(*est*) is, I think you would say that it isn't a name but a verb, although the argument has taught us that it is also a name.[37]

ADEODATUS: It's exactly as you say.

AUGUSTINE: Do you still doubt that other parts of speech are also names in the same way in which we have demonstrated [a   135
verb to be a name]?

ADEODATUS: I don't doubt it, insofar as I admit they signify something. Now if you should inquire what each of the things they signify is called (*i.e.*, what they are named), I can only reply that they are the very parts of speech we do not call 'names' — but

37. Augustine's point is that '*est*' is, strictly speaking, a verb. See the preceding note.

140   I see we're proven to be wrong [with this answer].[38]

[5.15]   AUGUSTINE: Aren't you at all troubled that there might be
someone who would make our argument totter by saying that
authority over *things* rather than *words* should be attributed to the
apostles? So the basis of our conviction[39] isn't as secure as we

145   think, because it may happen that Paul, although he lived and
taught most correctly, spoke less correctly when he says "in Him
was Yea," especially since he admits himself to be unskilled in
speech.[40] How then do you think this objector should be refuted?

ADEODATUS: I have nothing to say against him! Please find
150   someone among those to whom the most profound knowledge of
words is granted, by whose authority instead you might bring
about what you wish.

AUGUSTINE: Does the argument itself seem less adequate to
you once the authorities are put aside? It demonstrates that every
part of speech signifies something and that it is so called on this
155   basis. Yet if a part of speech is called something, then it is named;
if named, surely it is named by a name.

This is most easily recognized in the case of different languages. Anyone can see that if I should ask, "What do the Greeks
name what we name 'who'?" the answer given to me is τίς; and
160   likewise for 'I want' θέλω; for 'well' καλῶς; for 'written' τὸ
165   γεγραμμένον; for 'and' καί; for 'by' ἀπό; for 'alas' οἴ. Yet in all these
parts of speech I have just listed,[41] it can't be that anyone who asks
what they are in this way would speak correctly unless they were
names. We can therefore maintain by this argument that the
Apostle Paul spoke correctly, while putting aside the authority

38. Adeodatus's point seems to be that the other parts of speech are not
called 'names,' although the preceding argument has established that
they are in fact names.

39. The 'conviction' is the claim that other parts of speech are also
names, and the 'basis' for the conviction is the argument taken from St.
Paul.

40. II Corinthians 11:6.

41. The seven question-answer pairs above correspond to seven of the
eight parts of speech, respectively: pronoun, verb, adverb, adjective, conjunction, preposition, interjection. The other part of speech is the name,
which surely includes names, and so can be left out of Augustine's argument.

belonging to all eloquent people. What need is there to ask who   170
supports our view?

If there is someone slower or more impudent who still doesn't   [5.16]
give in, and asserts that he isn't going to give in at all except to
those authors who everyone agrees are paradigms of proper language[42] — what in the Latin language more excellent than Cicero   175
can be found? Yet in his noblest speeches he called 'in the presence
of' (*coram*) — which is a preposition, or rather in this passage is an
adverb — a name.[43]

Now perhaps I don't understand that passage from Cicero sufficiently well, and I myself or another person might explain it differently at other times. Yet there is, I think, another point to which   180
no reply can be made. The most eminent teachers of dialectic hand
it down that a complete sentence, which may be affirmed and
denied, consists of a name and a verb. (Cicero somewhere calls
this kind of thing a 'proposition.'[44]) When the verb is in the third
person, they say that the nominative case of the name ought to
accompany it. This is correct. If you should consider with me that   185
when we say "The man sits" or "The horse runs," I think you recognize that they are two propositions.

ADEODATUS: I do recognize that.

AUGUSTINE: You observe in each case that there is a single
name, 'man' in the one and 'horse' in the other, and that there is a   190
single verb, 'sits' in the one and 'runs' in the other.

42. "Authors who everyone agrees are paradigms of proper language":
literally "authors to whom the rules of usage (*verborum leges*) are attributed
by the consent of all." Augustine is referring to authors whose writing has
been taken to be a paradigm of correct style, such that their texts set the
standards that are then taught as the 'rules of usage': Cicero for rhetorical
and philosophical prose, Livy for historical prose, and Vergil for poetry.

43. When Cicero describes Verres's forgery of judicial records to make
it appear that Sthenius, tried *in absentia*, was instead present at the trial,
he writes: "Don't you see this whole name 'in the presence of' (*coram*) is
in the text where [Verres] put it?" (*viditisne totum hoc nomen coram ubi facit
delatum esse in litura?*, *The Action Against Verres* 2.2.104). Augustine admits
that he is unsure about his reading of the passage.

44. Cicero, *Tusculan Disputations* 1.7.14: "Every proposition (*pronuntia-
tum*) — at the moment it strikes me that I should render ἀξίωμα in this
way; I'll use a different term later if I find a better one — a proposition,
then, is what is true or false."

ADEODATUS: Yes.

AUGUSTINE: Then if I were to say only 'sits' or only 'runs,' you would correctly ask me "Who?" or "What?" To that question I would reply "the man" or "the horse" or "the animal" or anything else, so that a name, when added to the verb, could complete the proposition. That is to say, it could complete a sentence that can be affirmed and denied.

ADEODATUS: I understand.

AUGUSTINE: Pay attention to the rest: imagine that we see something far away and are uncertain whether it is an animal or a stone or something else, and I say to you: "Because it is a man, it is an animal." Wouldn't I be speaking carelessly?

ADEODATUS: Very carelessly. You clearly wouldn't be speaking carelessly if you were to say: "If it is a man, it is an animal."

AUGUSTINE: You're right. So the 'if' in your statement is acceptable to me and acceptable to you, whereas the 'because' in mine is unacceptable to both of us.

ADEODATUS: I agree.

AUGUSTINE: Now see whether these two sentences are complete propositions: "'If' is acceptable" and "'Because' is unacceptable."

ADEODATUS: They are complete.

AUGUSTINE: Now do this: tell me which are the verbs and which are the names in those sentences.

ADEODATUS: I see that there the verbs are 'is acceptable' and 'is unacceptable.' What else are the names but 'if' and 'because'?

AUGUSTINE: Then it has been adequately proved that these two conjunctions ['if' and 'because'] are also names.

ADEODATUS: Yes.

AUGUSTINE: Can't you derive for yourself the selfsame result in the case of the other parts of speech, so as to establish the same rule for them all?

ADEODATUS: I can.

[6.17] AUGUSTINE: Then let's move on from here. Now tell me whether it seems to you that, just as we have found that all words are names and that all names are words, so too all names are terms (*vocabula*) and all terms are names.[45]

45. Cledonius, *The Grammatical Art* (Keil [1868], p. 35.1–3): "Among the old [grammarians] there was this distinction between names and terms

ADEODATUS: I don't see what difference there is between 5
['name' and 'term'], aside from the different sound of the syllables.

AUGUSTINE: I don't raise any objection to your reply for the
time being. Although there is no lack of people who distinguish
them even by signification, there is no need to consider their view
now. Surely you're aware that we have now come to signs that 10
signify one another mutually, differing in nothing but sound, and
that signify themselves along with all the other parts of speech.[46]

ADEODATUS: I don't understand.

AUGUSTINE: Then don't you understand that 'name' is signified by 'term' and 'term' is signified by 'name' in such a way that 15
there is no difference between them, aside from the sound of their
letters? At least, so far as 'name' in general is concerned — for we
also say 'name' specifically as one of the eight parts of speech,
such that it does not contain the other seven parts of speech.

ADEODATUS: I understand.

AUGUSTINE: This is what I said: that 'term' and 'name' signify 20
each other mutually.

ADEODATUS: I understand that, but I'm asking what you meant [6.18]
when [you said]: "they also signify themselves along with the
other parts of speech" (6.17.11–12).

AUGUSTINE: Hasn't the argument above taught us that all parts
of speech can be called names as well as terms — that is to say, 25
they can be signified by both 'name' and 'term'?

ADEODATUS: That's true.

AUGUSTINE: What if I should ask you what you call name itself,
that is, the sound expressed by the single syllable ['*name*']? Won't
you correctly answer me 'name'? 30

ADEODATUS: Yes.

AUGUSTINE: When we say '*con-junc-tion*,' this sign that we
enunciate with three syllables doesn't signify itself in this fashion,

---

(*inter nomina et vocabula*): living things were denoted by names, whereas
inanimate things were denoted by terms. But this usage was confusing
and died out." The same view is apparent in Donatus, *The Grammatical
Art* (Keil [1868], p. 373.5): "Now 'name' is for a single man, 'appellation'
for a multitude, and 'term' for things." See Wijdeveld [1937], p. 152 for
other references.

46. See 5.11.1–3 above.

does it? The name ['conjunction'] can't be counted among the
things that it signifies.

35   ADEODATUS: I accept that.

AUGUSTINE: That is, [you accept] what has been said: that
'name' signifies itself along with the other things it signifies. You
also may understand this for yourself regarding 'term.'

ADEODATUS: Come on! That's easy. Yet now it strikes me that
40   'name' is said both generally and specifically, whereas 'term' isn't
taken to be among the eight parts of speech. Accordingly, I think
that ['name' and 'term'] also differ from one another in this
regard, aside from the difference in sound.

AUGUSTINE: Well, do you think that 'name' [*nomen*] and ὄνομα
differ from one another in any regard, aside from the sound by
45   which the two languages are also distinguished?

ADEODATUS: Here I see no other difference.

AUGUSTINE: Then we have arrived at signs: (*a*) that signify
themselves; (*b*) each of which is mutually signified by the other; (*c*)
wherein whatever is signified by the one is also signified by the
other; and (*d*) that differ from each other in nothing aside from
50   sound. To be sure we have discovered only (*d*), for (*a*)-(*c*) are also
understood for 'name' and 'word.'[47]

ADEODATUS: Absolutely.

[7.19]   AUGUSTINE: Now I should like you to review what we have
found out in our discussion.

ADEODATUS: I'll do so as best I can.

First, I remember that we spent some time inquiring why we
5   speak. It was found that we speak for the sake of teaching or
reminding, given that when we ask questions we do so only in
order that the person who is asked may learn what we wish to
hear (1.1.3–26).

Now in the case of singing, which it seems we do for pleasure
(and this is not a proper feature of speaking), and in the case of
praying to God, Who we cannot suppose is taught or reminded,
10   words are for the purpose either of reminding ourselves or that
others may be reminded or taught by us (1.1.27–1.2.77).

Next, since we were sufficiently in agreement that words are

47. The translation "as regards 'name' and 'verb'" is also possible, but
see 7.20.69–75, where Adeodatus remarks that 'name' and 'word' do not
mean the same although they mean 'just as much.'

only signs and that things not signifying anything can't be signs, you put forward a line of verse:[48]

If nothing from so great a city it pleases the gods be left...   15

and I undertook to show what each word in this line of verse signifies (2.3.1–20). Though the second word of this line of verse, ['nothing'], is familiar and obvious, in the end we didn't uncover what it signifies (2.3.21–27). Since it seemed to me that we don't use it pointlessly when we speak, but with it we teach something to the person who is listening, you replied that when one finds or   20
thinks oneself to have found that the thing one seeks doesn't exist, perhaps a state of mind is indicated by this word (2.3.28–42). Yet you avoided any depth there may be to the question with a joke and postponed it to be explained at another time (2.3.43–48) — don't think that I have forgotten your obligation too!

Then, since I was hard pressed to explain the third word in this   25
line of verse, ['from'], you urged me to show you not another word that had the same meaning but instead the thing itself signified by the word (2.4.50–72). Because I had said that we could not do this while engaged in discussion, we came to those things that are exhibited to people raising such questions by [pointing] a finger (3.5.1–11). I thought all these things were corporeal, but we   30
found that they are only the visible things (3.5.12–28).

From here we moved on — I don't know how — to the case of deaf people and actors, who signify with wordless gesturing not only things that can be seen, but many other things besides, and nearly everything that we talk about (3.5.29–38). Just the same, we found that gestures themselves are signs (3.6.39–46).

At that point we began again to inquire how we could show   35
without any signs the things themselves that are signified by the signs, since it was proved that even a wall, or color, or anything visible that is shown by aiming the finger is shown by a definite sign. Here I was mistaken since I had said that nothing of the sort could be found (3.6.47–52).

Eventually we agreed that we can point out without a sign   40
those things we aren't doing when we are asked about them but we can do after the inquiry. Yet it was apparent that speaking isn't

48. Vergil, *Aeneid* 2.659.

that kind of thing, given that when we're asked what speaking is while we're speaking, it's easy to illustrate speaking through itself (3.6.53–83).

[7.20]
45
After that, our attention was called to the fact that either [1] signs are exhibited by means of signs, or [2] things that we can do after a question [has been raised] are exhibited without a sign, or [3] other things, which are not signs, are exhibited with signs (4.7.1–11).[49] We undertook to consider and discuss carefully [1] (4.7.12–13).

50
In the debate [regarding (*a*)], it was revealed that on the one hand there are signs that could not in turn be signified by the signs they signify, as for example when we say the three-syllable word '*con-junc-tion*'; on the other hand there are signs that could in turn be signified by the signs they signify; for example when we say '*sign*' we also signify 'word' and when we say '*word*' we also sig-

55
nify 'sign' (for 'sign' and 'word' are both two signs and two words) (4.7.13–4.9.94).

However, in this class of signs that signify each other mutually, it was established that some mean not so much, some mean just as much, and some even mean the same.[50] The fact is that when we

49. Adeodatus gives [3] before [2] in his summary here; I have reversed the order to conform to Augustine's earlier presentation of the fundamental division.

50. The phrases 'not so much,' 'just so much,' and 'the same' are adverbial modifiers, describing the kind of signification possessed by terms. Adeodatus seems to be talking on the one hand about inclusion-relations among the class of significates, and on the other hand about sense (or intension). Let x and y signify each other mutually. The class of x-significates may be a subclass of the class of y-significates, so that x "means not so much" as y; or the class of x-significates and the class of y-significates may be the same, so that x and y "mean just as much." (Adeodatus does not mention the case in which the classes overlap, but neither is completely contained within the other.) The Latin term '*tantum*' indicates quantity, and suggests this extensional reading. However, the case in which terms "mean the same" is not a case in which the extensions are equal (that case is covered by terms that "mean just as much"). Adeodatus offers two ways in which terms can fail to mean the same: (*a*) they may have a sense that is derived from their initial use, revealed by etymology; (*b*) they are not interchangeable in ordinary contexts. Hence this case seems to include a difference in 'meaning' beyond the comparison of

say this one-syllable word *'sign,'* which makes a certain sound, it signifies absolutely everything by means of which anything is signified. Yet when we say *'word,'* it isn't a sign of all signs but only of signs uttered by an articulated sound. Accordingly, it's clear that although 'word' is signified by 'sign' and 'sign' is signified by 'word' — that is to say, the former syllable is signified by the latter and the latter syllable is signified by the former — 'sign' nevertheless means more than 'word' does, given that the former syllable signifies more things than the latter (4.9.95–4.10.158). [60]

Yet 'word' in general means just as much as 'name' in general. The argument has taught us that all the parts of speech are also names, since (*a*) pronouns can be added to [names] (5.13.58–73); (*b*) it can be said of all parts of speech that they name something (5.13.74–5.16.177); (*c*) there is no [part of speech] that can't complete a proposition by means of an added verb (5.16.178–219). [65]

Although 'name' and 'word' mean just as much, in that all things that are words are also names, they don't mean the same. We probably discussed sufficiently the reason some are called 'words' and others 'names,' if it has been ascertained that one of these is for marking out the striking of the ear, the other for marking out the mind's recollection (*commemorationem*) (5.12.54–57). Or perhaps the point can be understood on this basis, namely that when we want to commit something to memory, we speak most correctly when we say "What is this thing's name?" whereas we are not accustomed to saying, "What is this thing's word?"[51] [70] [75]

We found that 'name' and ὄνομα signify not only just as much but also exactly the same, and there is no difference between them aside from the sound of the letters (6.18.43–46). The point had really slipped my mind that in the class of signs that signify one another mutually we found no sign that doesn't also signify itself, among the other things that it signifies. [80]

I've recalled these things as best I could. You, I believe, haven't said anything in this discussion except with knowledge and assurance. Now see whether I have reviewed these matters properly and in order. [85]

AUGUSTINE: You have accurately recalled from memory all I [8.21]

---

significate-classes. Thus it appears to be a difference not in extension, but in intension or sense.

51. The argument given in this sentence is new.

wanted. I must admit to you that these distinctions now seem much clearer to me than they were when the two of us, by inquiry and discussion, unearthed them from whatever their hiding places were.

5   However, with so many detours, it's difficult to say at this point where you and I are trying to get to! Maybe you think we're playing around and diverting the mind from serious matters by some little puzzles that seem childish, or that we're pursuing some result that is only small or modest — or, if you suspect that this

10   discussion might issue in some important result, you want to know straightaway what it is (or at least to hear me say what it is!). Well, I'd like you to believe that I haven't set to work on mere trivialities in this conversation. Though we do perhaps play around, this should itself not be regarded as childish. Nor are we thinking about small or modest goods. Yet if I were to say that there is a

15   happy and everlasting life, and I want us to be led there under the guidance of God (namely Truth Himself) by stages that are suitable to our weak steps, I'm afraid I might seem laughable for having set out on such a long journey by considering signs rather than the things themselves that are signified.

20   So then, you'll pardon me if I play around with you at first — not for the sake of playing around,[52] but to exercise the mind's strength and sharpness, with which we're able not only to withstand but also to love the heat and light of that region where the happy life is.

ADEODATUS: Continue as you have begun! I would never think to belittle what you think ought to be said or done.

[Discussion of Division [2]][53]

[8.22]   AUGUSTINE: Then come now, let's consider the division [of
25   signs] where signs do not signify other signs but instead things,

52. There is some untranslatable wordplay here: *si praeludo tecum, non ludendi gratia.*

53. Division [2] deals with significates that are non-signs. More precisely, it deals with the extent to which things that may be signifiable (but are not themselves signs) can be known, either (*a*) in their own right or (*b*) through signs. Before Augustine and Adeodatus can address (*a*) and (*b*), a possible source of confusion has to be ruled out, namely the case in which a sign is used to exhibit itself *qua* sound (8.22–24). See 4.7 above.

which we call 'signifiables.' First tell me whether man is man.

ADEODATUS: Now I don't know whether you're playing around with me.

AUGUSTINE: Why so?

ADEODATUS: Because you think it necessary to ask me whether   30
man is anything but man!

AUGUSTINE: Then I believe you'd also think I was merely play-ing around with you if I were to ask whether the first syllable of this name ['man'] (*homo*) is anything but '*ho-*' and the second syl-lable anything but '*-mo.*'

ADEODATUS: Yes! I would!   35

AUGUSTINE: Yet those two syllables ['*ho-*' and '*-mo*'] conjoined are man (*homo*). Will you deny it?

ADEODATUS: Who could deny it?

AUGUSTINE: Then I ask the question: are you those two con-joined syllables?

ADEODATUS: Not at all, but I see where you're headed.

AUGUSTINE: Then you shall tell me, so you don't think I'm   40
being offensive.

ADEODATUS: You think it follows that I'm not a man.

AUGUSTINE: Well, don't you think the same thing? You grant that all those claims above, from which this conclusion has been deduced, are true.

ADEODATUS: I won't tell you what I think until I have first heard from you whether in your question about man being man   45
you were asking me about those two syllables [('*ho-mo*')] or about the very thing they signify.

AUGUSTINE: Reply to this instead: from what standpoint have you taken my question? If it's ambiguous, you ought to have guarded against this first, and not answered me before you made certain precisely how I put the question.   50

ADEODATUS: Why should this ambiguity be any obstacle, since I have replied to each? Man is certainly man: those two syllables ['*ho-mo*'] are nothing other than those two syllables, and what they signify is nothing other than what it is.

AUGUSTINE: Of course you know this. Yet why have you taken   55
only the word 'man' in each way, and not also the other words we have spoken?

ADEODATUS: On what grounds am I proven wrong not to have taken the others in this way too?

AUGUSTINE: To put aside other reasons — if you had taken that
60   first question of mine entirely from the standpoint in which the
syllables are mere sounds, you wouldn't have made any reply to
me, for I could have seemed not to ask you anything. Yet now,
given that I uttered three words — one of which I repeated in the
second and fourth place[54] — saying "whether man is man," you
clearly took the first word and the third word not as signs them-
65   selves but as the things they signify. This is obvious from the fact
that you were immediately certain and confident that the question
ought to be answered.

ADEODATUS: You're right.

AUGUSTINE: Then why did it suit you to take only the word in
the second and fourth place both according to what it sounds like
70   and according to what it signifies?

ADEODATUS: Look, now I take the whole thing only from the
standpoint of what is signified. I do agree with you that we can't
carry on a conversation at all unless the words we hear direct the
mind to the things of which they are the signs. So now show me
75   how I was misled by the line of reasoning in which it's deduced
that I'm not a man (8.22.27–41).

AUGUSTINE: Instead, I'll ask the same questions again, so that
you yourself may discover where you stumbled.

ADEODATUS: Fine!

[8.23]   AUGUSTINE: I won't repeat my first question, [namely whether
80   man is man], because now you haven't granted it. So, then, examine more carefully [my second question]: whether the syllable '*ho-*'
is anything but '*ho-*' and whether '*-mo*' is anything but '*-mo.*'

ADEODATUS: I don't see anything else here at all.

AUGUSTINE: See also whether man (*homo*) is not made from
these two syllables ['*ho-*' and '*-mo*'] in combination.

85   ADEODATUS: I should never have granted this! It was agreed,
and rightly so, that when a sign is given we should pay attention
to what is signified, and from the consideration of this to admit or
to deny what is said (8.22.72–74). Yet when the syllables ['*ho-*' and
'*-mo*'] are enunciated separately, it was granted that they are the
sounds themselves (8.23.83), since they are sounds without any
signification.

54. "In the second and fourth place": literally, 'in the middle,' since the
question is *utrum homo homo sit.*

AUGUSTINE: Then it is agreed, and firmly established in your 90
mind, that questions should be answered only on the basis of the
things signified by the words.

ADEODATUS: I don't understand why this is unacceptable — so
long as they *are* words.

AUGUSTINE: I'd like to know how you would refute the man
we often hear about while we're telling jokes, who drew the con- 95
clusion that a lion came out of the mouth of the person with whom
he was arguing. He had asked whether what we say comes out of
our mouth. His interlocutor couldn't deny it. He then easily contrived to make his interlocutor use the name 'lion' during the conversation. When this happened, he began to taunt his interlocutor 100
and ridicule him, saying that a man who wasn't a bad fellow
seemed to have vomited up a monstrous beast! For his interlocutor had admitted that whatever we say comes out of our mouth,
and he couldn't deny that he had said 'lion.'

ADEODATUS: Well, it wasn't difficult at all to refute this clown.
I wouldn't grant that whatever we say comes out of our mouth. 105
We signify the things that we say, and what comes out of the
speaker's mouth isn't the thing signified but the sign by which it
is signified — except when the signs themselves are signified, and
we discussed this class [of signs] a little while ago.

AUGUSTINE: In this way you would have been well armed [8.24]
against him. Yet what will you say to me upon being asked 110
whether man is a name?[55]

ADEODATUS: What except that it is a name?

AUGUSTINE: Well, do I see a name when I see you?

ADEODATUS: No. 115

AUGUSTINE: Then do you want me to say what follows?

ADEODATUS: Please don't! I declare for myself that I'm not a
man — for when you asked whether man is a name, I answered
that it *was* a name. As a matter of fact, we had already agreed to 120
grant or deny what is said based on the thing signified (8.23.85–
92).

AUGUSTINE: It seems to me, however, that you didn't fall into
this answer without grounds. The law of reason that is implanted

55. Here and in the next several paragraphs I have not inserted quotation marks, since Augustine's argument turns on blurring the distinction
between man and 'man.'

in our minds overcame your caution.[56] If I should ask what man
is, you probably would answer "an animal." If I were to ask what
125   part of speech man is, you could only answer correctly "a name."
So although man is found to be both a name and an animal, the
former is said from the standpoint in which it is a sign; the latter,
the standpoint in which it is signified.

If anyone asks me whether man is a name, then, I would
130   answer that it is nothing else, for he signifies well enough that he
wants to hear the answer from the standpoint in which it is a sign.
If he asks whether man is an animal, I would give my assent much
more readily. If without mentioning "name" or "animal" he were
to inquire only what man is, then in virtue of that agreed-upon
rule of language the mind would quickly move along to what is
signified by this syllable ['*man*'], and the answer would simply be
135   "an animal"; or even the whole definition, namely "a rational
mortal animal," might be stated. Don't you think so?

ADEODATUS: I do, entirely. Yet since we have granted that
[man] is a name, how shall we avoid the offensive conclusion in
which it's deduced that we aren't men?

140   AUGUSTINE: How do you think but by establishing that the
conclusion was not inferred from the standpoint in which we
agreed with the questioner?

On the other hand, if he were to admit that he draws the conclusion from this standpoint, then it isn't to be feared in any way.
Why should I be afraid to admit that I'm not *man* — that I'm not
that syllable?

145   ADEODATUS: Nothing is more true! Then why is saying "Hence
you are not a man" offensive to the mind, since according to what
we granted nothing more true could be said?

AUGUSTINE: Because as soon as the words [of the conclusion]
are uttered, I can't help thinking that what is signified by the syllable ['*man*'] is relevant to the conclusion, by virtue of the law that
150   naturally has the most power — so that once the signs are heard

56. The "law of reason" is to follow explicit contextual signs in disam-
biguating questions, which overcame Adeodatus's Rule always to inter-
pret questions from the standpoint of what is signified. Augustine
suggests in the next paragraph that Adeodatus's Rule comes into play in
the absence of contextual signs, and in 8.24.149–50 he perhaps suggests
that this is natural.

the attention is directed to the things signified.

ADEODATUS: I agree with what you say.

AUGUSTINE: Now then, I want you to understand that the [9.25] things signified should be valued more than their signs. Whatever exists on account of another must be worth less than that on account of which it exists[57] — unless you think otherwise.

ADEODATUS: It seems to me that assent shouldn't be given 5 lightly at this point. When we say 'filth,' for instance, I think the name is far superior to the thing it signifies. What offends us when we hear it isn't the sound of the word itself. When one letter is changed, the name 'filth' (*caenum*) becomes 'heaven' (*caelum*), but we see what a great difference there is between the things signified by these names ['filth' and 'heaven']! For this reason, I cer- 10 tainly wouldn't attribute to the sign ['filth'] what we so loathe in the thing it signifies, and hence I rightly prefer the former to the latter, for we're more willing to hear the sign than to come into contact with the thing it signifies by any of the senses.

AUGUSTINE: You're most certainly on your guard. Then it's false that all things should be valued more than their signs. 15

ADEODATUS: So it seems.

AUGUSTINE: Then tell me what you think the men who gave the name ['filth'] to so vile and loathsome a thing were aiming at, and whether you approve or disapprove of them.

ADEODATUS: For my part, I do not venture either to approve or 20 to disapprove of them, and I don't know what they were aiming at.

AUGUSTINE: Can't you at least know what *you* are aiming at when you enunciate this name?

ADEODATUS: Obviously I can. I want to signify, in order to teach or recall to the person I'm talking with, the thing I think he 25 should be taught or recall.[58]

AUGUSTINE: Well, the teaching or recalling (or being taught or

57. Call this "Augustine's Rule": if x exists on account of y, then y is more valuable than x. See Wijdeveld [1937], p. 163 for sources of this principle.

58. This awkward sentence has a simple meaning: Adeodatus uses the name 'filth' when he wants to talk about filth with someone — that is, to convey knowledge, which is a matter of either teaching or recalling, according to the start of the dialogue.

recalled) that you conveniently furnish by the name (or that is furnished to you by the name) — shouldn't it be held more valuable
30   than the name itself?

ADEODATUS: I do grant that the very knowledge that results
from the sign should be preferred to the sign, but I don't think that
therefore the thing should be.

[9.26]   AUGUSTINE: In this theory of ours, then, although it's false that
35   all things should be preferred to their signs, it's not false that anything existing on account of another is worth less than that on
account of which it exists.[59] The knowledge of filth, for the sake of
which the name ['filth'] was instituted, should be held more valuable than the name itself — and we found that this is in turn to be
40   preferred to filth. This knowledge is preferable to the sign we're
speaking about ([namely 'filth']) precisely because the latter
demonstrably exists on account of the former, and not the other
way around.

This [rule][60] also holds, for example, in the case of the glutton
and "worshipper of his stomach" (as the Apostle says[61]), who said
that he lived to eat: the temperate man who heard him protested
45   and said: "How much better that you should eat to live!"[62] Each
man, however, spoke according to this very rule. The only reason
the glutton evoked displeasure was that he valued his life so little
that he should lead it in a worthless fashion for the pleasure of his
palate, saying that he lived on account of meals. The only reason
the temperate man deserves praise is that, understanding which
50   of these two things should occur on account of the other (namely
which one is subordinate to the other), he gave the reminder that
we should eat to live rather than the other way around.

Likewise, if a talkative word-lover says "I teach in order to
talk," you and any other person judging things with some experi-
55   ence might perhaps respond to him: "Why don't you instead talk
in order to teach?"

Now if these things are true, as you know they are, surely you

59. That is, Augustine's Rule, initially stated at 9.25.1–4, still holds.

60. Augustine's Rule again.

61. Romans 16:18.

62. The story is an old one. The saying is reported in the Pseudo-Cicero's
Rhetoric for Herennius 4.28.39 and in Quintilian, *Oratorical Guidelines* 9.3.85;
it is attributed to Socrates by Aulus Gellius in *Attic Nights* 19.2.7.

see how much less words are to be valued than that on account of which we use words. The use of words should itself already be preferred to words: words exist so that we may use them. Furthermore, we use them in order to teach. Hence teaching is better than speaking to the same extent that the speaking is better than the words. The teaching[63] is, therefore, that much better than words.[64] I want to hear any objections you think perhaps should be offered against this. 60

ADEODATUS: I do agree that the teaching is better than words. I don't know whether any objection can be raised against the rule according to which everything that exists on account of another is said to be inferior to that on account of which it exists. [9.27] 65

AUGUSTINE: We'll discuss this more opportunely and more carefully at another time. Right now what you concede is sufficient for what I'm trying to establish. You grant that knowledge of things is more valuable than the signs of things, and for this reason knowledge of the things signified should be preferable to knowledge of their signs. Doesn't it seem so to you? 70

ADEODATUS: Surely I haven't conceded that knowledge of things is superior to the knowledge of signs, and not just superior to the signs themselves, have I?[65] So I have misgivings about agreeing with you on this score. The name 'filth' is better than the thing it signifies. What if knowledge of this name is then likewise to be preferred to knowledge of the thing, although the name itself 75

63. The earlier occurrences of 'teaching' have referred primarily to the activity (*ad docendum, docere*); here Augustine subtly moves to the distinguishing feature of the activity (or to its content): *doctrina*.

64. The argument in this paragraph rests on a double application of Augustine's Rule: words are for the sake of their use, and the use of words is for the sake of teaching; hence teaching is more valuable than the use of words (first application), and the use of words is more valuable than the words themselves (second application). Augustine's claim that the two comparative judgments are proportional involves a shift from ordinal to cardinal measures.

65. Adeodatus is hesitant about Augustine's inference from "the knowledge of things is better than the signs" to "the knowledge of things is better than the knowledge of signs." Adeodatus grants the former but has not yet been persuaded that the latter also holds (or that it follows from the former).

is inferior to that knowledge? There are obviously four things here:

    (*a*) the name
    (*b*) the thing
    (*c*) knowledge of the name
    (*d*) knowledge of the thing

Just as (*a*) surpasses (*b*), then, why shouldn't (*c*) also surpass (*d*)?
80   Yet even if (*c*) were not to surpass (*d*), surely (*c*) isn't then to be subordinated to (*d*), is it?

[9.28]   AUGUSTINE: I see with great admiration that you've held fast to what you conceded and explained what you thought. I think you understand, however, that the one-syllable name pronounced when we say '*vice*' is better than what it signifies, although knowl-
85   edge of the name ['vice'] itself is far inferior to knowledge of vices.[66] So although you may distinguish those four things and reflect upon them — the name, the thing, knowledge of the name, knowledge of the thing — we rightly prefer (*a*) to (*b*). For instance, when Persius says:[67]

    But this man is besotted with vice . . .

putting the name ['vice'] into the poem didn't do anything vicious
90   to his line of verse, but even embellished it. When, however, the very thing signified by the name ['vice'] is present in anyone, it compels him to be vicious. Yet we don't see that (*c*) surpasses (*d*) in this way. Instead, (*d*) surpasses (*c*), since knowledge of the name ['vice'] is worthless compared to knowledge of vices.

95   ADEODATUS: Do you think this knowledge should be preferred even when it makes us more miserable? Among all the punishments contrived by the cruelty of tyrants or meted out by their cupidity, Persius himself puts first the one that tortures men by forcing them to recognize vices they can't avoid.

100   AUGUSTINE: In the same way you also can deny that knowl-

---

66. As Augustine points out, here (*a*) is superior to (*b*), since the name 'vice' is preferable to an actual vice, but (*d*) is superior to (*c*), since knowledge of the vice is preferable to merely knowing the name 'vice.'

67. Persius, *Satires* 3.32.

edge of virtues itself should be preferred to knowledge of the name ['virtue']. Seeing virtue and not possessing it is a torment, one that the same satirist wished tyrants would be punished with.[68]

ADEODATUS: May God turn aside this madness! Now I understand that the items of knowledge themselves, with which the best   105
education of all has filled the mind, are not to be blamed. Instead, those men should be judged the most miserable — as I think Persius also judged them — who are afflicted with such a disease that not even so great a remedy provides relief for it.

AUGUSTINE: That's right. But what do we care whatever Persius's opinion may be? We aren't subject to the authority of these   110
men[69] in such matters. Consequently, it isn't easy to explain at this point whether some item of knowledge is to be preferred to another item of knowledge. I'm satisfied that we have shown that knowledge of things signified is preferable to the signs themselves, though not to knowledge of signs.

[Discussion of Division [2(a)]]

Therefore, let's now analyze more completely the class of   115
things we said can be exhibited through themselves, without signs, such as speaking, walking, sitting, lying down, and the like.[70]

ADEODATUS: I now recall what you're describing.

AUGUSTINE: Does it seem to you that all the things we can do   [10.29]
once we've been asked about them can be exhibited without a sign? Is there any exception?

ADEODATUS: Considering this whole class over and over again, I still don't find *anything* that can be taught without a sign —   5
except perhaps speaking, and possibly if someone should happen to ask the very question "What is it to teach?" — for I see that no

68. Persius, *Satires* 3.35–38: "Great Father of the Gods! When detestable lust attainted with dreadful venom has moved the souls of cruel tyrants, let it be your will to punish them in no other way but this: let them look upon virtue and pine away for leaving it behind!"

69. "Of these men": *horum*. It is unclear who Augustine means to single out here — satirists? poets? pagans?

70. These 'self-exhibiting actions' were introduced in 3.6.

matter what I do after his question so that he may learn, he doesn't learn from the very thing he wants exhibited to him.

10   For example, if anyone should ask me what it is to walk while I was resting or doing something else, as was said, and I should attempt to teach him what he asked about without a sign, by immediately walking, how shall I guard against his thinking that it's just the amount of walking I have done? He'll be mistaken if he thinks this. He'll think that anyone who walks farther than I have,

15   or not as far, hasn't walked at all. Yet what I have said about this one word ['walking'] applies to all the things I had agreed can be exhibited without a sign, apart from the two exceptions we made.[71]

[10.30]   AUGUSTINE: I agree with this point. Yet doesn't it seem to you that speaking is one thing and teaching another?

20   ADEODATUS: It does. If they were the same, nobody would teach except by speaking; but seeing that we also teach many things with other signs besides words, who would have any doubt that there is a difference?

AUGUSTINE: Well, is there any difference between teaching and signifying, or not?

25   ADEODATUS: I think they're the same.

AUGUSTINE: Anyone who says that we signify in order to teach is right, isn't he?

ADEODATUS: Completely right.

AUGUSTINE: Well, if someone else were to say that we teach in

30   order to signify, wouldn't he easily be refuted by the view given above?[72]

ADEODATUS: That is so.

AUGUSTINE: Then if we signify in order to teach, and we don't teach in order to signify, teaching is one thing and signifying another.

ADEODATUS: You're right. I was wrong in answering that they are the same.

35   AUGUSTINE: Now answer this: does the person teaching what

71. The two exceptions are speaking and teaching, which Adeodatus mentions in 10.29.5–7 (calling to mind the earlier discussion at 3.6.79–81).

72. "By the view given above": *superiore sententia*. The reference is unclear. Augustine could be referring to his immediately preceding statement that signifying is for the sake of teaching, or alternatively to the discussion in 9.36.55–62.

it is to teach do so by signifying, or in another way?

ADEODATUS: I don't see how he can do it in another way.

AUGUSTINE: Then you stated a falsehood a little while ago, namely that a thing can be taught without signs when the question is raised what teaching itself is. Now we see that not even this can be done without signification, since you granted that signify- 40 ing is one thing and teaching another: if they're different things, as they appear to be, and the latter is shown only through the former, then it isn't shown through itself, as you thought. So we haven't yet uncovered anything that can be exhibited through itself — except speaking, which also signifies itself, among other 45 things. Since speaking itself is also a sign, though, it isn't yet entirely apparent whether anything seems able to be taught without signs.

ADEODATUS: I have no reason for not agreeing.

AUGUSTINE: Then it has been established that nothing is taught [10.31] without signs, and that knowledge itself should be more valuable 50 to us than the signs by means of which we know, although not all things signified can be superior to their signs.

ADEODATUS: So it seems.

AUGUSTINE: I ask you — do you remember how circuitous was the path by which we finally reached such a slight result? Ever 55 since we started bandying words with one another, which we've been doing for a long time now, we have been working to find out these three things: whether anything can be taught without signs; whether certain signs should be preferred to the things they signify; and whether knowledge of things is itself better than the signs. Yet there is a fourth, and this I should like to know about 60 from you briefly: whether you think of these discoveries in such a way that you can't now have doubts regarding them.

ADEODATUS: I should hope that by these great detours and byways we have arrived at certainties! Yet somehow this question of yours disturbs me and keeps me from agreeing. I think you 65 wouldn't have asked me this unless you had an objection to offer, and the intricacy of these matters doesn't allow me to investigate the whole issue and answer with assurance. I fear there is something hidden in these great complexities that my mind is not keen enough to illuminate.

AUGUSTINE: I commend your hesitation; it bespeaks a circum- 70 spect mind, and this is the greatest safeguard of tranquility. It's

extremely difficult not to be perturbed when things we were holding with easy and ready approval are undermined by contrary
arguments and, as it were, are wrenched out of our hands.

75   Accordingly, just as it is right to yield to arguments that have been
thoroughly considered and scrutinized, so it is hazardous to
regard what is unknown as known. There is a danger that when
things we presume are going to stand firm and endure are regularly overturned, we fall into such a great hatred and mistrust of
reason[73] it seems that confidence should not even be had in the
plain truth itself.

[10.32]   Well then, let's straightaway reconsider now whether you were
80   correct in thinking that these things should be doubted. Consider
this example. Suppose that someone unfamiliar with how to trick
birds (which is done with reeds and birdlime) should run into a
birdcatcher outfitted with his tools, not birdcatching but on his
way to do so. On seeing this birdcatcher, he follows closely in his
85   footsteps, and, as it happens, he reflects and asks himself in his
astonishment what exactly the man's equipment means. Now the
birdcatcher, wanting to show off after seeing the attention focused
on him, prepares his reeds and with his birdcall and his hawk[74]
intercepts, subdues, and captures some little bird he has noticed
nearby. I ask you: wouldn't he then teach the man watching him
90   what he wanted to know by the thing itself rather than by anything that signifies?[75]

ADEODATUS: I'm afraid that everything here is like what I said
about the man who asks what it is to walk. Here, too, I don't see
that the whole of birdcatching has been exhibited.

AUGUSTINE: It's easy to get rid of your worry. I add that he's so
95   intelligent that he recognizes the kind of craft as a whole on the
basis of what he has seen. It's surely enough for the matter at hand
that some men can be taught about some things, even if not all,
without a sign.

73. "Hatred and mistrust of reason": possibly "hatred and mistrust of
argument" — in any event, a clear reference to Plato's discussion of 'mis-
ology' in *Phaedo* 89D–E. See also *Against the Academicians* 2.1.1.12–14.

74. Wijdeveld [1937], p. 171 regards the sudden appearance of a hawk
at this stage, previously unmentioned, as evidence that the formula *fistula
et accipetre* is an interpolation and we should instead read *arundine*.

75. "Rather than by anything that signifies": *nullo significatu*.

ADEODATUS: I also can add this to the other case! If he is suffi- ciently intelligent, he'll know the whole of what it is to walk, once walking has been illustrated by a few steps.   100

AUGUSTINE:[76] You may do so as far as I'm concerned; not only do I not offer any objection, I even support you! You see, each of us has established that some people can be taught some things without signs, and what seemed apparent to us a little earlier (10.29–31) — that there is absolutely nothing that can be shown without signs — is false. These examples already suggest not one   105 or another but thousands of things that are exhibited through themselves, without any sign being given.

Why, I ask you, should we doubt this? For example (passing over the performances of men in all the theaters who display things themselves without a sign), doesn't God or Nature show   110 and display to those paying attention, by themselves, this sun and the light pervading and clothing all things present, the moon and the other stars, the lands and the seas, and the countless things begotten in them?

•

[Discussion of Division [2(b)]][77]

Well, if we should consider this more carefully, perhaps you'll   [10.33] discover that nothing is learned through its signs. When a sign is   115 given to me, it can teach me nothing if it finds me ignorant of the thing of which it is the sign; but if I'm not ignorant, what do I learn through the sign?

For example, when I read:[78]

76. Here Augustine begins his closing monologue, which occupies the last quarter of the work.

77. Do we ever learn about non-signs through signs? That is the ques- tion of Division [2(b)], which Augustine answers in a lengthy monologue. The remainder of *The Teacher* is devoted to establishing and exploring the thesis he and Adeodatus had defended in 10.29–31, repeated here: "noth- ing is learned through its signs."

78. Daniel 3:94 (Vulgate) = 3:27 (Septuagint). (The Vulgate has *sarabala* rather than *sarabara*.) I have left *sarabarae* untranslated, since Augustine is employing a deliberately unfamiliar word to make his point. A good thing, too: the form and meaning of the word are extremely unclear. See the entry in Pauly-Wissowa [1920], 2.R.1 col. 2386 *s.v.* saraballa, and Knauer [1954].

. . . and their *sarabarae* were unchanged.

120   the word doesn't show me the thing it signifies. If certain head-
coverings are denominated by this name ['*sarabarae*'], have I
learned upon hearing it what the head is or what coverings are? I
knew these things before; my conception of them wasn't fashioned because they were named by others, but because I saw
125   them. The first time the syllable '*head*' struck my ears I was just as
ignorant of what it signified as when I first heard or read '*sarabarae.*' Yet since '*head*' was often pronounced, noting and observing when it was pronounced, I discovered that it was the term for
a thing already familiar to me by sight. Before I made this discov-
130   ery, the word was a mere sound to me; but I learned that it was a
sign when I found out of what thing it is the sign — and, as I said,
I learned this not by anything that signifies but by its appearance.
Therefore, a sign is learned when the thing is known, rather than
the thing being learned when the sign is given.
[10.34]   So that you may understand this more clearly, suppose that we
135   hear '*head*' now for the first time. Not knowing whether that utterance is a mere noise or also signifies something, we ask what
'*head*' is. (Remember we want to have a conception not of the
thing signified but of the sign itself, which we surely don't have as
140   long as we don't know what it's the sign of.) If, then, the thing is
pointed out with the finger after we raise the question, once it has
been seen we learn the sign, which we had only heard and didn't
know at that point.
Now there are two elements in the sign: the sound and the signification. We don't perceive the sound by the sign, but when it
strikes the ear. We perceive the signification, however, by seeing
145   the thing signified. Aiming with the finger can only signify what
the finger is aimed at, and it's aimed not at the sign but at the
bodily part called the head. Consequently, by aiming the finger I
can't know either the thing (which I knew already) or the sign (at
which the finger isn't aimed).
150   I don't much care about aiming with the finger, because it
seems to me to be a sign of the pointing-out itself rather than of
any things that are pointed out. It's like the exclamation 'look!'[79]

79. "It's like the exclamation 'look'": *sicut adverbium quod 'ecce' dicimus.*
Nothing turns on the part of speech in question.

— we typically also aim the finger along with this exclamation, in case one sign of the pointing-out isn't enough.

Most of all I'm trying to persuade you, if I'll be able to, that we 155 don't learn anything by these signs called words. As I have stated, we learn the meaning of a word — that is, the signification hidden in the sound — once the thing signified is itself known, rather than our perceiving it by means of such signification.

What I've said about 'head' I also might have said about 'cov- [10.35] erings' (and about countless other things!). Although I already knew them, I still don't yet know them to be *sarabarae*. If anyone 160 should signify them to me with a gesture, or represent them, or show me something similar to them, I won't say that he didn't teach me — a claim I might easily maintain should I care to speak a little longer — but I do state something close to it: he didn't teach me with words. Even if he happens to see them when I'm around 165 and should call them to my attention by saying "Look: *sarabarae!*" I wouldn't learn the thing I was ignorant of by the words that he has spoken, but by looking at it. This is the way it came to pass that I know and grasp what meaning the name has. When I learned the thing itself, I trusted my eyes, not the words of another — though perhaps I trusted the words to direct my attention, that is, to find 170 out what I would see by looking.[80]

To give them as much credit as possible, words have force only [11.36] to the extent that they remind us to look for things; they don't display them for us to know. Yet someone who presents what I want to know to my eyes, or to any of my bodily senses, or even to my mind itself, does teach me something.

From words, then, we learn only words — rather, the sound 5 and noise of the words. If things that aren't signs can't be words, then although I have already heard a word, I don't know that it is a word until I know what it signifies. Therefore, knowledge of words is made complete once the things are known. On the other hand, when words are [only] heard, not even the words are 10 learned. We don't learn words we know. Also, we have to admit

---

80. "To find out what I would see by looking": *ut aspectu quaererem quid viderim*. The grammar as well as the sense of this phrase is obscure; one family of manuscripts omits it entirely. Several conjectural emendations readily suggest themselves: *auditu* for *aspectu*, *audierim* for *viderim*, or the like.

that we learn words we didn't know only after their signification
has been perceived, and this happens not by hearing the mere
sounds uttered but by knowing the things signified. This is a
15   truthful and solid argument: when words are spoken we either
know what they signify or we don't; if we know, then it's reminding rather than learning; but if we don't know, it isn't even
reminding, though perhaps we recollect that we should inquire.
[11.37]   You may object: granted that (*a*) it's only by sight that we can
20   know those head-coverings, whose name ['*sarabarae*'] we only
take as a sound; and (*b*) we know the name itself more fully only
when the things are themselves known. Yet we do accept the story
of those boys — how they overcame King Nebuchadnezzar and
his flames by their faith and religion, what praises they sang to
God, and what honors they merited even from their enemy him-
25   self.[81] Have we learned these things otherwise than by words?

I reply to this objection that everything signified by those
words was already known to us.[82] I'm already familiar with what
three boys are, what a furnace is, what fire is, what a king is, and
finally what being unharmed by fire is, and all the other things
that those words signify. Yet Ananias, Azarias, and Misahel are
30   just as unknown to me as the *sarabarae*, and these names didn't
help me at all to know them, nor could they help me.

I do admit that I *believe* rather than *know* that everything we
read in the story happened then just as it is written. Those whom
35   we believe are themselves not unaware of the difference, for the
Prophet says:[83]

Unless you believe, you shall not understand.

81. Anaias, Azarias, and Misahel were cast into a fiery furnace by King
Nebuchadnezzar; because of their piety, God made the flames powerless
to harm them, whereupon they were hauled out, pardoned, and richly
rewarded by the king. This story is recounted in Daniel 3, where the word
'*sarabarae*' appears (Septuagint 3:21 and 3:94; Vulgate 3:21).

82. "Was already known to us": *in nostra notitiam iam fuisse*, literally
'was already in our conception.' The term *notitia* is often a technical term,
roughly synonymous with 'definition,' but it does not seem to bear the
technical sense in this passage.

83. Isaiah 7:9. The Vulgate has *permanebitis* in place of Augustine's *intel-
ligetis*.

He surely would not have said this if he had thought there was no difference. Therefore, what I understand I also believe, but not everything I believe I also understand. Again, everything I understand I know; not everything I believe I know. Hence I'm not unaware how useful it is to believe even many things I do not 40 know, and I also include in this usefulness the story of the three boys. Accordingly, although the majority of things can't possibly be known by me, I still know how useful it is to believe them.[84]

Regarding each of the things we understand, however, we [11.38] don't consult a speaker who makes sounds outside us, but the 45 Truth that presides within over the mind itself, though perhaps words prompt us to consult Him. What is more, He Who is consulted, He Who is said to *dwell in the inner man*,[85] does teach: Christ — that is, *the unchangeable power and everlasting wisdom of God*,[86] which every rational soul does consult, but is disclosed to anyone, 50 to the extent that he can apprehend it, according to his good or evil will.[87] If at times one is mistaken, this doesn't happen by means of a defect in the Truth consulted, just as it isn't a defect in light outside that the eyes of the body are often mistaken — and we admit that we consult this light regarding visible things, that it may 55 show them to us to the extent that we have the ability to make them out.

Now, on the one hand, regarding colors we consult light, and [12.39] regarding other things we sense through the body we consult the elements of this world, the selfsame bodies we sense, and the senses themselves that the mind employs as interpreters to know

84. Augustine expresses his point at the end of this paragraph obscurely. Briefly: knowledge and understanding entail belief, but not conversely; belief, even when unaccompanied by knowledge, can be useful (and one can know this last fact). The story of the three boys falls into the category of useful belief that is not knowledge.

85. Ephesians 3:16–17. See also *The True Religion* 39.72: "The Truth lives in the inner man."

86. I Corinthians 1:24. See *Against the Academicians* 2.1.1.26.

87. In his early works Augustine is attracted to the idea that wisdom depends on moral rectitude: see his *The True Religion* 3.3, *On Order* 2.8.25, and *Soliloquies* 1.1.2 (the last of which Augustine repudiates in his *Revisions* 1.4.2 for the obvious reason: non-Christians often seem to know quite a lot).

5   such things. On the other hand, regarding things that are under-
      stood we consult the inner Truth by means of reason. What then
      can be said to show that we learn something by words aside from
      the mere sound that strikes the ears?

      Everything we perceive, we perceive either by one of the bodily
      senses or by the mind. We name the former sensible, the latter
10   intelligible — or, to speak in the fashion of our authorities,[88] carnal
      and spiritual. When we are asked about the former, we answer, so
      long as the things we sense are present at hand. For example,
      while looking at the new moon we're asked what sort of thing it is
      or where it is. In this case if the person raising the question doesn't
      see the object, he merely believes our words (and often he doesn't
15   believe them!). He doesn't learn at all unless he himself sees what
      is described, where he then learns not from words but from the
      things themselves and his senses. Words make the same sounds
      for the one who sees the object as for the one who doesn't see it.

      When a question is raised not about things we sense at present
      but about things we sensed in the past, then we speak of not the
      things themselves but of the images impressed by them and com-
20   mitted to memory.[89] I don't know how we state truths even
      though we look upon these false [images],[90] unless it's because we
      report not that we are seeing or sensing [the things themselves],
      but that we have seen or sensed them. We carry these images in
      the recesses of our memory in this way as certain attestations of
      things sensed previously. Contemplating them in the mind, we
25   have the good conscience that we aren't lying when we speak. Yet
      they are proofs for us [alone]. If anyone hearing me was then
      present and sensed these things, he doesn't learn from my words
      but knows them again from the images stored away within him-
      self. If he hasn't sensed them, isn't it obvious that he merely
      believes my words rather than learns from them?

[12.40]   When we deal with things that we perceive by the mind,
30   namely by the intellect and reason, we're speaking of things that
      we look upon immediately in the inner light of Truth, in virtue of

      88. "Our authorities": the (inspired) writers of the Bible and the early
      Church Fathers.

      89. See Matthews [1965] for a discussion of this passage.

      90. The images are "false" in that they are not the things themselves, but
      mere representations of the things themselves.

which the so-called inner man is illuminated and rejoices.[91] Under these conditions our listener, if he likewise sees these things with his inward and undivided eye, knows what I'm saying from his own contemplation, not from my words. Therefore, when I'm stating truths, I don't even teach the person who is looking upon these truths. He's taught not by my words but by the things themselves made manifest within when God discloses them.[92] Hence if he were questioned, he could give answers even about these matters. What is more absurd than thinking that he's taught by my speaking, when even before I spoke he could explain these very matters were he questioned?

Now it often happens that someone denies something when questioned about it, and is brought around by further questions to admit it. This happens because of the weakness of his discernment. He can't consult that light regarding the whole matter. Yet he is prompted to do it part-by-part when he's questioned about the very parts that make up the whole, which he didn't have the ability to discern. If he's guided in this case by the words of his questioner, the words nevertheless do not teach him, but they raise questions in such a way that he who is questioned learns within, corresponding to his ability to do so.

For example, if I were to ask you about the very matter at issue, namely whether it's true that nothing can be taught by words, at first it would seem absurd to you, since you aren't able to examine it as a whole. It would therefore be necessary to ask you questions suited to your abilities to hear the Teacher within you. Thus I might say: "The things I'm saying that you admit to be truths, and that you're certain of, and that you affirm yourself to know — where did you learn them?" Maybe you would reply that I had taught them to you. Then I would rejoin: "What if I should say that I had seen a flying man?[93] Do my words then make you as certain as if you were to hear that wise men are better than fools?" Surely you would deny it and reply that you do not believe the former statement, or even if you did believe it that you do not know it; whereas you know the latter statement with utter cer-

35

40

45

50

55

91. See *Against the Academicians* 3.17.37.26–28.
92. See *Confessions* 11.3.5.
93. See *The Usefulness of Belief* 16.34.

60   tainty. As a result, you would then understand that you hadn't
learned anything from my words, neither in the former case
(where you did not know although I was asserting it) nor in the
latter case (where you knew quite well), seeing that when questioned about each case you would swear the former was unknown
and the latter known to you. Yet at that point you would be admitting the whole that you had [initially] denied. You came to know

65   that the [parts] in which it consists are clear and certain — namely,
that whatever we may say, the hearer either (*a*) doesn't know
whether it is true; (*b*) knows that it is false; or (*c*) knows that it is
true. In (*a*) he either believes it or has an opinion about it[94] or
doubts it; in (*b*) he opposes and rejects it; in (*c*) he bears witness to

70   the truth. Hence in none of these three cases does he learn. We
have established that the one who doesn't know the thing, the one
who knows that he has heard falsehoods, and the one who could
when questioned have answered precisely what was said, have
each clearly learned nothing from my words.

[13.41]   Consequently, even in the case of matters discerned by the
mind, anyone who can't discern them hears in vain the discourse
of one who does, save that it's useful to believe such things so long
as they aren't known.[95] Yet anyone who can discern them is

5   inwardly a student[96] of Truth and outwardly a judge of the
speaker, or rather of what he says. Often he knows what is said
even when the speaker doesn't know it. For example, if anyone
believing the Epicureans and thinking that the soul is mortal
should set forth the arguments for its immortality (discussed by
more prudent thinkers) in the hearing of someone able to look

10   upon spiritual things, then he judges that the speaker is stating
truths. The speaker is unaware that he's stating truths. Instead, he
holds them to be completely false. Should it then be thought that
he teaches what he doesn't know? Yet he uses the very same
words that someone who does know also could use.

[13.42]   Accordingly, words don't have even the minimal function of
15

94. See *The Usefulness of Belief* 11.25 and Wijdeveld [1937], p. 181.

95. This repeats the conclusion announced at the start of 12.40, namely
that nobody can teach anyone anything at all, qualified by a provision
about useful belief.

96. For "student" Augustine uses *discipulus*, derived from *discere* (to
learn): this connection is lost in the translation.

indicating the speaker's mind, since it's uncertain whether he
knows the truth of what he says. Moreover, in the case of liars and
deceivers it's easy to understand that their minds are not only not
revealed but are even concealed by their words. I don't by any
means doubt, of course, that the words of those who tell the truth
attempt to make the speaker's mind evident and somehow   20
declare it. They would accomplish this, everyone agrees, if liars
were not permitted to speak.

We have often had the experience in ourselves and in others,
however, of words being uttered that don't correspond to the
things thought about. I see that this can happen in two ways: (*a*)
when a speech that has been committed to memory and often run
through pours out of the mouth of someone thinking about other   25
things, as frequently happens to us while we're singing a hymn;
(*b*) when by a slip of the tongue some words rush out in place of
others against our will, and here too signs are heard that aren't
about the things we have in mind. (Liars also think of the things
they say, so that although we don't know whether they're speak- 30
ing the truth, we know that they have in mind what they're saying, should neither (*a*) nor (*b*) occur.)[97] If anyone contends that (*a*)
and (*b*) occur only occasionally and that it's apparent when they
occur, I make no objection, though they are often unnoticed and
they have often deceived me upon hearing them.

There is another class in addition to these, one that is wide-   [13.43]
spread and the source of countless disagreements and quarrels: 35
when the speaker does signify the selfsame things he's thinking
about, but for the most part only to himself and to certain others,
whereas he doesn't signify the same thing to the person to whom
he's speaking and again to several other persons.

For example, let someone say in our hearing that man is sur-   40
passed in virtue by some brute animals.[98] We immediately can't

97. The previous paragraph offered the case of liars and deceivers, who
mislead with words, to show that words don't even reveal the mind of the
speaker. Two replies might be made: first, we might prevent liars and
deceivers from speaking; second, liars and deceivers do think of their
lying and deceptive aims. Augustine offers (*a*) and (*b*) as stronger cases.

98. The speaker says: *ab aliquibus belvis hominem virtute superari*. The
ambiguity lies in *virtute*, which could mean 'virtue' or 'physical strength'
(as Augustine goes on to point out).

bear this, and with great vehemence we refute it as false and
harmful. Yet perhaps he's calling physical strength 'virtue' and
enunciating what he was thinking about with this name. He
45   would be neither lying nor in error about things. Nor is he reeling
off words committed to memory while turning something else
over in his mind. Nor does he utter by a slip of the tongue something other than he wanted. Instead, he's merely calling the thing
he's thinking about by another name than we do; we should at
once agree with him about it if we could look into his thinking,
which he wasn't yet able to disclose to us by the words he had
already uttered in expressing his view.

50   They[99] say that definitions can remedy this kind of error, so that
in this case if the speaker were to define what 'virtue' is, he would
make it plain, they say, that the dispute is over the word and not
the thing. Now I might grant this to be so. Yet how many people
can be found who are good at definitions? In any event, there are
55   many arguments against the system of definitions,[100] but it isn't
opportune to discuss them here; nor do I altogether approve them.

[13.44]   I pass over the fact that there are many things we don't hear
clearly, and we argue forcefully at great length about them as if
they were things we heard. For example, you were saying
recently, Adeodatus, that although I had asserted that *mercy* is signified by a certain Punic word, you had heard from those more
60   familiar with this language that it signifies *piety*. Well, I objected
to this, insisting that you completely forgot what you were told,
because it seemed to me that you had said *faith* rather than *piety* —
though you were sitting right next to me, and these two names
don't at all trick the ear by any similarity in sound. Yet for a long
time I thought you didn't know what was said to you, whereas it
65   was I who didn't know what you had said. If I had heard you
clearly, it would never have seemed absurd to me that piety and
mercy are named by a single Punic word.

These things often happen. Let's pass over them, as I said, so
that I not seem to be stirring up quibbles against words because of
70   the carelessness of hearing, or even of men's deafness. The cases

99. Augustine likely has in mind the Peripatetics here.

100. "The system of definitions": *disciplina definiendi*. Cicero, *Good and
Bad Goals* 2.2.4 says that Epicurus refused to give definitions; perhaps he
is the source of the "many arguments" Augustine alludes to here.

we listed above are more bothersome, where we can't know the thoughts of the speakers, though we speak the same language and the words are Latin and are clearly heard.

See here: I now give in and concede that when words are heard [13.45] by someone who knows them, he can know that the speaker had 75 been thinking about the things they signify. Yet does he for this reason also learn whether the speaker has stated truths, which is the question at hand?

Do teachers hold that it is their thoughts that are perceived and [14.45] grasped rather than the very disciplines they take themselves to pass on by speaking? After all, who is so foolishly curious as to send his son to school to learn what the teacher thinks? When the 5 teachers have explained by means of words all the disciplines they profess to teach, even the disciplines of virtue and of wisdom, then those who are called 'students'[101] consider within themselves whether truths have been stated. They do so by looking upon the inner Truth, according to their abilities. That is therefore the point at which they learn. When they inwardly discover that truths have 10 been stated, they offer their praises — not knowing that they are praising them not as teachers but as persons who have been taught, if their teachers also know what they are saying.[102] Men are mistaken in calling persons 'teachers' who are not, which they do because generally there is no delay between the time of speaking and the time of knowing; and since they are quick to learn 15 internally after the prompting of the lecturer, they suppose that they have learned externally from the one who prompted them.

At another time we shall, God willing, look into the whole [13.46] problem of the usefulness of words[103] — which, if considered properly, is not negligible! For the present, I have prompted you that we should not attribute more to words than is suitable. As a result, we should by now not only believe but also begin to under- 20 stand how truly it has been written on divine authority that we

---

101. "Students": *discipuli.*

102. The supposed 'teachers' are only persons who have been taught by the inner Truth what is true (provided they have been so taught); it is therefore out of place to praise them for their teaching. Augustine offers similar remarks in his *Letter* 19.1 (Augustine to Gaius).

103. Augustine never does so, though parts of *Christian Doctrine* and *The Trinity* discuss the usefulness of words.

should not call anyone on earth our teacher, since *there is one in heaven Who is the Teacher of all.*[104] Furthermore, He Himself will teach us what 'in heaven' is — He Who prompts us externally through men by means of signs, so that we are instructed to be
25   inwardly turned toward Him. To know and love Him is the happy life which all proclaim they seek,[105] although there are few who may rejoice in having really found it.[106]

Now I would like you to tell me what you think of this whole disquisition of mine. On the one hand, if you know that what has been said is true, then if you were questioned about each of the
30   points you would have said that you knew them. Therefore, you see from Whom you have learned these points. It isn't from me. You would have given all the answers to me were I to have questioned you. On the other hand, if you don't know that what has been said is true, neither I nor He has taught you — not I, since I can never teach; not He, since you still are not able to learn.

ADEODATUS: For my part, I have learned from the prompting
35   of your words that words do nothing but prompt man to learn, and that the extent to which the speaker's thought is apparent in his speaking amounts to very little. Moreover, I have learned that it is He alone who teaches us whether what is said is true — and, when He spoke externally, He reminded us that He was dwelling within. With His help, I shall love Him the more ardently the more I advance in learning.
40   However, I'm especially grateful for this disquisition of yours, which you delivered without interruption, for this reason: it has anticipated and resolved everything that I had been prepared to say against it, and you didn't overlook anything at all that had produced a doubt in me; that private Oracle answered me about
45   everything exactly as you stated in your words.

104. This citation is a compressed paraphrase of Matthew 23:9–10.
105. See *Against the Academicians* 1.2.5.13–14 and the note on that passage.
106. See *The Free Choice of the Will* 1.14.30 and 2.9.26.

Appendix 1:

The Happy Life 1.4

. . . From the time I was nineteen years old, after I became acquainted with Cicero's *Hortensius* in the rhetorician's school, I was inflamed with so great a love for philosophy that I immediately thought of devoting myself to it.

Yet there was no lack of clouds to confound my course and to lead me into error. For a long time, I admit, I looked up to stars that were setting in the ocean.[1] A certain childish superstition used to frighten me away from investigation itself. When I became more resolute I dispelled that darkness,[2] and I persuaded myself to submit to the men teaching me rather than to those who commanded me. I fell in with men to whom the very light that is seen by our eyes was taken to be among supremely divine objects to be revered. I didn't agree, but I thought they were hiding something important in those wrappings which they were going to reveal someday. When I left those men once I had investigated them,[3] the Academicians above all held my rudder for a long time in passing over this sea, fighting all the winds and in the midst of the waves.[4]

1. Augustine's phrase *labentia in Oceanum astra suspexi* derives from Vergil, *Aeneid* 3.515: *sidera cuncta notat tacito labentia caelo.*

2. Cicero, *Tusculan Disputations* 1.26.64: "He dispelled that darkness from his soul as though from before his eyes."

3. Augustine describes his cross-examination of Faustus the Manichaean in *Confessions* 5.6.11 and his disillusionment at the result in *Confessions* 5.7.12–13.

4. "And in the midst of the waves": *in mediis fluctibus*, alluding to the 'wavering' between alternatives that characterizes the Academician. See *Confessions* 5.14.25 (Appendix 4). The same events are described, with the same figure of speech, in *The Usefulness of Belief* 8.20: "But I had reason on my side and at that point I held a great deliberation in Italy — not whether to remain in the sect into which I was sorry to have fallen, but in what fashion the truth ought to be searched for; for my sighs over the love of the truth are known to You better than anyone else. Often it seemed to me not able to be found, and the great fluctuations of my thoughts were carried off into the view of the Academicians . . . and at length I decided to be a catechumen in the church I was entrusted to by my parents, until I either found what I wanted or was persuaded that I shouldn't search for it."

I then came to this part of the world, and here I learned of the North Star[5] to which I entrusted myself. For I often noted in the sermons of our bishop,[6] and sometimes in discussions with you, [Manlius Theodorus], that one shouldn't think about anything corporeal at all when thinking about God — or about the soul, since this is the one thing in the world nearest to God.[7]

But the attractions of a wife and of reputation held me back,[8] I admit, from flying swiftly to the bosom of philosophy. It was not until I had pursued these [attractions] that I at last sped away with full sails and all oars for that refuge — this is granted to but a few, who are the happiest men — and there to find repose. Having read a few treatises by Plotinus (of whom I hear you are an enthusiastic student) and comparing with these, as far as I was able, the authority of those who have passed along the divine mysteries,[9] I was so inflamed that I would have broken away from all my anchors, had not the prestige of some men made an impression on me.[10]

5. "The North Star": *septentrionem*. This word in classical times, in both singular and plural forms, referred to the constellation called the Wain (or the Seven Sisters), including the Polestar. The imagery of ships following the stars for their guides suggests that Augustine here intends only the only star that is the sailor's reliable guide, the Polestar. Yet it should be noted that the term could be used to denote the northern winds (though typically in plural form rather than as Augustine has it), which would fit the proximate imagery of the skeptical vessel fighting against all winds until it learns which one to trust. But why the *north* wind in that case? The metaphor of the 'guiding light' seems better suited to the tone of the whole paragraph. Most likely Augustine is following the star-imagery of Cicero, *Academica* 2.20.66.

6. "Our bishop": Ambrose, who was Bishop of Milan when Augustine joined the imperial court there as a rhetorician. See *Confessions* 5.13.23 and 6.3.4.

7. In *Confessions* 5.14.25 (Appendix 3) Augustine remarks on the difficulty he had in thinking of God as nonphysical. See also *Confessions* 5.10.19, 6.3.4, 6.11.18, 7.1.1, and the more extensive discussion in 7.1.2.

8. See *Confessions* 6.6.9 and the start of *Confessions* 8.1.2.

9. For the Plotinian treatises and Augustine's comparison of Plotinus to the Apostles, see *Against the Academicians* 2.2.5 and the associated notes.

10. In *Confessions* 6.11.19 Augustine describes the attractions of secular success and mentions that he has "plenty of influential friends" (*amicorum maiorum copia*), doubtless Manichaean patrons. Note that Augustine's

What else was left, then, but that a storm (thought to be unfavorable!) rescue me as I was lingering over trivialities? Consequently, so great a pain in my chest seized me that I was unable to carry the burden of my profession,[11] by which I was setting sail — perhaps to the Sirens. I threw everything overboard and brought my battered and weary vessel to the tranquility I desired.

Appendix 2:

The Happy Life 2.13–16

". . . Now I want you to feast freely on what it has suddenly entered your host's mind[12] should be brought in for you; if I'm not mistaken, it has been concocted and flavored with 'scholastic honey,' so to speak, like dessert."

As soon as they heard this they all reached out for the proffered dish, as it were, and insisted that I hasten to tell them just what it was.

"Well," I said, "don't you think that the whole business we undertook has been completed, except with the Academicians?"

Hearing this name, the three to whom this matter was familiar rose promptly and, as it were, stretching forth their hands, assisted their host in his serving with what words they could, showing that they were going to hear nothing with more pleasure.

I then posed the issue as follows: "It's clear that the person who [2.14] doesn't have what he wants isn't happy (which the argument demonstrated a little while ago[13]), but nobody searches for what he doesn't want to find. Now [the Academicians] are always searching for the truth — hence they want to find it, and so they want to have the discovery of the truth — but they don't find it. It follows that they don't have what they want. From this it also follows that they aren't happy. Yet no one is wise unless he is happy. Hence the Academician is not wise."

---

term for 'prestige' (*existimatio*) could mean 'judgment' or 'opinion' instead.

11. See *Against the Academicians* 1.1.3.71–72 and the note on that passage.

12. Augustine is speaking; he himself is the 'host' mentioned here.

13. Augustine is referring to the course of argument earlier in *The Happy Life*.

They all suddenly cried out at this point, as if grabbing up the whole morsel. But Licentius, listening more closely and carefully, feared to assent and interposed: "I have grabbed it up along with all of you, since I cried out when moved by that conclusion. But from now on I shall swallow nothing and save my helping for Alypius! He will either devour it along with me or advise me why it shouldn't be touched."

"Navigius should be more afraid of sweets," I remarked, "because of his diseased spleen."

"Such delicacies will surely be a cure for me!" [Navigius] replied while laughing. "The dish you have set before us is some-how subtle and intricate.[14] As one says of Hymettic honey,[15] it is 'bitingly sweet' and doesn't bloat the stomach. Accordingly, even if it stings my palate to some extent, I freely gobble the whole thing so far as I'm able. For I don't see how that conclusion can be refuted."

"Surely it can't in any way," asserted Trygetius. "Therefore, I'm glad that for a long time now I have undertaken hostilities against the Academicians. Impelled by some natural impulse or other — or, to speak more truthfully, by God — I was greatly opposed to them even while not knowing how they should be refuted."

[2.15]   Licentius said: "I shall not desert them yet."

"Then you disagree with us?" Trygetius asked.

"Do all of you disagree with Alypius?" he rejoined.

I said: "I have no doubt that if Alypius were here he would give in to this little argument. He wasn't able to entertain the absurdity that either (*i*) to him a person seems happy who doesn't have such a great good for the mind that he most ardently wants to have; or (*ii*) the Academicians do not want to find the truth; or (*iii*) the per-son who is not happy is nevertheless wise — for what you're afraid to taste has been concocted out of these three ingredients: honey, meal, and nuts, so to speak."

"Would Alypius give in to this small bait for children," Licen-

14. "Subtle and intricate": *contortum hoc et aculeatum*, a verbal echo of Cicero, *Academica* 2.24.75, *contorta et aculeata quaedam sophismata*.

15. Cicero, *Hortensius* frag.89. See also *Academica* 2.24.75. The sharp-tasting honey gets its name from Mt. Hymettus near Athens, from which it comes.

tius asked, "deserting the great copiousness of the Academicians? Their flood would overwhelm or wash away your little offering, whatever it may be!"

I said: "As though we were searching for something far away, especially against Alypius! He would nontrivially prove from his own body that small things provide sufficient strength and usefulness. But you have chosen, Licentius, to depend on his authority in his absence — which of (*i*)–(*iii*) don't you approve? That a person is not happy who doesn't have what he wants? Or do you deny that the Academicians want to have discovered the truth that they are eagerly searching for? Or does it seem to you that a wise man is not happy?"

"Surely a person is happy who does not have what he wants." He laughed peevishly.

When I ordered that this be written down, he exclaimed: "I didn't say that!"

After I again ordered that it be written down, he admitted: "I did say that." And I instructed once and for all that he say no word off the record. (In this way I kept the young man balanced between embarrassment and stubbornness.)

But while teasing Licentius with these words, as if we were urging him to eat his little helping, I noticed that the others, ignorant of the whole issue and wanting to know what was so pleasantly at stake between us, were watching us without smiling. As frequently happens, they seemed to me like people who, in dining with greedy and insatiable table companions, refrain from grabbing, either because of their dignity or because they are cowed by shame. And since I had invited them, and you, [Manlius Theodorus], have taught me how to take the role of a great man — even of a true man, to explain it fully — as a host at these banquets, the inequality and discrepancy at our table bothered me. [2.16]

I smiled at my mother. Bidding them to draw freely what they lacked out of her larder, so to speak, she said: "Now tell us and explain who these Academicians are and what they want for themselves."

After I explained to her briefly and clearly, so that nobody had to go away without knowing, she said: "These men are *stumblers*!" (This is the name colloquially used for people suffering from epilepsy.) She immediately got up to leave. And at this point all of us departed, amused and laughing, putting an end to our discussion.

Appendix 3:

Letter 1

[1] Hermogenianus:
   I would never dare, even while joking, to attack the Academicians — for when would the authority of such great men not influence me? — were I not to think them to hold a view far distant
from what is commonly believed. Accordingly, I've imitated [the
Academicians] as far as I was able, rather than overcome them,
which I'm completely unable to do. For it seems to me that it well
suited those times that, if any unadulterated stream were to flow
out of the Platonic spring,[16] it run through dark and thorny brambles[17] into the possession of a very few men rather than gushing
through the open fields — since it couldn't remain clear and pure
with the sheep running around in it everywhere! What is easier
for the common herd than that the soul be thought to be a body?
It was against men of this sort, I believe, that [the Academicians]
usefully devised their technique and method for concealing the
truth.[18] Yet if the view of the Academicians has deterred men from
the apprehension of things, by way of the ingeniousness of their
words — well, since there are no philosophers around nowadays,
other than those who go about all dressed up in the traditional
robes[19] (and I hardly think *them* worthy of this venerable name!),

16. Augustine speaks of "Platonic springs" in *Against the Academicians*
3.18.40.3.

17. Augustine uses the same image in *Against the Academicians* 2.2.6.79–80.

18. O'Meara [1950], p. 191, n. 49 asserts that the manuscript reading *Dei
veri artem* does not need to be emended as here (to *occultandi veri artem*),
since "the providential concealment of their doctrine by the Academics
was an *ars Dei*." Yet without emendation the main verb is *excogitatam
(esse)*: the Academicians surely did not devise God's art, and there is no
mention of concealment.

19. "Since there are no philosophers around nowadays, other than those
who go about all dressed up in the traditional robes": *cum iam nullos vide-
amus philosophos nisi forte clanculo corporis,* literally "since we don't see any
philosophers around nowadays, except perhaps by means of their bodily
covering" — alluding to the fact that philosophers wore special
clothes to set them apart from others and to indicate the philosophical
school to which each gave his allegiance.

it seems to me that men should be led back to the hope of discovering truth. Otherwise, what was appropriate at the time for getting rid of the deepest errors might now begin to be a hindrance to the knowledge to be grasped.

At that time, the ardor of the various sects [of philosophy] [2] blazed so greatly that nothing was more to be feared than the approval of a falsehood. Yet insofar as someone pushed away by those arguments from what he had believed himself to hold firm and steadfast was searching for something else carefully and systematically, the assiduousness of his character was to that extent greater, and the truth, most profound and intricate, was felt to be hiding in the nature of things and souls. At the present time, on the other hand, there is such a great avoidance of work and neglect of the liberal arts that, as soon as it sounded like it seemed to the sharpest philosophers that nothing can be apprehended, some people[20] renounce the use of their minds and close them forever. They don't dare to believe themselves more energetic than those [philosophers]. As a result, it seems to them that even with so much study, ingenuity, leisure, and so much and varied learning — and, in the end, during a very long life — Carneades was at a loss! But if, struggling for even a little bit against slothfulness, they read the selfsame books in which it is 'shown' that perception [of the truth] is denied to human nature, they will fall into such a deep sleep that not even Gabriel's horn would awaken them!

Consequently, since I have your obliging and trustworthy [3] judgment about my [three] little books [of *Against the Academicians*], and since I rely so much on you, in order that error cannot enter into your practical judgment nor deception into our friendship, I beg you to consider this point more carefully and write back to me: do you give your approval to what at the end of the third book I thought should be believed?[21] Perhaps it's more of a

20. Presumably those who avoid work and neglect the liberal arts, who have heard that it seems to the sharpest philosophers that nothing can be apprehended. See *Against the Academicians* 2.1.1.6–17, where Augustine lists several reasons why people give up on the search for truth.

21. Augustine is referring to his discussion in *Against the Academicians* 3.17.37.3–3.20.43.8, where he describes the 'secret' view of the Academicians and how it came to be secret.

suspicion than a certainty, yet I think it's more useful than hard to believe. Well, whatever may be the case with that work, it doesn't please me as much that I have "overcome the Academicians," as you write — you write this with perhaps more affection than truth! — than that I have broken through a restraint most hateful to me, because I was held back from philosophy's breast[22] on account of my despair over truth, which is the soul's nourishment.

Appendix 4:

On Dialectic 5.7–8

[7]   A *word* is a sign of any given thing, which can be understood by a hearer, and is uttered by a speaker. A *thing* is anything sensed, understood, or concealed. A *sign* is what shows itself to sense and something beyond itself to the mind. *Speaking* is giving a sign by means of an articulated sound. (By 'articulated' I mean one that can be gotten hold of with letters.)

The text in which the art of definitions is treated will indicate whether all these things that have been defined are defined properly and whether the words heretofore belonging to the definition will have to be followed up in other definitions. Right now take what stands as given.

Every word makes a sound. When it is in writing, it isn't a word but rather a sign of a word. For this reason, when the letters are being looked at by a reader, what would issue forth in vocal sounds occurs to his mind. Written letters show nothing but themselves to the eyes, whereas vocal sounds show [something] beyond themselves to the mind. Just a little while ago we declared that a sign is what shows itself to sense and something beyond itself to the mind. Hence the things we read are not words but signs of words. Now although a letter is itself the minimal part of an articulated sound,[23] we still misuse this term in calling something a 'letter' even when we see it written down, for then it is completely silent and is no part of an utterance; it appears as a

---

22. Augustine uses the same image in *Against the Academicians* 1.1.4.84–85.

23. According to this definition a 'letter' is what we would call a phoneme — roughly, a single vowel or consonant — and not an individual written element.

sign of part of the utterance. In the same way, something is called a 'word' when it is written down, although it is the sign of a word; *i.e.,* it manifests itself not as a word but as the sign of a significant utterance.

Therefore, as I was beginning to say, every word makes a sound. But making sounds is irrelevant to dialectic. The sound of a word is in question when we inquire about or pay attention to how it is softened by the arrangement of vowels or stretched out by their emphatic repetition, or again how it is thickened by the insertion of consonants or sharpened by their concentration; how many and what kind of syllables it consists in; its poetic meter and rhythm. These matters, pertaining to the ears alone, are dealt with by grammarians. Yet when there is a dispute about them, it is in the province of dialectic, for this is the science of disputation.

But although words are signs of things whenever they get hold [8] of them, the words by which we dispute about [words] are signs of words. For since we can only talk about words by means of words and we don't talk unless we talk about some things, we realize that words are signs of things in such a way that they do not cease to be things.

Therefore, [1] when a word is uttered, if it's uttered for itself — *i.e.,* so that something is in question or in dispute regarding that very word — then surely it is the thing that is the subject of the disputation and the questioning, but the thing itself is called a 'word' (*verbum*). Furthermore, [2] whatever the mind rather than the ears perceives on the basis of the word and holds within the mind is called a 'sayable' (*dicibile*). However, [3] when a word is uttered not for itself but for signifying something else, it is called a 'saying' (*dictio*). But [4] the thing itself, which is not now a word nor a mental conception belonging to a word — whether it has a word by which it can be signified or not — is called nothing else but a 'thing' (*res*) in the strict sense of the name.

Therefore, let these four items be kept distinct: [1] the word; [2] the sayable; [3] the saying; [4] the thing. What I have called a 'word' is a word and also signifies a word. What I have called a 'sayable' is a word, yet it doesn't signify a word but rather what is understood in the word and contained in the mind. What I have called a 'saying' is a word and it signifies [1]–[2] together, that is, both the word itself and what is brought about in the mind by

means of the word. What I have called a 'thing' is a word that signifies whatever is left apart from [1]–[3].

But I recognize that [1]–[4] should be illustrated with examples.
Suppose, then, that a boy is questioned by some grammarian or
other as follows: "What part of speech is *weapons*?"[24] What [the
grammarian] has said — 'weapons' — has been said for the sake
of itself, that is, the word for the sake of the word itself. The other
[words] that he said — 'what part of speech' — were said not for
themselves but for the word 'weapons,' whether they be sensed
by the mind or spoken by the voice. Now when they are sensed by
the mind, prior to utterance, they will be sayables; whenever they
burst forth into voice they are rendered sayings, according to
what I have stated above. And while 'weapons' is a word here [in
the grammarian's question], when it was pronounced by Vergil it
was a saying, since it was spoken not for itself but so that either
the wars that Aeneas waged or his shield (or other [weapons] Vulcan fashioned for this hero) might be signified by it.

Now these wars or weapons that are waged or worn by Aeneas
— the very same that were seen when they were waged and
existed; if they were present now we could either exhibit by
[pointing] a finger or touch, and, even if they were not thought
about, it wouldn't thereby happen that they did not exist — are of
themselves neither sayables nor sayings, therefore, but rather
things so called in the strict sense of the name.

Hence we should discuss words, sayables, sayings, and things
in this part of dialectic. In all these cases, although sometimes
words are signified and sometimes non-words, there is still nothing about which it is not necessary to discuss with words. Thus let
us first of all discuss these items by means of which, everyone
agrees, discussions about all other matters take place.

Appendix 5:

Confessions 5.14.25

At this point I directed all my mind's efforts to whether I could by
some decisive proofs somehow convict the Manichaeans of fal-

24. The context makes it clear that Augustine has picked the first word of
the first line of Vergil's *Aeneid* (*Arma virumque cano . . .*).

sity. Now if I had been able to think of spiritual substance, all their devices would have immediately been undone and cast out of my mind. Yet I wasn't able to.

Considering it more and more and reflecting on it, however, I concluded that most philosophers understood much more plausible things about this material world and about every nature to which the senses of the flesh reach [than the Manichaeans did]. Accordingly, doubting everything and wavering about everything[25] in the fashion of the Academicians, as they are held to do,[26] I resolved that the Manichaeans should be abandoned, thinking at that time of doubt that I shouldn't remain in this sect since I was already putting some philosophers above it.[27]

Yet I completely refused to commit the healing of my weak soul to these philosophers, since they were without Christ's saving name. I therefore decided for the time being to be a catechumen in the Catholic church I was entrusted to by my parents, until some certainty would shine forth by which I might direct my course.[28]

25. "Wavering about everything": Augustine is alluding to the suspension of judgment produced by equipoise between two opposing arguments.

26. "As they are held to do": Augustine uses this phrase because he believes the skepticism of the Academicians to be merely a cover for their secret doctrines. See also the passage cited in the next note.

27. See the beginning of *Confessions* 5.10.19: "There also arose in me the thought that those philosophers whom they call 'Academicians' were more prudent than the rest, since they maintained that one should doubt everything, and they held that man can't apprehend any truth. They seemed to me clearly to have thought so, as they are popularly thought to do, even to one not yet understanding their intention."

28. Augustine gives a similar description of his motives for becoming a catechumen in *The Usefulness of Belief* 8.20: "I held a great deliberation in Italy — not whether to remain in the sect into which I was sorry to have fallen, [the Manichaeans], but in what fashion the truth ought to be searched for. My sighs over the love of the truth are known to You better than anyone else. Often it seemed to me that [the truth] was unable to be found, and the great waverings of my thoughts were carried off into the view of the Academicians. . . . At length I decided to be a catechumen in the Church I was entrusted to by my parents, until I either found what I wanted or was persuaded that I shouldn't search for it."

Appendix 6:

The Trinity 15.12.21

First, as for the very knowledge with regard to which our thoughts are formed truly[29] when we speak about the things we know — of what sort and how much of it can come to a man, however expert and learned? Putting aside what comes into the mind from the bodily senses, for so many of these are otherwise than they seem to be that a man who is overly impressed by their truthlikeness seems sane to himself but really is not sane — and in consequence the Academic philosophy has so prevailed that in doubting everything it is so much the more wretchedly insane — putting aside, then, what comes into the mind from the bodily senses, how many things are left that we know in the same way we know that we're alive? In this case, we're completely without fear of perhaps being in error on account of some truthlikeness, since it's certain that even he who is in error is alive. This isn't reckoned among those appearances that come from outside, so that the eye might be in error about it, as it is in error when the oar in the water seems to be bent, when towers seem to move to those sailing by, and a thousand other things that are otherwise than they seem: this [truth] isn't discerned by the eye of our flesh.

The knowledge by which we know that we're alive is the most inward knowledge of all, located where the Academician can't give even this objection: "Perhaps you're sleeping and don't know it and you're seeing things in your dreams! Doesn't everyone know that the things seen by people who are asleep are very like the things seen by people who are awake?" Yet anyone certain of the knowledge of his own life doesn't maintain in it "I know that I'm awake" but "I know that I'm alive"; therefore, whether he be asleep or awake, he is alive. Nor can he be in error in his knowledge through dreams, since both sleeping and seeing things in dreams are features of someone who is alive.

Nor can the Academician give this objection against such knowledge: "Perhaps you're insane and don't know it! The things

29. Augustine held that our minds or our thinking 'conforms itself' to knowledge when we know something: the knowledge itself determines whether our thinking is of the sort.

seen by people who are insane are very like the things seen by people who are sane." Yet anyone insane is alive. Nor does [such knowledge] maintain "I know that I'm not insane" against the Academicians, but "I know that I'm alive." Therefore, anyone who says he knows that he's alive can never be deceived nor speak a falsehood. Thus let a thousand kinds of deceptive appearances come to someone who says "I know that I'm alive"! He won't fear any of them when even the one in error is alive.

If such things alone fall under the heading of human knowledge, however, they are very few in number — except because in any one kind they are multiplied so that they not only aren't few in number but are even found to extend to an infinite number. The person who says "I know that I'm alive" says that he knows one thing. Next, if he were to say "I know that I know that I'm alive," there are now two things. Now the fact that he knows these two things amounts to knowing a third thing. He can add a fourth in this manner, and a fifth, and innumerable others, so long as he holds out. Yet since he can't apprehend an innumerable number by adding one at a time, or say it innumerable times, he apprehends this fact with complete certainty and he says that it is true and so innumerable that he truly cannot apprehend or say its infinite number.[30]

The same point can also be noted in the case of a will that is certain. Wouldn't it be impudent to reply "Perhaps you are in error!" to anyone who says: "I want to be happy"? If he were to say "I know that I want this" and "I know that I know this," then he can add a third thing to these two, namely that he knows these two; and a fourth, that he knows himself to know these two; and he can go on to an infinite number.

Again, if anyone were to say "I want not to be in error," then,

30. Augustine's point seems to be that that the potentially infinite iteration of knowledge-claims is knowable, though inexpressible; and recognition of both its knowability and its inexpressibility comes from the same feature: the statement of each single iteration is possible and takes up some of our finite amount of time. Such iteration follows from $Kp \rightarrow KKp$, the thesis Augustine maintains above. (Since Augustine accepts $Kp \rightarrow p$, these theses together entail $Kp \equiv KKp$ and hence the logical equivalence of all iterations.) See his remark about this requiring an "awkward expression" (*non commoda elocutione*) below.

whether he be in error or not, won't it be true that he wants not to be in error? Wouldn't it be overly impudent to reply "Perhaps you are in error!"? For surely whenever he is in error, he is nonetheless *not* in error in wanting not to be in error. If he were to say that he knows this, he adds any number he wishes of things known, and he sees that the number is infinite. In fact, the person who says "I want not to be in error," and "I know that I want not to be [in error]" and "I know that I know this" can already display an infinite number from this source, though with an awkward expression.

There are other examples [of knowledge] that work effectively against the Academicians, who maintain that nothing can be known by man, but we should limit our discussion — especially since we haven't undertaken this task in the present work. We wrote a book on the subject, [*Against the Academicians*],[31] in the early days of our conversion. The many arguments that have been devised by the Academicians against the perception of truth will surely have no influence at all on anyone who wants to and can read it and who understands it once he has read it.

Although there are two kinds of things that are known — (*a*) the things that the mind perceives through the bodily senses; and (*b*) the things that it perceives through itself — these philosophers[32] have babbled much against the bodily senses, but they have never been able to call into doubt the most solid perceptions of true things the mind has through itself, such as the one I mentioned: "I know that I'm alive."

Yet far be it from us to doubt the truths that we have learned through the bodily senses! Through them we learned about the heaven and the earth, and the things in them that are known to us, insofar as He who fashioned both us and them wanted us to know them.

Far be it from us, too, to deny that we know what we have learned from the testimony of others! Otherwise we don't know that there is an Ocean; we don't know that the places and cities that widespread report describes to us exist; we don't know that the men and the works of theirs we learned about by reading his-

31. Augustine refers to "three books on the subject" here, *i.e.*, the three books of *Against the Academicians*.

32. "These philosophers": the Academicians.

tories have existed; we don't know the news brought to us daily from all over and confirmed by the agreement of informants and witnesses; and, finally, we don't know where or from which persons we sprang — for we believe all these things on the testimony of others.[33] But if it's supremely ridiculous to say this, then it should be granted that not only our senses but those of other people contributed greatly to our knowledge.

Appendix 7:

Enchiridion 7.20

. . . I'm not going to try now to untie the knotty question that plagued the cleverest Academicians: whether the wise man ought to give his approval [to anything], lest he fall into error if he were to give his approval to falsehoods as truths — since all things, the Academicians affirm, are either hidden or uncertain. Accordingly, I wrote *Against the Academicians*[34] at the beginning of my conversion, so that the things they said in opposition wouldn't be a hindrance to us upon entering [the Christian life]. The despair over finding the truth, despair that seemed to be strengthened by their arguments, surely had to be eradicated. Thus, with the Academicians, every error is thought to be a sin, which they maintain can only be avoided if all assent is suspended. They say that anyone who assents to uncertain things is in error, and they argue in clever but shameless debates that there is nothing certain in men's sights, because of the indistinguishable likeness to falsehood[35] — even if what seems to be so were perhaps true! With us, however, *the just man lives by faith*.[36] But if assent were taken away faith is taken away, since without assent

33. A similar list of reliable testimonies is given in *Confessions* 6.5.7, though Augustine does not mention the Academicians there.

34. Augustine only mentions "three books" here, *i.e.*, the three books of *Against the Academicians*.

35. The Academicians maintained what appears to be true cannot be reliably distinguished from what is false since the true and the false closely resemble each other, the view to which Augustine is cryptically alluding here.

36. Romans 1:17; see also Habakkuk 2:4 and Hebrews 10:38.

nothing is believed. And there are truths that, although they do not seem to be so, must be believed for anyone to be able to reach the happy life (which is eternal). I don't know whether we should talk to those who don't know not only that they are going to live throughout eternity but that they are alive at present — or rather, they claim not to know what they cannot fail to know. For nobody is allowed not to know that he is alive, seeing that he can't even fail to know something if he isn't alive! Failing to know, as well as knowing, are features of the living. But clearly by not assenting that they are alive, they seem to guard themselves against error, even though by being in error they are proven to be alive, since the one who is not alive cannot be in error. Therefore, just as it is not only true but also certain that we are alive, so are many things both true and certain to which we should not fail to give our assent, to merit the name 'wisdom' rather than 'madness'!

Appendix 8:

The City of God 11.26

We recognize in ourselves an image of God, that is, an image of the supreme Trinity. This image isn't equal to God — rather, it falls far short of Him: it isn't co-eternal [with God] and, to put it briefly, it isn't of the same substance as God. Yet there is nothing closer to God in nature among all the things made by Him, though it still needs to be perfected by refashioning[37] so that it also be closest to God in likeness. For we exist, and we know that we exist, and we take delight in the fact that we exist and know it.

Now in these three statements, we aren't confused by any falsity that is like the truth. We don't come into contact with them by any bodily sense, as we do with things outside us: colors by seeing, sounds by hearing, odors by smelling, flavors by tasting, hard and soft things by touching. We do turn in our thoughts to images of these sensible [qualities], images that are quite like them, but these images aren't corporeal. We keep them in our memory, and through them we're stirred into the desire for these

---

37. "It still needs to be perfected by refashioning": *adhuc reformatione perficiendam*, with the suggestion of 're-forming' (taking on a new form).

things.[38] Yet without any deceptive imagination of real or unreal appearances,[39] I'm completely certain that I exist and that I know and delight in it.

Where these truths are concerned I fear none of the arguments of the Academicians when they say: "What if you're in error?" If I'm in error, I exist.[40] Someone who doesn't exist surely can't be in error! In light of this fact, I exist if I'm in error. Therefore, since I exist if I'm in error, how can I be in error about my existing, when it's certain that I exist if I'm in error? Because I would have to exist if I were in error, then, even if I were in error, I am therefore undoubtedly *not* in error about knowing that I exist. It also follows that I'm not in error about knowing that I know. For just as I know that I exist, so too I know this very fact — that I know it.

When I delight in these two things, then to the things that I know I also add the selfsame delight as a third thing which is equal to them.[41] I'm not in error about being delighted, since I'm not in error about the things in which I delight: even if they were falsehoods, it would still be true that I delight in falsehoods. How could I correctly be criticized and prevented from delighting in falsehoods, if it were false that I delighted in them? Since they are true and certain, does anyone doubt that when delight is taken in them the delight is itself true and certain? Furthermore, as nobody wants not to exist, so nobody wants not to be happy. How can anyone be happy if he is nothing?

38. That is, the images in our memory may stimulate desire for the things of which they are the images.

39. "Without any deceptive imagination of real or unreal appearances": *sine ulla phatasiarum vel phantasmatum imaginatione ludificatoria,* literally 'without any deceptive imagination of [mere] fantasies or of [genuine] appearances.' Augustine stigmatizes such "real appearances" as deceptive since they are representations, albeit accurate representations.

40. "If I'm in error, I exist": *Si fallor, sum.*

41. That is, Augustine knows (a) that he exists, (b) that he knows that he exists, and (c) that he is delighted about (a) and (b). In the remainder of this passage Augustine refers to the content of (a)–(b) as "the things he knows." He insists on the 'equality' of the three truths since he takes them to be an image of the Trinity, where the Persons are equal.

Appendix 9:

On Christian Doctrine 1.2.2

All doctrine[42] is about either things or signs, but things are learned
through signs. Now I strictly call those items 'things' that are not
employed for signifying anything, as for example a tree, a stone, a
sheep, and things of this sort — but not the tree of which we read
that Moses cast it into bitter waters to remove the bitterness,[43] nor
the stone that Jacob placed at his head,[44] nor the sheep that Abra-
ham sacrificed in place of his son,[45] for these are things in such a
way that they are also signs of other things. Yet there are other
signs whose whole use is in signifying, as for example words;
nobody uses words except for the sake of signifying something.
What I call 'signs' is understood on this basis, namely those things
that are employed for signifying something. Thus every sign is
also some thing, for what is no thing is nothing at all. But not every
thing is also a sign. Hence in this distinction between things and
signs, when we speak of things let us speak in such a way that
even if some of them can be employed for signifying, they will not
interfere with the classification according to which we first examine things and afterwards examine signs. Let us keep in mind that
in the case of things we are now to consider what they are, not
what else they also signify beyond themselves.

Appendix 10:

On Christian Doctrine 2.1.1–2.4.5

[2.1.1]   When I was writing about things (*res*) I put first the warning that
no one should consider anything in them except the fact that they
are, even if they signify something else beyond themselves. Likewise, examining the case of signs I state this: no one should consider in them the fact that they are but rather that they are signs,

42. The term rendered 'doctrine' here — *doctrina* — derives from *docere*
(to teach), and so could be rendered 'teaching.'
43. Exodus 15:25.
44. Genesis 28:11.
45. Genesis 22:13.

i.e., that they signify.

A *sign* is a thing that of itself causes something else to enter into thought beyond the appearance it presents to the senses. For example, having spotted a track we think an animal to have passed by whose track it is; seeing smoke we know that fire is close at hand; hearing the voice of a living creature we atttend to its mental emotion; when the trumpet sounds the soldiers know they must advance or retreat, and whether the battle demands anything else.

Some signs are natural and others are conventional. The natural ones are those that of themselves cause something beyond themselves to be known, without wanting or having any desire to signify. For example, smoke signifies fire. It does this without wanting to signify; instead, by observation and by attention to familiar matters, it is known that fire is close at hand, even if only the smoke is apparent. The track of a passing live creature belongs to this class [of signs], and the face of someone who is angry or sad signifies his mental emotion, even without the wish of the angry or sad person, even as any other mental impulse is revealed by our facial expression without our acting to reveal them. But examining this whole class [of natural signs] is not part of my task. However, since it falls under our classification it couldn't be completely passed over; it will be sufficient that we have taken this notice of it. [2.1.2]

Conventional signs are those that living creatures give to themselves and to each other for showing one another, so far as they are able, their mental impulses or whatever they have sensed or understood. The only reason for our signifying, *i.e.*, giving signs, is to bring forth and to transfer into another's mind what is happening in the mind of the person giving the sign. [2.2.3]

We have, then, set out to discuss and consider the signs belonging to this class to the extent that it involves men, since the conventional signs from God that are contained in the Holy Writ are presented to us through the men who wrote them. Brute animals also have certain signs among themselves by which they reveal their desires. The rooster who finds his feed gives a sign with his voice to his hen, so that she runs to him; the dove calls to his mate with a cry or is called in turn by her; and many cases of this kind are usually pointed out. Whether these [signs], like the facial expression or scream of someone in pain, follow upon a mental impulse without the will to signify, or whether they are truly given for signifying, is another question and irrelevant to the issue dealt with here. We shall drop this part from this work as superfluous.

[2.3.4]   Some of the signs by which men communicate to one another what they have sensed pertain to sense belonging to the eyes, most to that of the ears, and very few to the other senses.

When we nod we give a sign only to the eyes of the person whom we want to make by this sign a participant in our wishes. Some people signify a great many things by the movement of their hands: actors give certain signs with the movements of all their limbs to those who understand, as though they were telling the tale to the eyes [of their audience]. Banners and military standards indicate through the eyes the will of the captains. These are all, so to speak, 'visible words.'

But those [signs] that, as I have said, are the great majority pertain to the ears, especially in the case of words. For the trumpet and the flute and the guitar give the most not only pleasant but also significant of sounds — but in comparison with words, all these [signs] are very few. Words have surely gained the first place among men for signifying whatever the mind conceives (if anyone wants to reveal them). Now the Lord gave a sign by the perfume of the unguent with which His feet were anointed;[46] He signified what He wanted to through taste in the sacrament of His body and blood;[47] and something was signified when the woman was healed by touching the hem of His garment.[48] But the countless multitude of signs with which men express their thoughts consists in words. I was able to describe by means of words all those signs whose kinds I have briefly touched upon, but I couldn't describe words at all by means of those signs.

[2.4.5]   But because vibrations in the air rapidly vanish and last no longer than their sound, signs of words have been devised through letters. Thus utterances are shown to the eyes — not through themselves but rather through certain signs of them. These signs could not be common to all peoples because of the sin

46. John 12:3–7.
47. Luke 22:19–20.
48. See Matthew 9:21.

of human dissension when someone snatches the leadership for himself; the sign of this pride is that Tower [of Babel] built up to Heaven, where impious men deserved to have not only their minds but also their voices made dissonant.[49]

Appendix 11:

Revisions 1.1.1–4

When I had renounced the worldly ambitions I had achieved and those that I wanted to achieve, I devoted myself to retirement in a Christian life. Even before I was baptized, I first wrote *Against the Academicians* (or *On the Academicians*). Their arguments cause many people to despair of finding the truth. They forbid the wise man to assent to anything and to give his approval to anything whatsoever as clear and certain, since everything seems unclear and uncertain to them. Since these arguments were troubling me, I meant to rid my mind of them by the strongest reasoning I could. This was done with the Lord's mercy and assistance.   [1.1.1]

I regret that in *Against the Academicians* I so often used the name 'fortune.'[50] Of course, I didn't intend any goddess to be understood in this name, but rather the fortuitous outcome of events for good or evil, either in our bodies or outside them. Accordingly, there are words we have no scruple about using: 'perhaps,' 'perchance,' 'by chance,' 'mayhap,' 'fortuitously.'[51] All this is nevertheless to be traced back to divine providence. I wasn't silent on this point in my work, saying (1.1.1.15–17):   [1.1.2]

> Perhaps what is commonly referred to as 'fortune' is governed by some hidden order, and we only call 'chance' those events in the world whose reason and cause is concealed. . . .

I did indeed say this, but I still regret having so named 'fortune'

49. Augustine is referring to the confusion of tongues when the Tower of Babel was cast down: see Genesis 11:1–9.

50. Augustine uses the term 'fortune' in *Against the Academicians* 1.1.1.9, 1.1.1.25, 1.7.20.27, 2.1.1.3, 2.1.1.9, 3.2.2.9–13, 3.2.4.49, and 3.2.4.55.

51. Augustine takes the word *fortuna* to be etymologically linked to the words *forte, forsan, forsitan, fortasse,* and *fortuitu.*

in this work, seeing that men have the deplorable habit of saying "It's the will of fortune" where they should say "It's the will of God."

Furthermore, in a certain passage I said (1.1.1.6–8):

> However, either because we deserve it or because it's necessary by nature, it has been ordained that the harbor of wisdom never gives entry to our divine spirit while it is united to our mortal bodies. . . .

Either none of these two reasons should have been mentioned (because the sense could also be complete without them), or it was enough to say "because we deserve it" (insofar as it is true that our unhappiness is derived from Adam) and not to add "or because it's necessary by nature" (since the stern necessity of our nature deservedly stems from the preceding iniquity).[52]

Again, when I said (1.1.3.75–77):

> Nothing whatsoever that is discerned by mortal eyes, or that any of the senses comes into contact with, should be worshipped. Instead, everything of the sort must be despised.

Some words should be added to this so it says: "that any of the senses *of our mortal body* comes into contact with": there is also a sense that belongs to the mind. At the time I was accustomed to speak in the manner of those who say that sense only belongs to the body and that things able to be sensed are only corporeal. Consequently, whenever I spoke in this fashion, the ambiguity isn't sufficiently avoided except among those persons who are accustomed to this manner of speaking.

Again, I said (1.2.5.23–24):

> What else do you think living happily is, if it isn't living in accordance with what is best in man?

I explain what I meant by 'that which is best in man' slightly later (1.2.5.26–30):

52. When Augustine speaks of "our unhappiness derived from Adam" he is referring to original sin (Romans 5:12), which is the "preceding iniquity": if our nature is (deservedly) flawed by original sin, Augustine holds, further reasons are unnecessary.

> Who would doubt that what is best in man is anything but the ruling
> part of his spirit? Anything else there is in man ought to comply with
> it. Furthermore, this part — lest you demand another definition — can
> be called 'mind' or 'reason.'

This is true. As far as man's nature is concerned, there is nothing
better in him than mind and reason. Nevertheless, it isn't in accordance with mind and reason that one who wants to live happily
should live; for, in that case, he lives in accordance with man,
whereas to be able to attain happiness *one should live in accordance
with God.*[53] To reach happiness, our mind ought not be content
with itself but rather should subordinate itself to God.

Again, in replying to my interlocutor, I said (1.4.11.34–35):

> You're clearly not in error on this point! I sincerely hope this will be a
> good omen for you of what follows.

Though this was said in jest rather than seriously, I still would
rather not use the word 'omen.' I don't remember reading it in our
Sacred Scriptures[54] or in the works of any ecclesiastical writer.
However, the word 'abomination,' which is derived from 'omen,'
is often found in the Holy Writ.[55]

Now in Book 2, the 'allegory' of Philocalia and Philosophy is   [1.1.3]
completely inept and tasteless. I said that they are "sisters born of
the same father" (2.3.7.6–7). Actually the so-called Philocalia is
either only concerned with trivialities and so isn't for any reason
a sister to Philosophy, or, if the name is to be honored since it signifies 'love of beauty' when translated, and the true and highest
beauty belongs to wisdom, then Philocalia is exactly the same as
Philosophy in the case of the highest incorporeal things, and they
aren't in any way two 'sisters.'

In another passage, while dealing with the human spirit, I said
(2.9.22.21):

> The spirit will return more safely to Heaven. . . .

53. I Peter 4:6.

54. Augustine is mistaken. The word 'omen' is found in III Kings 20:33
("The men took this for an omen . . .").

55. In Deuteronomy, for example, the word 'abomination' occurs no
fewer than fourteen times.

Well, I might have spoken more safely by saying "go" rather than "return," on account of those people who think that human spirits have fallen from or been cast out of Heaven and are forced to enter bodies in punishment for their sins. I didn't hesitate to put it this way since I used the expression "to Heaven" as though it were "to God (Who is the author and maker of Heaven)." In the same way the blessed Cyprian had no qualms about saying:[56]

> Since we have a body that comes from Earth and a spirit from Heaven, we ourselves are Earth and Heaven.

It is also written in Ecclesiastes [12:7]:

> Let the spirit return[57] to God, who gave it.

(To be sure, this should be understood so that it is compatible with the Apostle's remark that *those who are yet unborn have done no good or evil*.)[58] It is beyond question, therefore, that the original region of the spirit's happiness is God Himself. He certainly didn't engender it from Himself, but He made it out of no other thing, just as He made the body out of the Earth.[59] For, with regard to the origin of the soul — how it comes to pass that it is in the body; whether it is derived from the one who was created at first, when *man was made into a living soul*,[60] or whether likewise each soul comes to be for each person — I didn't know then, nor do I know now.[61]

[1.1.4]   In Book 3, I said (3.12.27.8–10):

> If you're asking what *seems* so to me, I think that the highest good of man is in the mind.

56. Cyprian, *The Lord's Prayer* 16 (278.10–12).

57. Where Augustine has "return" (*revertatur*) the Vulgate has "go" (*redeat*), as he recommended above.

58. Romans 9:11.

59. In Genesis 2:7 God is said to have "fashioned man from the mud of the Earth" (the Latin expression used in the Vulgate, *ex limo terrae*, may have a stronger meaning — from slime or filth — but not a weaker one).

60. I Corinthians 15:45.

61. Augustine never came to a settled view about this question; see O'Connell [1987] for a discussion.

I might have said "in God" more truly. The mind enjoys Him as its greatest good so that it may be happy.

I also regret this remark I made: "I'm ready to swear by everything holy" (3.16.35.35).

Again, I regret having said about the Academicians that they had known the truth, the likeness of which they called 'truthlike,' and also that I called the truthlike itself, to which they gave their approval, false (3.18.40.11–12). What I said was wrong for two reasons. First, it was wrong because I said that something that was truthlike in some fashion was false: this too is true in its own way. Second, it was wrong because I said that the Academicians gave their approval to these falsehoods they called 'truthlike': they didn't give their approval to anything and asserted that the wise man doesn't give his approval to anything.[62] I happened to say this about them since they also gave the name 'plausible' to the truthlike.[63]

I also have reason to regret having praised Plato and the Platonic philosophers, or Academicians,[64] to a degree not suitable for impious men — especially since Christian doctrine is to be defended against their great errors!

My remark that in comparison with the arguments Cicero employed in his *Academica*, mine, by which I refuted his arguments with the most certain reasoning (3.20.45.49–51), were trifling — well, although I said this in jest and above all with irony, I still shouldn't have said it.

---

62. See *Against the Academicians* 2.6.14.25.

63. Augustine's reason here is lost in translation: 'the plausible' (*probabile*) is linked with giving approval (*[ap]probare*).

64. Augustine is here likely thinking of 3.17.37, but see also 2.10.24.

Textual Notes

For *Against the Academicians* I have used the Latin text given in Green [1970a], with the following corrections and emendations (some are taken from Doignon [1981]):

1.1.2.59	adding *ex aliqua parte bene* after *ita*
1.2.6.47	*est* for *es*
1.3.7.16	*excedisse* for *excedsse*
1.6.17.16	*diu* for *diua* (!)
1.7.19.1	*Hic ego primo inquam* for *Hic ille primo inquit*[1]
1.8.22.12	*frustraque* for *frutraque*
1.8.22.19	*a* for *sa*
2.2.3.7	adding *pergrina* after *ad*
2.2.3.12	*inlustrioris* for *inlustrios*
2.2.3.13	adding *soli* after *tibi*
2.2.5.67	*cautissime* for *castissime*[2]
2.2.6.72	*pomaria* for *pomeria*
2.3.8.28	*disciplinis* for *discipulis*
2.7.17.32	*legerant* for *lgerant*
2.9.22.3	*Academicos* for *Acdemicos*
2.13.29.7	*tuae* for *suae* [following β and R[1]]
2.13.30.37	*Quaeritur* for *Quaeriter*
3.3.6.56	*reclamante* for *reclmante*
3.9.21.61	*iudico* for *uidico*
3.11.24.6	*est* for *es*
3.11.26.67	*dixi* for *diui* (!)
3.13.29.38	*istorum* for *isotrum*
3.14.30.18	*tenebrascens* for *tenebras tegens* [following β and μ]
3.18.40.9	*ergo nihil* for *enim*
3.18.40.11	*approbabant* for *approabant*
3.18.41.43	*maxime* for *mauime*

1. Doignon [1981], pp. 74–78 argues for this reading, which ascribes the lengthy discussion of Albicerius to Augustine rather than Trygetius. To his arguments I would add that the *character* of the reply is too sophisticated for Trygetius as otherwise represented in *Against the Academicians*, and that we know Augustine endorsed at least the 'demonic' explanation from elsewhere.

2. See O'Donnell [1992], Vol. 1, p. liii, n. 104; Doignon [1981], pp. 71–73; O'Meara [1950], p. 178, n. 25.

3.19.42.18   *recipere* for *resipiscere*
3.20.44.37   *posset* for *potest*   [following μ and κ]
3.20.45.51   *iste* for *ista*

I have consulted the English translations of Garvey [1942], Kavanagh [1943], and O'Meara [1950], as well as the French translation of Jolivet [1939]. For *The Teacher* I have used the Latin text given in Daur [1970], with the following corrections and emendations (some are taken from Madec [1976]):

1.2.65   *videtur* for *videretur*
2.3.47   *tamen* for *tandem*
3.6.71   *enim* for *etiam*
4.9.122   *ea* for *et*
4.9.127   *omne* for *omno*
5.15.152   *minusne* for *minus enim*
5.16.218   *ducere* for *docere*
8.23.88–89   *sonuere* for *sonuerunt*
9.25.17   *arbitreris* for *arbitraris*
9.26.72   *cognitione* for *cognitioni*   cfr. 9.28.114
10.35.169   *oculis* for *oculus*
13.41.12   *eisdem* for *isdem*
13.43.52   adding *ita esse* after *concedam* (accidentally omitted by Daur)
14.46.30   *dixisses* for *dixisse*

I have altered Daur's punctuation in two ways that affect the sense of the translation. First, in 5.12.41, 5.12.54, 6.18.28, and 9.27.74 Daur treats an initial *Quid* as exclamatory, but I do not. Second, in 7.20.75 I have added a semicolon after *compertum*. I have consulted the English translations of Leckie [1938], Colleran [1950], and Burleigh [1953], as well as the French translation of Madec [1976].

The Appendices are drawn from several sources. I have used the following editions of the Latin texts (with emendations noted):

Appendix 1:   *The Happy Life* 1.4
               Green [1970b]
Appendix 2:   *The Happy Life* 2.13–16
               Green [1970b] (reading *scriberetur* for *seriberetur* at p.
               74, line 228)
Appendix 3:   *Letter 1*
               Goldbacher [1895] (reading *clanculo* with the manuscripts at p. 2.2 rather than Goldbacher's conjecture *amiculo*: see the note on this passage)

Appendix 4:   *On Dialectic* 5.7–8
               Jackson & Pinborg [1975]
Appendix 5:   *Confessions* 5.14.25
               O'Donnell [1992], Vol.1
Appendix 6:   *The Trinity* 15.12.21
               Mountain [1968]
Appendix 7:   *Enchiridion* 7.20
               Evans [1969]
Appendix 8:   *The City of God* 11.26
               Dombart & Kalb [1955]
Appendix 9:   *On Christian Doctrine* 1.2.2
               Martin [1962]
Appendix 10:   *On Christian Doctrine* 2.1.1–2.4.5
               Martin [1962]
Appendix 11:   *Revisions* 1.1.1–4
               Mutzenbecher [1984]

When other works of Augustine are cited in the notes and no source is given, I have used the most recent edition, determined by searching in this order: the *Corpus christianorum series latina*; the *Corpus scriptorum ecclesiasticorum latinorum*; the *Bibliothèque Augustinienne*; and, if all else failed (and only then), the *Patrologia latina*.

Biographical Index

Adeodatus   [Interlocutor in *The Teacher*]: Augustine's son.
Aesop   Aesop († 564 B.C.): Fabulist who lived as a slave on the island of Samos. He is remembered for his moral tales presented in the form of animal stories.
Aetius   Aetius (*fl.* 1st or 2nd c. A.D.): Eclectic writer who summarized opinions of Greek philosophers on natural philosophy.
Albicerius   Albicerius (*fl.* 4th c.): All information about Albicerius comes from *Against the Academicians*.
Alypius   [Interlocutor in *Against the Academicians*]: Wealthy native of Thagaste and close friend of Augustine thoughout their lives, probably a kinsman of Romanianus. Alypius studied with Augustine in Carthage, and was Augustine's companion in Rome, Milan, Cassici-

acum, and their joint return to Africa. He followed Augustine into Manichaeanism and thereafter into Christianity, and spent most of his life after returning to Africa as the bishop of Thagaste.

Ambrose   Ambrose (*c*.339–397 A.D.): Born at Trier, Ambrose was a Christian platonist who became bishop of Milan in 374, overseeing Augustine's conversion and baptism in 386. His literary works are considered the first models of Christian eloquence. He had a deep influence on Augustine.

Ammianus   Ammianus Marcellinus (330–395 A.D.): Historian of the later Roman empire; born at Antioch.

Antiochus   Antiochus of Ascalon († 68 B.C.): Sometimes considered the founder of the Fifth Academy, he argued against the skeptical tendencies of his predecessors and reverted to the teaching of the Old Academy.

Apuleius   Apuleius of Madaura (*c*.123–??? A.D.): African philosopher, poet, and rhetorician.

Arcesilaus   Arcesilaus of Pitane (316–242 B.C.): Head of the Academy in the middle of the third century, Arcesilaus is said to have given it a skeptical turn.

Carneades   Carneades (214–129/128 B.C.): Born in Cyrene. The founder of the New Academy (also called the Third Academy). Generally considered the author of "probabilism," which Augustine discusses at length in *Against the Academicians*. See the Introduction for a description.

Catiline   Lucius Sergius Catilina (108–62 B.C.): Leader of an abortive revolution against the Roman republic.

Celsus   Aulus Cornelius Celsus (*fl.* 14–37 A.D.): Roman author of an encyclopedia comprising agriculture, medicine, military science, rhetoric, philosophy, and probably jurisprudence.

Chrysippus   Chrysippus (280–207 B.C.): Successor to Cleanthes as the head of the Stoic school.

Cicero   Marcus Tullius Cicero (106–43 B.C.): Roman orator and statesman whose immensely influential writings were taken to be the paradigm of rhetorical, expository, and philosophical prose. Author of the *Academica*, the work from which Augustine derives his knowledge of skepticism.

Cledonius   Cledonius (5th c. A.D.): Grammarian who taught in Constantinople and wrote a work that explains the grammatical textbook of Donatus (*q.v.*).

Democritus   Democritus of Abdera (*fl.*430–390 B.C.): Philosopher. Democritus is the founder of atomism, the doctrine that all things are composed of minute indivisible bodies.

Donatus   Aelius Donatus (4th c. A.D.): Roman grammarian, the most famous of the fourth century. Wrote *The Art of Grammar* and commentaries on Terence and Vergil.

Epicurus   Epicurus (341–270 B.C.): Philosopher; his distinctive doctrines included a version of Democritean atomism and the thesis that the supreme good is pleasure.

Epiphanius   Epiphanius (315–403 A.D.): Monk and later bishop of Salamis on Cyprus.

Gellius   Aulus Gellius (*c*.130–*c*.180 A.D.): Roman grammarian and antiquarian. Author of the *Attic Nights*.

Hermogenianus   Hermogenianus (*fl*. 4th c.): Addressee of Augustine's *Letter* 1. Nothing else is known of him.

Iamblichus   Iamblichus (*c*.250–*c*.325 A.D.): Platonist philosopher and mystic, from Syria.

Justin Martyr   Justin Martyr (*c*.100–*c*.165 A.D.): Early Christian thinker, the first to be influenced by platonism; intellectual predecessor of Augustine.

Lartidianus   Cousin of Augustine and member of the household at Cassiciacum, interlocutor in some of the dialogues written there.

Licentius   [Interlocutor in *Against the Academicians* and *The Happy Life*]: Born in Thagaste, Licentius was the son of Romanianus and educated by Augustine. He was a young man, perhaps sixteen years old, while studying with Augustine at Cassiciacum. A later exchange of letters between Augustine and Licentius survives in which Augustine chides Licentius for showing more interest in composing poetry than in Christ; it isn't clear whether Licentius was simply less than devout or had become a pagan. There are also letters from Paulinus of Nola about Licentius. There is some evidence that he became a Roman senator before his death.

Lucilianus   Lucilianus (perhaps Lucianus or Lucinianus:*fl*. 4th c.): Mentioned in Augustine's correspondence. He is otherwise unknown.

Monnica   [Interlocutor in *The Happy Life*]: Augustine's mother.

Navigius   [Interlocutor in *The Happy Life*]: Navigius was Augustine's brother and also appears in the *Confessions* at the death of their mother Monnica; he may be the father of Augustine's nephew Patricius. He apparently had a diseased spleen. Apart from Augustine's testimony nothing else is known of him.

Origen   Origen (*c*.185–*c*.254 A.D.): Early Christian thinker, influenced by platonism and an intellectual predecessor of Augustine.

Persius   Aulus Persius Flaccus (34–62 A.D.): Roman poet and satirist, follower of the Stoics.

Pherecydes   Pherecydes of Syros (*fl*. 550 B.C.): Author of a cosmogonic myth.

Philo   Philon of Larissa (160–80 B.C.): The last undisputed head of the Academy.

Plato   Plato (429–347 B.C.): Philosopher; disciple of Socrates and teacher of Aristotle. Founder of the Academy.

Plautus   Titus Maccius Plautus († 184 B.C.): Roman dramatist. Author of
    many comedies.
Plotinus   Plotinus (205–269 A.D.): Philosopher. One of the leaders of the
    'neoplatonic revolution' in philosophy of the third century. He may
    have been the author of the 'platonist books' read by Augustine; in any
    event, Augustine was familiar with at least some of his works.
Polemo   Polemon of Athens († 270 B.C.): Third head of the Academy,
    from 314 B.C. until his death.
Porphyry   Porphyry (232–c.305 A.D.): Born at Tyre. Philosopher, scholar,
    and student of religions. Edited the works of Plotinus. Composed an
    influential treatise *Against the Christians*. He may have been the author
    of the 'platonist books' read by Augustine.
Quintillian   Marcus Fabius Quintillianus (*c*.30–??? A.D.): Roman rhetori-
    cian, author of an influential handbook of rhetoric.
Romanianus   [Dedicatee of *Against the Academicians*]: Wealthy native of
    Thagaste and Augustine's early patron and apparently convinced by
    him to become a Manichaean. Most of what we know about Roma-
    nianus derives from Augustine, but if we accept the conjecture of
    Gabillon [1978] that Augustine's *Letter* 259 was about him — the evi-
    dence depends on taking Romanianus's name to have been Cornelius
    on the basis of a fragmentary inscription from Thagaste — then a much
    fuller account is available. See O'Donnell [1992], Vol. 2, p. 382 for a dis-
    cussion.
Rusticianus   Cousin of Augustine and member of the household at Cas-
    siciacum, interlocutor in some of the dialogues written there.
Sallust   Gaius Sallustius Crispus (86–35 B.C.): Roman historian; he wrote
    a history of Catiline's rebellion against the Roman republic.
Tacitus   Cornelius Tacitus (*c*.56–??? A.D.): Roman historian, considered
    one of the masters of historical writing.
Terence   Publius Terence Afer (*c*.190–159? B.C.): Roman dramatist from
    North Africa. Author of many comedies.
Theodore   Manlius Theodorus (*fl.* 4th c.): Dedicatee of *The Happy Life*.
    Milanese platonist.
Trygetius   [Interlocutor in *Against the Academicians* and *The Happy Life*]:
    Trygetius, born in Thagaste, was educated by Augustine. He was a
    young man, perhaps sixteen years old, while studying with Augustine
    at Cassiciacum. Nothing else is known of him apart from the evidence
    in Augustine's dialogues of this time.
Verecundus   Verecundus (*fl.* 4th c.): Grammarian and owner of the
    country-house at Cassiciacum.
Vergil   Publius Vergilius Maro (70–19 B.C.): Roman poet, author of the
    Aeneid. Vergil's works were taken to be the paradigm of Latin poetry,
    and formed the basis of all later Roman 'classical' education.
Victorinus   Marius Victorinus (*fl.* 4th c.): Platonist who was eventually

converted to Christianity. Likely the translator of the 'platonist books' read by Augustine.

Zeno   Zeno of Citium (335–263 B.C.): Founder of the Stoic school of philosophy.

Zenobius   Zenobius (*fl.* 4th c.): Dedicatee of Augustine's *On Order*. Milanese platonist.

Recommended Reading

For more detail about Augustine's life and times, the place to start is with his own autobiographical work, the *Confessions*. It is one of the classics of Western literature; the recent translation of Chadwick [1992] is admirable and readable. Turn to Brown [1967] for a biography that situates Augustine firmly in his social and historical surroundings. O'Donnell [1985] and Chadwick [1986] are general overviews of Augustine's life and thought; Bonner [1967] pays more attention to Augustine's philosophical views. O'Meara [1954] is an intellectual biography up to 386, the year in which Augustine composed *Against the Academicians*. For those able to read French, Holte [1962] is a good treatment of Augustine's conception of 'wisdom,' while Testard [1958] and Lévy [1992] discuss his indebtedness to Cicero.

For ancient skepticism, a survey such as Stough [1969] or Long [1974] will do, and there are more technical articles collected in Schofield [1980] and Burnyeat [1983]. There is no introductory survey of ancient philosophy of language, but the specialized studies of Sedley [1982] and Markus [1972b] are accessible and well worth consulting.

Augustine is seen against classical philosophy in Armstrong [1967] and against mediaeval philosophy in Spade [1985]. The best general introduction to Augustine's philosophy is still Gilson [1967]. Markus [1972a] is a useful collection of articles on several topics. Matthews [1992] talks about the issues raised in *Against the Academicians* and *The Teacher*. For an analysis of Augustine's theory with regard to modern philosophy of language see Burnyeat [1987] and Kirwan [1989]. Nash [1969] is a very useful discussion of the theory of illumination, also discussed in Bubacz [1981] and O'Daly [1987].

Select Bibliography

Armstrong [1967]   A. H. Armstrong (editor), *The Cambridge History of Later Greek and Early Medieval Philosophy*. Cambridge University Press, 1967.

Bardy [1950]   *Oeuvres de Saint Augustin*, Première serie: Opuscules tom. XII: Les Révisions. Bibliothèque Augustinienne. Texte de l'édition Bénédictine, introduction, traduction, et notes par Gustave Bardy. Paris: Desclée de Brouwer et Cie, 1950.

Bonner [1986]   G. I. Bonner, *St. Augustine of Hippo: Life and Controversies*. Canterbury Press, 1986.

Brown [1967]   Peter Brown, *Augustine of Hippo: A Biography*. University of California Press, 1967.

Bubacz [1981]   B. Bubacz, *St. Augustine's Theory of Knowledge: A Contemporary Analysis*. Texts and Studies in Religion 11. New York/Toronto, 1981.

Burleigh [1953]   J.H.S. Burleigh, "St. Augustine on the Teacher" (translation), in *Augustine: Earlier Writings*. The Westminster Press, 1953.

Burnyeat [1983]   Myles F. Burnyeat (editor), *The Skeptical Tradition*. University of California Press, 1983.

Burnyeat [1987]   Myles F. Burnyeat, "Wittgenstein and Augustine *de Magistro*" in *The Proceedings of the Aristotelian Society*, supplementary volume for 1987.

Chadwick [1986]   Henry Chadwick, *Augustine*, in the "Past Masters" Series from Oxford University Press, 1986.

Chadwick [1992]   Henry Chadwick, *Saint Augustine: Confessions* (translation), The World's Classics, Oxford University Press, 1991.

Collaert [1971]   J. Collaert, "Saint Augustin grammairien dans le «De magistro»" *Revue des études augustiniennes* 17 (1971), pp. 279–92.

Colleran [1950]   Joseph M. Colleran, "St. Augustine: The Teacher" (translation), in *Ancient Christian Writers*, Vol. 9. The Newman Press, 1950.

Crosson [1989]   Frederick J. Crosson, "The structure of the *De magistro*." In *Revue des études augustinennes* 35 (1989), pp. 120–27.

Daur [1962]   *Corpus christianorum series latina* tom. XXXII: Aurelii Augustini opera, pars IV.1: Turnholti, Typographi Brepols editores Pontificii 1962. De vera religione, liber unus, cura et studio Klaus-Detlef Daur, pp. 187–260.

Daur [1970]   *Corpus christianorum series latina* tom. XXIX: Aurelii Augustini opera, pars II.2: Turnholti, Typographi Brepols editores Pontificii 1970. De magistro, liber unus, cura et studio Klaus-Detlef Daur, pp. 157–203.

Divjak [1981]   J. Divjak, Aurelii Augustini epistolae ex duobus codicibus nuper in lucem prolatae, *Corpus scriptorum ecclesiasticorum latinorum* tom. 88 (1981).

Doignon [1981]   Jean Doignon, "Leçons méconnues et exégèse du texte du «Contra Academicos» de saint Augustin." *Revue des études augustiniennes* 27 (1981), pp. 67–84.

Doignon [1984]   Jean Doignon, "L'apologue de Philocalie et de Philosophie chez saint Augustin (*C. Acad.* 2, 3, 7)." *Revue des études augustiniennes* 30 (1984), pp. 100–6.

Dombart & Kalb [1955]   *Corpus christianorum series latina* tom. XLVII–XLVIII: Aurelii Augustini opera, pars XIV.1–2: Turnholti, Typographi Brepols editores Pontificii, 1955. De civitate Dei. curaverunt B. Dombart & A. Kalb (ex editione teubnerianae paucis emandatis mutatis additis). Libri I–X (tom. XLVII), libri XI–XXII (tom. XLVIII).

Ebert [1987]   Theodor Ebert, "The Origin of the Stoic Theory of Signs in Sextus Empiricus." In *Oxford Studies in Ancient Philosophy*, Vol. 5 (1987), pp. 83–126.

Evans [1969]   *Corpus christianorum series latina* tom. XLVI: Aurelii Augustini opera, pars XIII.2: Turnholti, Typographi Brepols editores Pontificii 1969. Enchiridion ad Laurentium de fide et spe et caritate, cura et studio E. Evans, pp. 23–114.

Frede [1987]   Michael Frede, *Essays in Ancient Philosophy*. University of Minnesota Press, 1987.

Gabillon [1978]   Aimé Gabillon, "Romanianus *alias* Cornelius: Du nouveau sur le bienfateur et l'ami de saint Augustin." *Revue des études augustiniennes* 24 (1978), pp. 58–70.

Garvey [1942]   Mary Patricia Garvey, *Saint Augustine Against the Academicians* (translation). Marquette University Press, 1942.

Gilson [1967]   Étienne Gilson, *The Christian Philosophy of St. Augustine*. Translated by L.E.M. Lynch. New York: Random House, 1967.

Goldbacher [1895]   A. Goldbacher, Aurelii Augustini epistolae. Pars 1/2: epp. 1–30/31–123. *Corpus scriptorum ecclesiasticorum latinorum* tom. 34 (1985).

Goldbacher [1904]   A. Goldbacher, Aurelii Augustini epistolae. Pars 3: epp. 124–84A. *Corpus scriptorum ecclesiasticorum latinorum* tom. 44 (1904).

Goldbacher [1911]   A. Goldbacher, Aurelii Augustini epistolae. Pars 4: epp. 185–270. *Corpus scriptorum ecclesiasticorum latinorum* tom. 57 (1911).

Goldbacher [1923]   A. Goldbacher, Aurelii Augustini epistolae. Praefatio et indices. *Corpus scriptorum ecclesiasticorum latinorum* tom. 58 (1923).

Greco [1992]   Anna Greco, *Cognitive Instability, Unpersuadability of the*

Knower, and the Deceptiveness of the World: A Study in Plato's Epistemology. Ph.D. dissertation, University of Pittsburgh, 1992.

Green [1970a]   *Corpus christianorum series latina* tom. XXIX: Aurelii Augustini opera, pars II.2: Turnholti, Typographi Brepols editores Pontificii, 1970. Contra Academicos, libri tres, cura et studio W. M. Green, pp. 3–61.

Green [1970b]   *Corpus christianorum series latina* tom. XXIX: Aurelii Augustini opera, pars II.2: Turnholti, Typographi Brepols editores Pontificii 1970. De beata vita, libri quattuor, cura et studio W. M. Green, pp. 65–85.

Heil [1972]   J. Heil, "Augustine's Attack on Skepticism," in *Harvard Theological Review* 65 (1972), pp. 99–116.

Holte [1962]   Ragnar Holte, *Béatitude et sagesse*. Études Augustiniennes: Paris, 1962.

Jackson & Pinborg [1975]   *Augustine: De dialectica.* Translated, with introduction and notes, by B. Darrell Jackson, from the text newly edited by Jan Pinborg. Synthese Historical Library, Vol. 16. D. Reidel: Dordrecht/Boston 1975.

Jolivet [1939]   *Oeuvres de Saint Augustin*, Première serie: Opuscules tom. IV: Dialogues philosophiques I — Contra Academicos, De beata vita, De ordine. Bibliotheque Augustinienne. Introduction, traduction, et notes de Régis Jolivet. Paris: Desclée de Brouwer et Cie, 1939.

Kavanagh [1943]   Denis J. Kavanagh, *Answer to Skeptics* (text and translation). Cosmopolitan Science & Art Service Company, New York, 1943.

Keil [1864]   H. Keil, ed. *Grammatici latini.* Vol. 4: Leipzig 1864. Reprinted by Georg Olms, Hildesheim, 1961.

Keil [1868]   H. Keil, ed. *Grammatici latini.* Vol. 5: Leipzig, 1868. Reprinted by Georg Olms, Hildesheim, 1961.

Kirwan [1989]   Christopher Kirwan, *Augustine* (in "The Arguments of the Philosophers" series). Routledge and Kegan Paul: London/New York, 1989.

Knauer [1954]   G. N. Knauer, "*Sarabara* (*Dan.* 3, 94 [27] bei Aug. *mag.* 10, 33–11, 37) in *Glotta. Zeitschrift für griechische und lateinische Sprache* 33 (1954), pp. 100–18.

Leckie [1938]   George G. Leckie, "Concerning the Teacher" (translation), in *St. Aurelius Augustine: Concerning the Teacher and On the Immortality of the Soul*. D. Appleton-Century Company, Inc., 1938.

Lévy [1992]   Carlos Lévy, *Cicero Academicus: Recherches sur les Académiques et sur la philosophie cicéronienne*. Collection de l'école française de Rome, Palais Farnèse, 1992.

Long [1974]   A. A. Long, *Hellenistic Philosophy*. Scribner's: New York, 1974.

Madec [1976]   *Oeuvres de Saint Augustin*, Première serie: Opuscules tom.VI: Dialogues philosophiques III — De magistro, De libero arbitrio. Bibliothèque Augustinienne. Troisième édition. Introductions, traduction, et notes par Goulven Madec. Paris: Desclée de Brouwer et Cie, 1976.

Madec [1986]   Goulven Madec, "L'historicité des *Dialogues* de Cassiciacum." *Revue des études augustiniennes* 32 (1986), pp. 207–31.

Markus [1972a]   R. A. Markus (editor), *Augustine: A Collection of Critical Essays*. Macmillan: London, 1972.

Markus [1972b]   R. A. Markus, "St. Augustine on Signs" in Markus [1972a], pp. 61–91.

Martin [1962]   *Corpus christianorum series latina* tom. XXXII: Aurelii Augustini opera, pars IV.1: Turnholti, Typographi Brepols editores Pontificii 1962. De doctrina christiana, libri quattuor, cura et studio Joseph Martin, pp. 1–167.

Matthews [1965]   Gareth Matthews, "Augustine on Speaking from Memory," *American Philosophical Quarterly*, Vol. 2 (1965), pp. 157–60. Reprinted in R. A. Markus (ed.), *Augustine: A Collection of Critical Essays*. Macmillan: London, 1972, pp. 168–75.

Matthews [1992]   Gareth Matthews, *Thought's Ego in Augustine and Descartes*. Cornell University Press, 1992.

Mosher [1981]   David L. Mosher, "The Argument of St. Augustine's *Contra Academicos*" in *Augustinian Studies* 12 (1981), pp. 89–113.

Mountain [1968]   *Corpus christianorum series latina* tom. L-LA: Aurelii Augustini opera, pars XVI.1–2: Turnholti, Typographi Brepols editores Pontificii, 1968. De Trinitate, cura et studio W. J. Mountain, auxiliante Fr. Glorie. Libri I–XIII (tom. L), libri XIV–XV (tom. LA).

Mourant [1966]   J. A. Mourant, "Augustine and the Academics" in *Recherches augustiniennes* 4 (1966), pp. 67–96.

Mutzenbecher [1984]   *Corpus christianorum series latina* tom. LVII: Aurelii Augustini opera: Turnholti, Typographi Brepols editores Pontificii, 1984. Retractationum libri duo, edidit Almut Mutzenbecher.

Nash [1969]   R. H. Nash, *The Light of the Mind: St. Augustine's Theory of Knowledge*. Lexington, Kentucky, 1969.

Nehamas [1985]   Alexander Nehamas, "Meno's Paradox and Socrates as a Teacher" in *Oxford Studies in Ancient Philosophy* 3 (1985), pp. 1–30.

O'Connell [1987]   Robert J. O'Connell, *The Origin of the Soul in St. Augustine's Later Works*. Fordham University Press, 1987.

O'Daly [1987]   Gerard O'Daly, *Augustine's Philosophy of Mind*. London: Duckworth & Company, 1987.

O'Donnell [1985]   James J. O'Donnell, *Augustine*. Twayne's World Authors Series: Latin Literature. TWAS 759. Boston: Twayne Publishers, 1985.

O'Donnell [1992]   James J. O'Donnell, *Augustine: Confessions*. Vol. 1: Introduction and Text. Vol. 2: Commentary on Books 1–7. Vol. 3: Commentary on Books 8–13 and Indexes. Oxford: The Clarendon Press, 1992.

O'Meara [1950]   John J. O'Meara, "St. Augustine Against the Academics" (translation). In *Ancient Christian Writers*, Vol. 12. The Newman Press, 1950.

O'Meara [1954]   John J. O'Meara, *The Young Augustine: The Growth of St. Augustine's Mind Up to His Conversion.* New York: Longmans, Green & Co., 1954.

O'Meara [1992]   John J. O'Meara, *Studies in Augustine and Eriugena.* Catholic University of America Press, 1992.

Parsons [1951]   Sister Wilfrid Parsons, translator, "Saint Augustine: Letters, Volume 1 (1–82)" in *The Fathers of the Church,* Vol. 12. New York, 1951.

Parsons [1953a]   Sister Wilfrid Parsons, translator, "Saint Augustine: Letters, Volume 2 (83–130)" in *The Fathers of the Church,* Vol. 18. New York, 1953.

Parsons [1953b]   Sister Wilfrid Parsons, translator, "Saint Augustine: Letters, Volume 3 (131–64)" in *The Fathers of the Church,* Vol. 20. New York, 1953.

Parsons [1955]   Sister Wilfrid Parsons, translator, "Saint Augustine: Letters, Volume 4 (165–203)" in *The Fathers of the Church,* Vol. 30. New York, 1954.

Parsons [1956]   Sister Wilfrid Parsons, translator, "Saint Augustine: Letters, Volume 5 (204–70)" in *The Fathers of the Church,* Vol. 32. New York, 1956.

Robertson [1958]   D. W. Robertson, *On Christian Doctrine* (translation). The Library of Liberal Arts, Vol. 50. Macmillan, 1958.

Schofield [1980]   Malcolm Schofield, Myles Burnyeat, Jonathan Barnes (editors). *Doubt and Dogmatism: Studies in Hellenistic Epistemology.* Oxford University Press, 1980.

Sedley [1982]   David N. Sedley, "On Signs," in J. Barnes, J. Brunschwig, M. F. Burnyeat, and M. Schofield, eds., *Science and Speculation.* Cambridge University Press, 1982.

Spade [1985]   Paul Spade, *A Survey of Mediaeval Philosophy*, Version 2.0, 29 August 1985. Privately circulated by the author.

Stough [1969]   Charlotte Stough, *Greek Skepticism: A Study in Epistemology.* University of California Press, 1969.

Testard [1958]   Maurice Testard, *Saint Augustin et Ciceron.* Études Augustiniennes, Paris, 1958.

Wijdeveld [1937]   G. Wijdeveld, *Aurelius Augustinus De magistro, ingeleid, vertaald en toegelicht door.* Amsterdam, 1937.